PRAISE FOR *REINVENTING BANKING AND FINANCE*

'A compelling narrative of the history, forces, threats and opportunities that are reshaping the financial industry. The experience of the authors shines through in their confident and accessible writing, as well as in their cross-continental overview of the key institutions and people that are enabling better ways for all of us to manage our money in the mobile and data-centred world we live in.'
Josh Bottomley, Global Head of Digital, HSBC

'With the emergence of fintech the banking industry is being dragged into the digital age kicking and screaming. This book describes how this transformation is taking place and how different parts of the globe are responding differently to the change. The authors' perspectives, derived from their first-hand knowledge of digital transformation in banking, make it a compelling read.'
Paolo Zaccardi, Co-Founder and CEO, Fabrick and President, Hype

'A must-read for every forward-thinking banking executive. The radically simple neobank model outlined is one all banks should consider as part of their transformation to a customer-centric organization, while the thorough global review of fintech hubs will bring any seasoned innovator right up to date. What makes the sharp perspectives shared in this book so credible is the industry experience both authors bring. Developed through extensive first-hand knowledge running banks and advising a whole host of fintechs, the rigorous point of view is rare in a book like this.'
James Haycock, General Manager, Idean UK

'In this book the authors describe the impact digital adoption is having on banking and financial services across the globe. A must-read for anyone seeking to know more about how a fundamental industry is transforming.'
Matthew Chen, Group CEO, Sunline Holding

'Provides an insider's perspective on how technology is transforming financial services. Particularly enjoyable are the historical context, the concept of the ideal neobank and the profiles of the fintech hubs across the globe.'
Elias A Baltassis, Partner and Director, Data and Analytics, Boston Consulting Group

'Delivers great insight on the global fintech ecosystem with the profiles of both the fintech hubs and what they call the fintech tribes. An enjoyable and thoughtful book for anyone looking for an insider's perspective on banking innovation.'
Shachar Bialick, Founder and CEO, Curve

'If you want to understand why "digital banking" is not just a buzzword and how this movement is changing finance, this is the book for you. Fintechs are powering a disruption that takes us back to the origins of banking, where personal outcomes and tailored services were the norm. The authors do an exemplary job of explaining the banking revolution of our time, placing it within the historical context of the industry and showing how new ideas are helping to recover foundational concepts.'
Professor Deeph Chana, Centre for Financial Technology, Imperial College London

'This book provides some fascinating insights into why there has never been a more exciting time to be innovating in the banking industry. Regulators and financial institutions are paving the way for a new digital-based economy – a faster, more transparent and secure banking industry!'
Diana Paredes, Co-Founder and CEO, Suade

'Thanks to the authors' experience, this book provides an insider view on what's next and an extensive analysis of how technology, data and a new approach can reshape banking services.'
Paola Papanicolaou, Executive Director and Group Head of Innovation, Intesa Sanpaolo

'A compelling book looking at how banking is being transformed at its core by technology, changing customer expectations and evolving regulation. It provides a global perspective on fintech, explaining how – unlike other tech innovations – it is not a US-centric phenomenon, with Europe and Asia being home to some of the more innovative businesses in the sector. A good book to read if you are keen to understand what is happening to banking around the world and how it will affect you.'
Laurent Nizri, CEO, Paris Fintech Forum and Chair, ACSEL

'This book could not be more timely as our financial institutions and economic models are severely disrupted and tested due to the Covid-19 outbreak. As digitized operations are forcibly accelerated and new tools integrated, the authors help us rethink traditional models and share a blueprint of the bank of the future, the neobank. This book is an important guide for understanding what to focus on going forward, shaped by customer needs, technology capabilities and business realities.'
Sophie Wade, author and CEO, Flexcel Network

Reinventing Banking and Finance

Frameworks to navigate global fintech innovation

Helene Panzarino and Alessandro Hatami

KoganPage

First published in Great Britain and the United States in 2021 by Kogan Page Limited

2nd Floor, 45 Gee Street
London
EC1V 3RS
United Kingdom
www.koganpage.com

122 W 27th St, 10th Floor
New York, NY 10001
USA

4737/23 Ansari Road
Daryaganj
New Delhi 110002
India

Kogan Page books are printed on paper from sustainable forests.

ISBNs

Hardback   978 1 78966 412 6
Paperback   978 1 78966 409 6
Ebook   978 1 78966 410 2

British Library Cataloguing-in-Publication Data

A CIP record for this book is available from the British Library.

Library of Congress Cataloging-in-Publication Data
Names: Panzarino, Helene, author. | Hatami, Alessandro, author.
Title: Reinventing banking and finance : frameworks to navigate global
    fintech innovation / Helene Panzarino, Alessandro Hatami.
Description: 1 Edition. | New York : Kogan Page Inc, 2020. | Includes bibliographical references and index.
Identifiers: LCCN 2020011627 (print) | LCCN 2020011628 (ebook) | ISBN 9781789664096
    (paperback) | ISBN 9781789664126 (hardback) | ISBN 9781789664102 (ebook)
Subjects: LCSH: Banks and banking–Technological innovations. | Financial
    services industry–Technological innovations.
Classification: LCC HG1709 .P36 2020 (print) | LCC HG1709 (ebook) | DDC 332.1–dc23
LC record available at https://lccn.loc.gov/2020011627
LC ebook record available at https://lccn.loc.gov/2020011628

Typeset by Integra Software Services, Pondicherry
Print production managed by Jellyfish
Printed and bound by CPI Group (UK) Ltd, Croydon CR0 4YY

A special thanks goes to my family who indulged and supported me, sometimes making do without me being present during the many months of writing. HP

I dedicate this book to Nina, Katayoun and Anahita for their inspiration, guidance and support. AH

CONTENTS

LIST OF FIGURES AND TABLES

ABOUT THE AUTHORS

HELENE PANZARINO

Originally a commercial banker, Helene is a highly experienced fintech programme director, exited entrepreneur, educator and author. Her most recent role was MD of the global Rainmaking Colab FinTech Programme, a world-first, post-accelerator programme for Series A+ fintechs and Tier 1 financial institutions. Responsible for the inaugural programme of education and events for Innovate Finance, Helene is also an Associate Director of the LIBF Digital Banking Centre, the Lead Fellow and creator on a world-first FinTech Pathway in a Masters in Tech Entrepreneurship Degree for UCL, and co-creator and lead delivery partner on the Imperial College FinTech Executive Education Programme.

Her specialist subject areas are Digital Banking and Alternative Finance (SMEs). She is also the CEO of the Banking Lab (London) enabling community banks and building societies to engage with the global fintech community. A regular judge, speaker and moderator for the banking and fintech awards and conferences, Helene was a BSI fintech representative for the UK in Brussels and was named on the *Computer Weekly* 100 Women in Tech Award 2018–19. (Twitter @HPanzarino)

ALESSANDRO HATAMI

Alessandro is the managing partner of Pacemakers, a research and strategy firm dedicated to supporting large firms in delivering successful digital change.

He has been a practitioner of digital innovation in financial services for over 15 years, at firms like GE Capital, PayPal, PayPoint and Lloyds Banking Group.

Alessandro is a mentor of several fintech startups working with established incubators and VCs. He is also an investor in several early-stage technology and fintech companies and a board member and adviser.

He holds a BSc from Georgia Tech, an MSc from Sapienza University of Rome and an MBA from INSEAD. He lives in London with his wife and two daughters. (Twitter @hatami; www.pacemakers.io ; LinkedIn aehatami)

FOREWORD

The perennial gale of creative destruction is the centrepiece of modern business school thinking. It is also the single most daunting challenge for established businesses across the globe. What does disruptive innovation mean to my industry? How would digital disruption affect my products, services and business as a whole? Among the various companies I have had the pleasure of teaching and working with over the past decades, executives in the financial industry often stand out in their pursuit for considered guidance in the face of digital disruption. They will find a thoughtful companion in this book.

In *Reinventing Banking and Finance*, Helene Panzarino and Alessandro Hatami offer a unique perspective on the revolution in banking that is currently underway. These two financial industry veterans bring a wealth of experiences and a breadth of thought that will enrich any executive who is thinking about the topic. They travel the past and present of the financial industry and advance illuminating insights into the future bank. Building on years of experiences working within and alongside traditional banks, the authors make the case for transformation; exploring how banks might evolve from retailers to enablers. A notable virtue of the book is that it marries a rich discussion of consumers' needs and how they might be enabled through modern technologies along with a keen eye for banks' structure and the organizational impediments. It is here that the reader will benefit from the breadth of perspectives. Along with numerous examples covering the experiences of traditional banks, the book brings complementary perspectives – including that of celebrated fintech innovators as well as large technology companies – and highlights the opportunities to engage and leverage relationships with such newcomers to the financial industry.

The future of traditional banks in the face of digital disruption may seem as terra incognita to many. The work of Helene Panzarino and Alessandro Hatami will prove an invaluable companion to anyone who wants to chart the direction of the revolution in banking. It offers a detailed account of the challenges facing traditional banks and some keen insights on how they might navigate them.

Gary Dushnitsky
Associate Professor of Strategy & Entrepreneurship
London Business School

AUTHORS' NOTE

The 2020 Covid-19 crisis hit as we were counting down to the formal publication of this book. One by one, countries in Asia started locking down. Europe, the Americas and the rest of the world soon followed suit. By late April 2020, a third of the world's population was in some form of lockdown. As the disease spread, hundreds of thousands of people lost their lives – nature emphatically reminding us of our vulnerability.

In addition to the thousands of lives lost, millions of livelihoods were destroyed with people being laid off and businesses failing across the globe. Governments worldwide tried to mitigate the catastrophe, but we will feel the repercussions of the coronavirus crisis for many years to come.

In addition to the financial costs that we will bear, we can be reasonably sure that we will also see substantial societal and behavioural changes, not all of them negative. Many businesses, forced to ask their employees to work from home, have realized that remote working is a viable alternative to expensive office space and to international business travel. Businesses and consumers are seeing that video conferencing can be just as good and sometimes even better than traditional face-to-face meetings. Retailers, media companies and financial institutions are seeing a huge uptake in their digital offerings while travel, hospitality, commercial real estate and transportation firms are facing a (hopefully temporary) collapse of their businesses. Moreover, people are able to enjoy blue skies and a markedly cleaner environment than they have seen for many decades.

As we write this note, across the world countries are cautiously lifting their lockdowns, but we can be certain that we are not going to go back to the same world we were living in before the pandemic. The 'New Normal' will be different.

Over the best part of the last two decades, technology has profoundly changed society. This transformation was sustained not just by technological capability but also by the acceptance of new ways of doing business by companies and consumers. Industries such as retail, travel, music and news are virtually unrecognizable from what they were like just 10 years ago. Personal interactions have also transformed as smartphones and social media platforms reshape our conversations with each other.

Perhaps surprisingly, financial services providers have been largely immune to this transformation, due in part to the complexity of the regulation they are subject to, but also to the inertia of their customers. Until quite recently, bank customers felt that their banks were trustworthy managers of their money and that using digital channels was something unfamiliar and complex. The financial crisis of the late 2000s landed a big blow to the perceived 'trustworthiness' of banks, leading to the rise of finance technology businesses (aka fintechs). The Covid-19 crisis will further accelerate this digital adoption, as customers realize that using digital channels is easier, faster and often more secure than going to a bank branch.

The spark of the idea for this book came about as a natural extension of over 30 years' work in digital innovation in financial services. We approached fintech innovation from two different directions: one of us has a track record of looking at fintech innovation from the standpoint of the disrupting innovators, while the other comes from the perspective of the disrupted incumbent. We decided to pool our years of experience to provide a reasoned analysis of the changes that are happening and, more importantly, why we should care.

However, the book that we actually wrote took a slightly wider berth than we anticipated. We thought it was important to remind ourselves of how the banking sector got to the age of digital and fintech. So, we discussed the role of banks in society and through the ages – from biblical times to the rise of Silicon Valley.

We also took a look at the drivers behind fintech disruption, looking at talent, capital and regulation but not forgetting customer appetite. We dissected the ideal 'neobank', describing what a bank would probably look like if we had no legacy issues or expectations to worry about.

Circling back to our core objectives, we delved into how digital innovation is actually being implemented across the globe, creating distinctive geographic hubs, and establishing global communities of like-minded companies solving the same financial problems, while making the most of their markets, challenges, and opportunities.

Finally, we felt that a book on fintech disruption would not be complete without a review of some of the most important global fintech hubs. In the second half of the book, the chapters are structured by regional hubs to give the reader an overview of the individual ecosystems of London, Paris, New York, Tel Aviv, the Gulf and Shenzhen. We reached out to our networks across the globe to get insiders' perspectives on how the fintech hubs across the globe are structured and are operating. We share this with our readers, with the caveat that even though we have tried to be as up-to-the minute as possible, fintech is evolving so rapidly that there will inevitably be some information that needs to be updated.

Ultimately, our goal is to share our passion for and fascination with the changes finally transforming one of the pillars of society: banking. It is the means through which a society can reward both prudence and entrepreneurship, enriching the community in the process. This was very much the case before industrialization led banks to become increasingly detached from their customers and their needs. Unfettered growth, faceless expansion, complacency and possibly arrogance are a recipe for disaster. In this book, we address the impact of digital transformation in banking and finance on all stakeholders, sifting out the runners and riders, and inevitably along the way the winners and losers.

During the many months of writing this book, we developed a heightened awareness of the speed of change in digital disruption and of the incredible work being done by pioneering entrepreneurs, courageous incumbents, dedicated academics, visionary investors and supportive public institutions – work that sometimes goes unnoticed on the global stage. It certainly reminded us to think more laterally and maintain our peripheral industry vision, as it is easy to forget that financial services are a global industry. It is collectively stronger than its individual parts when it comes to solving shared problems. Just as the boundaries between nation states are blurring, so are the boundaries to finding solutions in this fascinating, interconnected sector.

In reading this book, we hope that you will find your own passion for the topic and continue to learn with us.

Alessandro Hatami
Helene Panzarino

ACKNOWLEDGEMENTS

We are deeply indebted to a number of incredibly receptive, giving and supportive professional networks who shared their experiences and insights with us, and now with you.

In particular we would like to thank Matthew Chen, Sabrina Del Prete, Yair Fonarov, James Haycock, Laurent Herbillon, Laurent Nizri, Susi Reitan, Francesco Scarnera, Omar Shaikh and Professor Nir Vulkan.

LIST OF ABBREVIATIONS

ABC	Agricultural Bank of China
ACPR	Autorité de contrôle prudentiel et de résolution
ADGMA	Abu Dhabi Global Market Authority
AI	Artificial intelligence
AMF	Autorité des Marchés Financiers
AML	Anti-money laundering
API	Application programming interface
ASIFMA	Asia Securities Industry and Financial Markets Association
B2B	Business-to-business
B2C	Business-to-consumer
BAT	Baidu, Alibaba and Tencent
BAU	Business as usual
BBB	British Business Bank
BOC	Bank of China
BOCOM	Bank of Communications (China)
BVCA	British Venture Capital Association
C2C	Consumer-to-consumer
CASS	Current Account Switching Service (UK)
CBB	Central Bank of Bahrain
CBI	Confederation of British Industry
CCB	China Construction Bank
CFPB	Consumer Financial Protection Bureau
CFTC	Commodities Future Trading Commission (USA)
CMA	Capital Market Authority (Saudi Arabia)
CMIS	Commissioner of the Capital Markets, Insurance and Savings (Israel)
CPA	Cost-per-action
CPC	Cost-per-click
CVC	Corporate venture capital
DFS	Department of Financial Services (NY)
DFSA	Dubai Financial Services Authority
DIEDC	Dubai Islamic Economy Development Centre
DLT	Distributed ledger technology

EBA	European Banking Authority
EBF	European Banking Federation
EC	European Commission
ECZ	Special Economic Zone (China)
EIS	Enterprise Investment Scheme (UK)
ESMA	European Securities and Markets Authority
EU	European Union
EVCA	Invest Europe (formerly European Private Equity & Venture Capital Association)
FCA	Financial Conduct Authority (UK)
FDIC	Federal Deposit Insurance Corporation
FISCO	Financial Blockchain Shenzhen Consortium
FPC	Financial Policy Committee (UK)
FSA	Financial Services Authority (UK)
FSMA	Financial Services and Markets Act 2000 (UK)
FSMR	Financial Services and Markets Regulations (Abu Dhabi)
GAFA	Google, Apple, Facebook, Amazon
GCC	Gulf Cooperation Council
GDPR	General Data Protection Regulation (EU)
GFIN	Global Financial Innovation Network
GSMA	Global System for Mobile Communications Association
HKMA	Hong Kong Monetary Authority
ICBC	Industrial and Commercial Bank of China
ICO	Initial coin offering
IDF	Israeli Defense Forces
IF	Innovate Finance
IFGS	Innovate Finance Global Summit
IFPI	International Federation of the Phonographic Industry
IIT	Indian Institutes of Technology
IMPA	Israeli Money Laundering and Terror Financing Prohibition Authority
IPO	Initial public offering
ISA	Israeli Security Authority
KAFD	King Abdullah Financial District
KYC	Know your customer
LBS	London Business School
LIBF	London Institute of Banking and Finance
LSE	i) London Stock Exchange; ii) London School of Economics and Political Science

M&A	Merger and acquisition
MAS	Monetary Authority of Singapore
MENA	Middle East/North Africa
MIFiD2	Markets in Financial Instruments Directive 2004 (EU)
MIT	Massachusetts Institute of Technology
ML	Machine learning
MVP	Minimal viable product
NBB	National Bank of Bahrain
NCTA	The Internet and Television Authority (USA)
NYC	New York City
OCC	Office of the Controller of the Currency (USA)
OECD	Organisation for Economic Co-operation and Development
ONS	Office of National Statistics (UK)
P2P	Peer-to-peer
PBoC	People's Bank of China
PE	Private equity
POC	Proof of concept
POS	Point of sale
PRA	Prudential Regulatory Authority
PSD2	Second European Payment Services Directive
QR	Quick Response (code)
R&D	Research and development
SaaS	Software-as-a-service
SAMA	Saudi Arabian Monetary Authority (SAMA)
SCA	Securities and Commodities Authority (UAE)
SCGC	Shenzhen Capital Group
SEC	Securities and Exchange Commission (USA)
SEIS	Seed Enterprise Investment Scheme (UK)
SFC	Securities and Futures Commission (China)
SME	Small and medium-sized enterprise
SNC	Start-up Nation Central (Israel)
SOAS	School of Oriental and African Studies
STEM	Science, technology, engineering and mathematics
SZIFA	Shenzhen Internet Finance Association
UCL	University College London
UCLA	University of California, Los Angeles
UKCFA	UK Crowdfunding Association
UKIFC	UK Islamic Finance Council

UKRI	UK Research and Innovation office
USP	Unique selling proposition
UX	User experience
VC	Venture capital
WEF	World Economic Forum

01

The History of Banking

For most people, banking is part of their everyday modern lives, whether that's sending money, paying bills or tapping a contactless pad to pay for a coffee or public transport. Rarely does anyone stop to think about how our modern banking system, with all its bells and whistles, came to be or how the impact of technology, economic forces and changing demographic behaviours brought us to the current state of global banking that is a part of our everyday personal and professional lives.

When you start to dig deeper, it becomes apparent, and perhaps as a surprise, that banking, and delivering innovation in financial services, is almost as old as human civilisation itself.

As far back as 2000 BC, the Sumerians and Ancient Egyptians lent money to each other in expectation of a fair return for their risk in the transaction. The Bible recognizes that the Israelites lent money to each other as well as to other groups, but that they could only charge interest to foreigners (Deuteronomy 23:20, 21). Roman citizens used promissory notes to support commercial deals. As if to serve as a reminder of our ancient financial past, one of these promissory notes which dates from 57 AD was recently discovered under the Bloomberg Building in the City of London, not far from where this book was written. In it, Tibullus, the freedman (former slave) of Venustus (his former master) acknowledged a debt of 105 denarii to Gratus, the freedman of Spurius (Smith, 2016).

The origins of the modern bank

Although banking itself has its roots in ancient times, the origins of what we have come to know as the 'modern bank' lie in the early part of the 13th century in Italy, when, following the end of the Roman Empire, the country underwent a metamorphosis and became an aggregate of smaller states. These states were often led by educated, commercially savvy and extremely competitive individuals. War between these individuals was not uncommon and resulted in huge financial losses at the state level.

To help navigate this precarious financial landscape, in central and northern Italy locals took the initiative and started offering each other financial services akin to what we would recognize as banking today. These services were often delivered by the bankers in key cities like Genoa, Siena, Florence and Venice, and often in very public surroundings. In Florence and Siena, for example, a banker would sometimes place a table (a *banco* in Italian) in the main market and potential customers would go to them with their financial needs; the relationship between banker and customers was very much out in the open. For example, should the customer default on a loan, the whole town would know. Similarly, if the bank did not deliver what they had committed to, the local ruler would send the militia to punish the banker. The punishment could take many forms, but the most visible manifestation of the banker's failure was that their table, or *banco*, would be publicly destroyed – *rotto* in Italian – resulting in a *banco rotto*: a great shame for the banker and the origin of the modern term 'bankrupt'. Extreme by modern standards, but very effective, nevertheless.

The Relationship Bank

The continued evolution in servicing the financial needs of the nation state resulted in what we might recognize as the roots of Relationship Banking, where client and banker built a relationship based on understanding each other's goals and trust that both parties would honour their commitments. Arguably the first advocate of this style of banking was Compere di San Giorgio (later known as the Banco di San Giorgio), established in Genoa in 1252 by a number of local wealthy merchants, in order to be able to pool their resources and offer a financial lifeline to the troubled Republic of Genoa weakened by a succession of wars (Hoggson, 1926). This was a bank created to serve one client: the Republic of Genoa. In the process of helping their Republic, the members of the Compere created the rulebook for many of the activities that centuries later would come to be known as 'banking'. Their offering was based on a one-to-one relationship of trust with their customer, a deep understanding of the customer's situation and a proposition that was designed and delivered to meet their needs. So, deep trust, customer insight and products designed for a 'segment of one'.

The Banco di San Giorgio, founded by one of the ancestors of the Grimaldi family of the Principality of Monaco (which is still a banking hub today), and which counted Christopher Columbus as a customer (Columbus, 2016), is no longer active today, having closed in 1805, after over 500 years of service to the community, when Napoleon invaded the country. However, a slightly later entrant into the market and currently the oldest bank still in operation, is the Monte dei Paschi di Siena, founded in 1472 whose aim was to service the Sienese feudal landlords.

TRULY CUSTOMER-CENTRIC

This deeply customer-centric approach of the relationship bank caught on and was replicated across the globe. Innovative products like demand deposits (where customers earn a return on funds handed to the bank) and payments accounts also took hold. In 17th-century merchant nations like the Netherlands and England, the range of products was expanded substantially but these were still created for a specific customer (Hoggson, 1926). In these early relationship banks, the banker was salesperson, risk manager, relationship manager and, perhaps most importantly, trusted adviser to the customer. They were also almost always the owner of the bank, risking their own net worth every time they provided the customer with the means to achieve their goals and ambitions. This business model remained the status quo for many centuries.

In Genoa, Florence and Venice banking was about protecting the independence of the state. Similarly, a few centuries later, matters of the state and finance came together again in Northern Europe. By making the Netherlands a global hub for trade and related financial services, Dutch bankers played a significant role in enabling the country to maintain a relative independence while being surrounded by very large and aggressive empires. For the early banks, playing a political role was an important *raison d'être*. The Industrial Revolution changed all that.

The Industrial Bank

The Industrial Revolution created cataclysmic changes in all areas of society, bringing with it the emergence of an affluent 'middle' class placed between the working and wealthy classes. Unlike the well-heeled demographics of the past, the new middle classes were often self-made and their fortunes recently attained. They were a relatively sophisticated customer group, but needed help in paying people, protecting what they had earned or borrowing to fund new ventures. They required more modest facilities than the rich, but there were many more of them. The sheer volume of customer numbers meant that the traditional one-to-one approach in banking was no longer viable, as it could not scale. A new approach was needed to serve this new, large and profitable segment – this led to the industrialization of banking.

The industrial bank was a consequence of industrialization of the economy and urbanization of society. It signalled a fundamental change in the banking business model, and saw banks become the resellers of products and propositions created at the centre of the bank and delivered at scale via the branches. The earlier banker's aim of being the means for the customer to achieve an end was abandoned in favour of becoming a seller of a portfolio of products aimed at making profit for the bank. In this new type of banking the banker that engaged with the customer had little leeway in adapting the product they sold to a customer need – pricing was within a range, product servicing had a framework and the guarantees required by the customer were tightly defined. The branch was able to influence pricing and terms to a certain extent, but this flexibility was possible only within a narrowly defined range.

PRODUCT VS OUTCOME

This upside of this new mass banking model allowed banks to grow, expand geographically, and serve many more customers than previously possible. The downside was that the customer was no longer offered an outcome but rather a product. That said, these products could still be slightly adapted to suit the customer needs if the banker felt that it was appropriate. Alongside this limited pricing flexibility, the bank branch staff had the time and motivation to engage with the customer to help them understand the different products and which ones best fit their needs. This personal exchange in what was becoming an increasingly impersonal approach to banking made customers feel that buying a financial product was a dialogue with a trusted adviser. This type of banking continued right up until the 1950s and is what today's older customers nostalgically refer to when they say that in the past their local branch manager 'listened to them'.

The industrial bank was a product of its age. Customers gained broader access to finance, but they paid a high price in personalization and focus. The scope of the bank changed – it slowly became more egalitarian and less political. In England and Scotland, both important centres in the Industrial Revolution, banking was about creating infrastructure to support a changing society and economy. The fact that a substantial number of entrepreneurs suddenly appeared in the market to demand both credit and decent returns for the capital they had accumulated created the need for bankers to become creative in their delivery model.

The Industrial Revolution was about changing operating models. Innovation in the manufacturing industry led to the creation of the concept of standardization. For example, before the Industrial Revolution when someone wanted a pair of boots and could afford to pay for them, they would go to a shoemaker who would make them a pair of boots that was designed for them. They did not ask for size 9 boots; they asked for boots made for their feet. Everything was bespoke; materials and quality were different, but every shoe was made for the customer paying for it. The same principle applied to banking. When Christopher Columbus asked for a loan from Banco di San Giorgio, he was not offered a set of prices and conditions. He engaged in a negotiation ending with him and his banker agreeing amounts, terms and prices.

BANKING FOR EVERYONE

With the Industrial Revolution banking changed. Demand increased dramatically and bankers realized that to support this new environment they needed to change also. Banking (like shoemaking) also became standardized. In 1717, the Bank of England introduced the first printed cheques – pieces of paper that were recognized across the land (Cheque & Credit Clearing Company, nd). These new standardized products led to modern financial products such as savings accounts, personal loans and eventually current accounts. These were aimed not at the very rich but at the emerging affluent middle classes. When the aristocracy needed banking they still engaged with their personal banker – often an owner of the bank – to provide them with a personalized product. When this wealthy customer wanted to raise funds to buy, say, a shipyard, the conversation with their banker would not be too dissimilar to one that would have been had at a medieval bank in Italy. Terms, rates, amounts and conditions were all negotiable and tailored to meet the exact needs and risk profile of the customers – like a cobbler making a bespoke pair of boots.

The story was different for less affluent customers. The former workman of the shipyard aiming to buy tools to set up a workshop would go to the industrial bank to ask for help. This entrepreneur would not speak to an owner of the bank, but to the manager of their closest branch. This manager had the authority to offer a limited range of facilities with prices, terms and conditions set by the bank's ownership. So the customer would get a product that was not designed for them but was good enough. They would get the banking equivalent of an off-the-shelf boot.

The bank manager would only have had limited discretion on terms and conditions as the technology of the day did not allow for risk underwriting for smaller facilities to be managed centrally. The bank manager would therefore develop a relationship with the customer, making the banker an integral part of the community they were operating in. This method of banking continued for many years. As banks became more successful, this business model proved very successful with banking groups emerging across the globe, some of which are still successful today: banks such as Barclays Bank in the UK, established in 1690, Bank of New York (BONY) in the United States, established in 1784 and the Daishi Bank, established in Japan in 1788, are just a few examples.

This approach became obsolete with the first wave of technology profoundly changing the industry: the advent of modern communication and computing. This led to the birth of the Information Technology Bank (IT Bank).

The IT bank

For many decades, the industrial bank reigned supreme, cementing the bank-centred relationship dynamic in the psyche of the customer as well as in industry. By the early 20th century things started to change. Two key developments were responsible for what would become a revolution in the banking system: modern communication and computers.

In the late 19th century, as providers of financial services started expanding their offerings, they realized that one of their customers' primary needs was to pay people in faraway places. Companies such as the American Express Company would take money from customers in New York and physically move the cash to San Francisco – fighting bandits along the way. The advent of the telegraph made it possible for the movement of cash to happen along a wire. The New York and San Francisco branches would simply move money from one customer's accounts to another's in branch without physical cash moving around, to the disappointment of highway robbers.

The possibility that characteristics of a financial product offered to a customer could be decided at a location other than the branch pushed large banks to increasingly centralize the decision-making away from the branches, into regional or even national hubs. The consequence of this was significant. This centralized decision-making enabled the big banks to offer a wide range of financial products very efficiently, managing their exposure to risk and fraud by setting up strict limits, guidelines and processes. This increase in volume resulted in banks having to manage the processing and monitoring of a huge volume of new transactions, in turn leading to huge bottlenecks, and it became commonplace for bank branches to be forced to close early to process all of a day's transactions. Banks were still industrial banks – only a bit more efficient.

CENTRALIZATION

This changed profoundly with the advent of computers. Until this point banks still had to rely on substantial local processing to run their business. The advent of computers enabled the extreme centralization of banking. Products could be not only defined at HQ, they could be managed from the same place; risk criteria, pricing, terms and conditions could be defined and then pushed onto the whole of branch network. The IT bank, combining the industrial bank with modern information and technological capabilities, had several effects.

First, volumes. Productivity and therefore profitability increased substantially. The banks were able to serve huge numbers of customers profitably, enabling the banks to grow rapidly. As banks could only sell through branches, the IT bank led to explosive growth in branch numbers. Branches could now be rolled out everywhere as the profitability hurdles were substantially reduced.

Secondly, as products were strictly controlled at a central location, the branch staff needed to have more sales skills and fewer banking skills, eliminating the need for skilled, experienced (and costly) bankers. Staff remuneration moved from salary to bonuses directly linked to sales targets. Branch staff slowly became less informed on what they sold and what the implications of the product could be to customers.

COMPUTER SAYS NO

Thirdly, this standardization led to an increase in rigidity in the way the banks operated. These centralized rules had to be strictly implemented to be effective. This made it extremely hard to introduce change. So, the owners of the banks' processes became very risk averse and resistant to change as every change had repercussions across all bank branches. As a result, the approach adopted by banks was, in practical terms, not to retire a product but to introduce a product change as if it were an entirely new product. This resulted in the banks' systems holding a huge number of products that needed to be serviced by an ever-growing IT and operations infrastructure.

To make things more complicated, at this stage in the 20th century banks saw the resulting economies of scale as a great incentive to acquire or merge with rivals. Although there were positive benefits in terms of customer numbers and products being sold, often this did not result in an optimization of the IT platforms. What actually happened was that the systems of the acquired banks were often not merged but were left as stand-alone independent entities simply linked to each other with bespoke interfaces, further increasing the complexity of the platforms and making change even more difficult. It was at this stage that the IT function went from a champion of change to a defender of stagnation.

This standardization led to a fundamental change in the relationship with customers. Most banks started thinking of their customers as a retailer would. Banks began adopting technology and adapting their product offering to suit the powerful but inflexible mainframe computer. They became the providers of services that were rigidly designed at a central location and delivered in branch with no discretionary leeway in conditions, terms or pricing. Unlike the industrial bank, the IT bank did not offer the branch staff any flexibility in adapting products sold to their customers' needs. The mammoth mainframes analysed data from remote locations and used a narrowly defined and rigid data set to profile and underwrite customers. These data were fewer than those available to both the banker in the Renaissance and in the post-Industrial Age, but the technology of predictive algorithms was able to deliver more precise risk management, lower-cost delivery and huge numbers of financial products sold.

HQ AND THE LOCAL BRANCH

As the mainframe was unable to consider any parameters other than those it was programmed for, so the 'relationship' aspects of banking were largely wiped out. 'The computer says no', a phrase popularized in *Little Britain*, a well-known BBC comedy programme (Bird, 2009), became a common response to customers, leading to the now all-too-familiar disconnect in the relationship between the customer and the bank. In addition, a number of management practices further eroded the trust between the bank and the customer. Branch staff were not only disempowered from meeting customer needs, they were also incentivized to sell certain products rather than others, frequently resulting in customers being sold inappropriate products.

The branch staff member became even less of an adviser and more of a salesperson. Some branch staff found themselves more motivated by the sales targets they were given than the welfare of the customer. This change of attitude was not lost on customers, and particularly on those who grew up in the system when bank managers knew them by name as opposed to their account number. Some of the highly publicized mis-selling scandals across the globe are the outcome of these practices. The advent of the age of mainframe computing may have made things quicker and potentially more accurate, but it was a formidable blow to the bank–customer relationship.

The IT bank, launched in 1950 by Bank of America, soon became the model followed by all other banks across the globe. Computers allowed banks to process transactions at a pace impossible before – resulting in even bigger banks, as IT banks could provide services that were vastly superior to their lesser rival banks. The IT banks enjoyed decades of unbridled success before they were caught off guard by the digital innovation that would change everything.

The Digital Bank

The telegraph led to the telex (a one-to-one text data messaging device), the telex then morphed into the Arpanet (the Advanced Research Projects Agency Network) and eventually to the internet and the world wide web (thanks, Tim Berners-Lee). The internet changed the world we live in by (at least theoretically) allowing everyone to connect to everyone else (Internet Society, 1997). One by one, the internet changed every aspect affecting society today. The financial sector was late in joining the digital revolution, but is now firmly in the middle of profoundly transformational evolution.

In the late 1980s, banks across the globe began offering digital access to business customers with limited success. In France, the Minitel (a videotext online service accessible through telephone lines) was launched in 1982 by the PTT, the French postal service (Schofield, 2012) and by the early 1990s it started offering banking services to consumers. Then, in 1994, the Stanford Credit Union in Palo Alto started offering online banking over the internet, bringing the world of banking into the Digital Age (Sarreal, 2019).

FROM A NEW CHANNEL TO A NEW KIND OF BANKING

The IT banks were suddenly faced with the internet revolution. At first the banks saw the internet as a communications tool. In fact, to start with many online banking services were driven by marketing. With the dawn of the dotcom era the public began getting used to doing things online, and customers started asking for banking on their computers.

Banks obliged by reluctantly replicating some of the things they did in branch on the web. Their reluctance was born out of fear that online engagement would reduce profitability, as it would be harder to cross-sell other products while simultaneously adding to the costs of managing and building a new channel. And initially they were right. Banks were not selling complex and more profitable products online (mortgages, investments, etc) and people did not need to go to the branches for everything. To make matters worse, the IT systems that were designed to be queried only when customers actually went to branch were feeling the strain of being queried much more frequently by customers online. This dramatically increased the load on the banks' systems, causing occasional blackouts and leading to a huge increase in IT spend to grow and maintain service levels.

The fintech disruption

While incumbent banks were grappling with changing customer demands and IT systems creaking under the strain of hugely increased workloads, the mid-2010s saw the arrival of what was initially seen, at best, as a mild nuisance – or even an opportunity – and gradually came to be seen as a mortal threat: the Fintech Startup.

These fintechs were smaller, more agile, focused new businesses that used technology to provide a specific financial service better than the banks could. They were created to challenge the status quo by offering a cheaper, more transparent, user-friendly financial proposition through the creative use of apps (applications), platforms and websites. They started to capture the public's imagination and slowly some of the incumbents' custom. These fintechs split the world of banking in two: on one side the existing banks with their digital solutions (the incumbents), and on the other the new businesses challenging the existing banks (the challengers). While incumbent digital banks provided a more holistic set of services and could, by and large, replace a traditional bank in fulfilling all of a customer's financial needs, fintechs focused on providing one specific technology-based service such as payments, advice etc. The incumbents could replace branches with digital services, a made-for-digital bank or a group of fintechs working together.

Around 2012–13, entrepreneurs and investors started thinking that, as in the fields of transport, travel, retail, entertainment and many other industries,

FIGURE 1.1 The evolution of banking

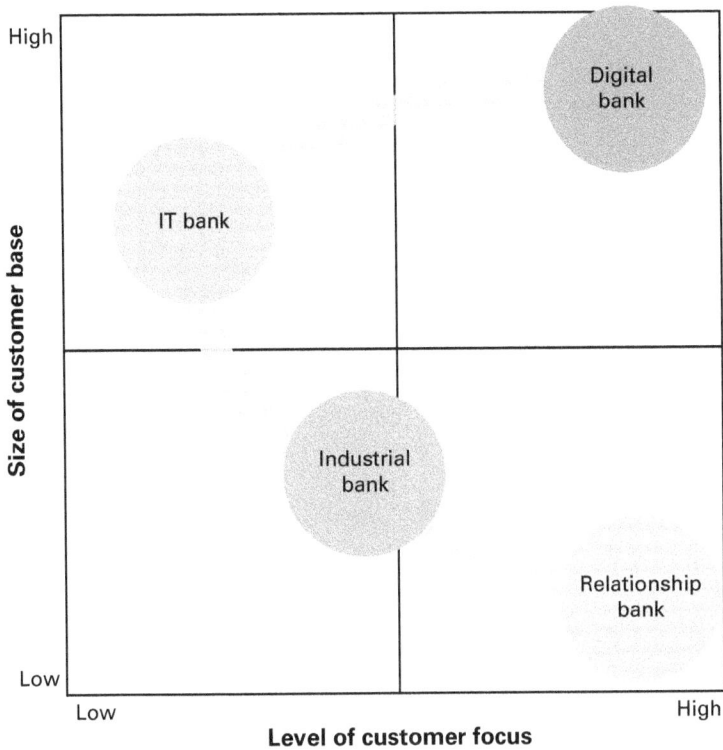

the banking industry was ready for disruption. So, startups aiming to challenge the incumbent banks began appearing across the globe. Investment in fintech startups went from $8 billion to $40 billion between 2014 and 2018 (CB Insights, 2019). The incumbent banks started seeing their offering being pushed aside in favour of a simpler, cleaner proposition by an ever-increasing number of new challenger banks or specialist providers.

Re-thinking banking

The offering of these challenger banks is not just a better version of what the incumbents deliver; they are re-thinking banking in order to completely revolutionize the industry. The fintech version of banking is taking banking away from products and bringing it back to outcomes. Many challengers start their relationship with customers by just focusing on one thing that they do very well or at least better than the incumbent. The incumbents tend to forget that very few of their customers wake up in the morning craving a credit card or a mortgage – they want to go on holiday or want to have a home. When a customer uses a challenger like TransferWise (a peer-to-peer (P2P) international payments challenger based in the UK) they are not ordering an international bank transfer; they are getting ready for a family holiday abroad. When a customer signs up to Betterment (a US wealth and investment adviser) they are not buying funds; they are buying a return. This targeted and well-informed focus on outcome is key to their success in serving customers better than the incumbent. With them, customers get the impression that they are understood and listened to. Yes, it's still a computer but it's not just saying no!

The digital bank and related products bring together the best of all the previous banking models and adds new dimensions to it (see Figure 1.1). The digital bank is not just a different version of the IT bank; it's a real evolution. Free from the shackles of decades of outdated technology and driven by the customer experience rather than profit margins, the fintech revolution is using technology to achieve what the incumbent banks thought impossible – profitable, personalized banking at huge scale.

DIFFERENT COST BASE

One of the most striking differences in the operations of these streamlined newcomers is that they can serve multitudes of customers at a fraction of the cost of the IT bank. Most incumbent banks suffer from what they call 'legacy issues' relating to costly technology that delivers products and services to customers in ways that are often obsolete. These were designed for a very different world, where customers had different expectations, regulation was different and technology had different limitations. Most incumbent banks offer digital interfaces to often obsolete delivery models.

These legacy issues are not just an IT problem; they run much deeper. Banking IT systems often consist of banking modules that were coded in another era, often brought together under one roof as a result of an acquisition. These modules often have little or no documentation on the coding, use programming languages from the 1960s and 1970s that are no longer in active use, and very frequently the people who wrote them are no longer with the banks – not just because they have retired but in some instances because they have passed away. These IT platforms were designed to run costly and time-consuming processes that are no longer fit for purpose today. As Anne Boden the CEO of Starling Bank (a UK-based challenger bank) often says: 'The big banks are increasing their cost base all the time, and they won't be able to compete because our cost of delivery here is very low' (Riddy, 2018). This lower cost base is not only the result of better technology and better processes but it also reflects the fact that most digital banks have done away with owning branches.

Customers of the digital bank need fewer branches, so as banks across the globe are becoming more digital, they are also closing branches – according to the European Banking Authority (EBA), the EU in 2017 had 20 per cent fewer branches than in 2007. But the number of EU citizens using digital banking surpassed 51 per cent in the same period, suggesting that the incumbent banks with branch services are sustaining the cost of a capability that the majority of their customers do not need (EBF, 2018). Managing a branch network is a cost that most digital banks do not have to bear. And if customers still want to deposit cash or a cheque, many digital banks are partnering with retailers and post offices to provide this facility.

The marginal cost of adding a new customer is close to nil for a digital bank, so when these acquire the customers of the incumbent banks, they do this with negligible incremental costs – so one could say that every new customer makes them more efficient.

A DIFFERENT OUTCOME

Many challenger banks are creating engagement models with their customers that are very different from those of the incumbent banks: the incumbents' aim is to sell, the challengers' aim is to build a relationship. The challenger banks are developing new ways of engaging with their customers, moving from a transactional model to one based on outcomes. They are not a supermarket where a customer goes in to buy a service; they are the means through which customers can achieve their goals. For example, the personal financial management tools (tools that use customer bank data to provide insight into spending patterns, budgeting and forecasting) offered by the challenger banks are not just a nice feature; their objective is to give customers the perception that their digital bank is giving them insight and control over their finances. Challenger banks say that if in the process of managing their finances their customers decide to buy a product, that would be great, but what is foremost in importance is the relationship – the sale of other products is of secondary importance. This is because the digital banks clearly see that the most valuable asset in banking is the relationship with the customer. The challenger bank's business is centred on monetizing the customer relationship.

The digital user experience (UX) offered by many incumbent banks mimics the experience in branch where a customer is endlessly cross-sold products. Let us be controversial here. Many traditional banks do not see their customer base as a community of individuals and organizations with distinct needs and aspirations. Many banks see their customers as a database of buyers to whom the bank has to cross-sell more bank products. Provided that customers can afford the product, the banks will sell it to them. Most banks still measure their success on the basis of how many bank products they sell. The best challenger banks of course also aim to be profitable, but most try to do this as an outcome of their relationship with their customers, not as a corporate strategic goal. They see profitability as an outcome of the relationship – a business mindset not too dissimilar to that of the big global social networks. That said, challenger banks will need to be able to show profitability soon to retain the support of investors, regulators and customers.

The most innovative digital bank is the Mobile Bank. Mobile banking took off with the launch of the smartphone by Apple in 2007. Banks began noticing that many customers logged into their desktop sites via their mobiles. The main difference between this and traditional banking is that with branches, call centres and even websites the customer has to *go* somewhere to bank. With mobile banking the bank is in an app within a device that is *always with you*. Customers are finally able to engage with their bank at their own convenience. Mobile opens a whole new world of opportunities for the challenger banks. Timing their services right to meet a customer need as it arises can be a powerful tool. Alerting customers when they cannot afford a purchase, or when they are about to be overdrawn, or asking whether they would like to push a few pence into their savings account are things that become much more meaningful if triggered at the right time on the customer's phone.

Incumbents have not ignored digital banking. Many have apps that can be accessed via a smartphone, and increasingly incumbents are launching their own stand-alone digital bank, such as Mettle and Bo from RBS. Interestingly, today the offering of the challenger banks and the more advanced incumbent bank digital offerings is not that dissimilar. The best incumbent banks offer spending categorization, budgeting tools, 24-hour customer service, card blocking and most of the other services provided by the challengers. But the incumbents are not marketing these with the verve of the challengers. This suggests that the incumbents still see these services as nice-to-have product features while the challengers see these as need-to-have relationship builders.

This focus on product is because the incumbent banks still often operate as product silos where profit and loss is measured along discrete product lines and not customer groupings or segments. This is a legacy from the past, and is possibly the greatest challenge faced by incumbent banks. Many incumbent banks are seeking to address this challenge with initiatives like customer-centricity or single customer view, but their siloed operating model is in direct contradiction of these approaches. The best digital banks were designed based on these principles; the incumbents see this, but the changes would need to be structural and deep. It would require a major redesign of the banks' operating models. Today, banks see product lines as profit centres with their own P&L. The redesign would turn these product lines into cost centres and service providers, with the P&L being held at the customer segment level. This is very hard to do, especially for established businesses that are still very profitable.

A DIFFERENT TYPE OF TRUST

The one customer behaviour that has baffled challenger bank innovators is customer inertia when it comes to switching banks. Customers do not seem to want to switch their main banking relationship to a challenger even if it is clear that their existing provider is not delivering what they want. Incumbent banks attribute this to reputation. Customers (especially retail banking ones) also feel that changing banks is hard work even though regulators across the globe are pushing to make moving a bank account as simple as possible. Nevertheless, historically most people remain with the bank where they opened their first bank account (van der Cruijsen and Diepstraten, 2017).

Papers, social media, customer advocates and shopping comparison sites have convinced most customers that their bank is not always their best friend. This resulting mistrust was further compounded by recurring banking crises and mis-selling scandals. In the EU, the majority of customers do not trust their banks (Bame, 2017).

In reality, account switching inertia is due to another factor. It is not about perceived trustworthiness; it is about perceived solidity. The reason that many challenger bank customers do not deposit their salaries in their account is that the incumbent appears more solid or real than the challengers. The incumbents often have branch networks and have stood the test of time. Customers often feel that challengers may not be around in a few years' time and that their deposits may be at risk. But this is a phenomenon that will erode with time and as challengers build their own reputations – as firms like Amazon and Google have done in a few short decades – customers will have little cause to stay with the incumbents if they do not do better.

A DIFFERENT TRANSPARENCY

Digital banking is bringing about a fundamental change in the banking industry: it is making providers of financial services transparent. This means that all pricing, product characteristics and operational conditions become open, completely visible to customers and prospects. Historically, banks have been able to 'arbitrage' their services by using the asymmetry between what the bank knows about the customer vs what the customer knows about the bank. The banks have been able to use this asymmetry to their advantage by directing their customers to products that were not necessarily bad, but sometimes were not what the customer really wanted – they were what the bank wanted to sell.

In the recent past, identifying the characteristics of different products required hard work on the part of the customer, so most relied on the advice of trusted bank managers. These managers would provide a list of the products relevant to the customer and then sometimes they would provide advice on which one to choose. In the digital banking world, all banks showcase all their products online and a customer can, with a few clicks, get a complete picture of a bank's product range, terms and pricing. They can do this relatively easily across several banks. If they then decide to use a comparison service, they can not only gather the data, they can get an (almost) whole-of-market perspective of products compared with each other and even rated by other customers or a specialist. In the past customers had limited means to challenge their bank's 'advice'. In the age of digital banking, with a few clicks customers can get a relatively complete picture of a bank's product offering, what other customers think of that product, and what other competitive products are present in the market.

This availability of data further enhances the perception that all banks are alike and that it does not matter which bank sells you the product, and that all sell the same thing. Taken to an extreme this would make it very hard for a bank to charge a premium on its product and price would soon become the main differentiator. This could result in a fast race to the bottom for the banks where the cheapest provider wins. Furthermore, if big tech firms like Google, Apple, Facebook and Amazon decided to enter the financial services space it is very likely that they would further compress prices.

This is terrible news for the incumbent banks. Industry insiders say that an incumbent bank has to make in the region of $200–400 a year per customer to break even, and each new account adds significant marginal cost. For a challenger bank, even including product development, customer acquisition and so on, the equivalent figure is around $50–60, and the marginal cost of maintaining each extra account is close to zero (*Economist*, 2019).

The challenger banks' strategy of building and nurturing a relationship with the customer is a good antidote to a price-driven marketplace as personal engagement is the one thing that could incentivize a customer not to decide on a purchase solely on costs. The incumbent banks' have often relied on the strength of their brand to drive customer affiliation. As the value of this brand is eroding in customers' eyes, unless incumbent banks pivot their approach to focus more on relationships, their fears of becoming 'dumb pipe' providers of a utility product may be unavoidable.

Back to the origins of banking

Perhaps the most interesting aspect of the digital banking revolution is that it could be taking banking back to its origins. The new digital challenger banks could usher in an era where banking is a service provided by a trustworthy entity that aims to help its customers achieve an outcome with a solution that is uniquely designed to their exact requirements.

This entity knows and cares about the customers and their financial success.

This entity would be able to treat every customer as if they belonged to a segment of one.

They would operate on the basis of the same principles of the first banks in Italy and the Netherlands, only with the ability to be always there for the customer and to be able to serve millions of customers with the highest quality.

Ironically, the future for digital banks and their customers is potentially a reflection of an innovative system from a bygone era that served its community well and may be exactly what modern-day banking needs.

References

Bame, Y (2017) Trust in Banks Is Not Universal, YouGov, 11 May, today.yougov.com/topics/international/articles-reports/2017/05/11/trust-banks-not-universal (archived at https://perma.cc/2YBH-2U7V)

Bird, J (2009) Computer says no but we need our say; Behind the headlines, The Free Library, www.thefreelibrary.com/Computer says no but we need our say; BEHIND THE HEADLINES.-a0214819160 (archived at https://perma.cc/M9QD-TEFX)

CB Insights Research (2019) Global Fintech Report Q1 2019, www.cbinsights.com/research/report/fintech-trends-q1-2019/ (archived at https://perma.cc/JRM6-QQH4)

Cheque and Credit Clearing Company (nd) Cheque Dates Through the Ages, www.chequeandcredit.co.uk/information-hub/history-cheque/cheque-dates-through-ages (archived at https://perma.cc/DE62-DZUX)

Columbus, C (2016) *Authentic Letters of Columbus,* Hansebooks, www.bookdepository.com/authentic-Letters-Columbus-Christopher-Columbus/9783743324329 (archived at https://perma.cc/6JZW-QBLM)

Deuteronomy 23:20-21, NIV/KJV, *BibleGateway*, www.biblegateway.com/passage/?search=Deuteronomy+23:20-21&version=NIV;KJV (archived at https://perma.cc/74YV-YY2Y)

Economist (2019) Neobanks Are Changing Britain's Banking Landscape, www.economist.com/special-report/2019/05/02/neobanks-are-changing-britains-banking-landscape (archived at https://perma.cc/5SZA-QUHH)

European Banking Federation (EBF) (2018) Banking in Europe: EBF publishes 2018 facts & figures, 5 September, www.ebf.eu/ebf-media-centre/banking-in-europe-ebf-publishes-2018-facts-figures/ (archived at https://perma.cc/PNZ2-BNGU)

Hoggson, NF (1926) Banking through the Ages: *Internet Archive*, archive.org/details/bankingthroughhag00hogg (archived at https://perma.cc/JVD9-JYN8)

Internet Society (1997) Brief History of the Internet, www.internetsociety.org/internet/history-internet/brief-history-internet/ (archived at https://perma.cc/4K4M-2TZ6)

Riddy, A (2018) Anne Boden: Big banks 'won't be able to compete' in a digital future, *New Statesman*, 8 April, www.newstatesman.com/spotlight-america/2018/04/anne-boden-big-banks-won-t-be-able-compete-digital-future (archived at https://perma.cc/TK4S-L23X)

Sarreal, R (2019) History of Online Banking: How Internet Banking Went Mainstream, *GOBankingRates*, Toggle Navigation Back, 21 December, www.gobankingrates.com/banking/banks/history-online-banking/ (archived at https://perma.cc/H8CL-RXQN)

Schofield, H (2012) Minitel: The Rise and Fall of the France-Wide Web, *BBC News*, 28 June, www.bbc.com/news/magazine-18610692 (archived at https://perma.cc/WQG6-5PPU)

Smith, R (2016) Ancient Roman IOUs Found Beneath Bloomberg's New London HQ, *National Geographic*, 1 June, www.nationalgeographic.com/news/2016/05/ancient-rome-London-Londinum-Bloomberg-archaeology-Boudicca-archaeology/ (archived at https://perma.cc/3ATM-KNUU)

van der Cruijsen, C and Diepstraten, M (2017) Banking Products: You *can* take them with you, so why don't you? *SpringerLink*, Springer US, 5 May, link.springer.com/article/10.1007/s10693-017-0276-3 (archived at https://perma.cc/M72A-DUA9)

02

The Digital Threat

From tabloids to television, the press in the UK in 2019 were incensed over the unusually large numbers of stores closing on the British high street. These closures were not the result of a financial downturn, but the outcome of a fundamental change in the mechanisms that consumers use to spend their money. According to Local Data Company, a UK market research firm, the UK has seen the closure of 33,000 stores between 2013 and 2018 (Local Data Company, 2018). In 2018, the largest number of closures was in one category: banks. In 1988, the UK had 20,583 branches; today that number stands at fewer than 8,000. During the same period, the number of banks serving UK customers went up by 60 per cent (Baringa, 2016).

Far from being financial Armageddon, this is just a simple indication that customers are using banks differently to the way they did in the past. As with other previously disrupted industries such as retail, media, travel, entertainment and so on, customers are opting to engage via digital rather than physical channels in order to get the goods or services they want. What is surprising is why it took so long for financial services to face their potential Kodak or Blockbuster moments (Satell, 2018).

It is generally accepted that the impact of digital change hit these two firms without them realizing they were being upended. The truth is that the CEOs of both firms realized that their business was being profoundly impacted. Like the captain of a tanker on course to collide with an iceberg, they tried to steer their businesses in the right direction – but ultimately failed to do so in time to save their firm (the passengers). The story of one such captain of industry, John Antioco, and his experience running Blockbuster is particularly relevant. Antioco's article for the *Harvard Business Review* is especially revealing. He and his management team saw how the internet was eroding their business and took measures to address this. It is widely believed that Antioco, somewhat optimistically, thought that the fact that he had doubled Blockbuster's revenue since joining would give him some sway with the board and shareholders with regard to his digital threat response. However, this influence was not to be. His planned investments in digital delivery were stonewalled by the board and he was eventually shown the door in 2007. The tangible results of this decision-making process: Blockbuster stopped trading three years later. Claiming an infamous place in business (management) folklore, Blockbuster is often mentioned in the roster of cautionary tales when discussing the perils of digital innovation.

The inevitability of digital disruption

For most industries, digital disruption is inevitable. Digital is not about adapting to a new marketing channel, a new customer base or a different tech platform – it is about re-imagining and re-thinking the business. The leadership and investors of an impacted business face a very difficult quandary: should we disrupt a well-tested, well-known business model to adopt one that is unfamiliar and uncertain? Most 'well-run' businesses will not take the gamble. The paradox is that when the business accepts that digital is the new way forward it is often too late to adapt. One by one, well-established industries with operating models that have successfully stood the test of time are being challenged, with new players replacing the incumbent businesses. After travel, media, retail, entertainment, photography and many more industries, financial services and banking is just the latest industry to be impacted. The question now is: Will the demise of great champions in other industries prove a source of enlightenment for the finance industry and provide a model of what not to do when responding to digital disruption? With a bit of luck and intelligence, being a relatively late 'victim' of digital change could prove to be the salvation of existing finance industry champions.

In order to be on the winning side of digital disruption, it is important to understand what drives digital disruption in banking and financial services (see Figure 2.1). Far from it being an overwhelming and confusing landscape,

FIGURE 2.1 What is driving digital innovation?

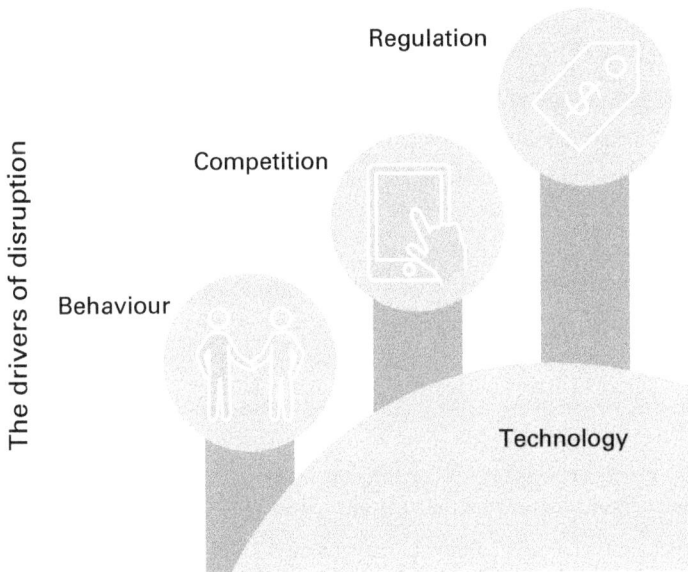

we can break it down into clearly segmented categories, and group the catalysts of change into four major groups:

- **Technology** – The ability of digital technology to revolutionize financial services delivering customer outcomes that are superior to those offered in branch and through traditional means.

- **Behaviour** – Change in how customers engage with their financial services providers; accepting that they can (and want to) bank online but with a service level expectation that is derived from their experience with other digital providers, a service level that the incumbent providers are seemingly unable to deliver.

- **Competition** – The emergence of thousands of new players that are re-thinking the industry with propositions that address and exceed customers' expectations using the new technological capabilities and that are funded by an increasing amount of venture capital (VC).

- **Regulation** – Increasingly friendly regulators that are supportive of innovation and are providing an environment that helps fintechs deliver products and services that serve their customers better than the banks and traditional financial services providers have in the past.

Let us take a closer look at each one.

Technology

In March 1989, Tim Berners-Lee proposed his vision for a networked messaging system to the leadership of CERN (the European Organization for Nuclear Research) as a means of improving communication between nuclear scientists globally (W3.org, 1989). This proposal led to the creation of the world wide web and shortly thereafter the digital revolution. Much more than just a messaging system, a better way of looking at the world wide web (and its connective tissue the internet) is as a set of rules and protocols that allow information to be created and distributed from one to many efficiently and with no degradation in quality or integrity. The web, plus a whole series of innovations built on the back of it, proceeded to make the web operate as the connective tissues of our society's thinking – a neural net for human thought.

When the internet first launched, connecting to it was complex and difficult. Once the connection was made, the speed was frustratingly low compared to today's standards. According to the NCTA (The Internet & Television Association), between 1992 and 2016 the speed of the internet went from 28 kbps to 2 gbps – that's an increase of over 7,000 per cent (NCTA, 2016). Four aspects of technology impacted digital financial services the most: data, applications, hardware and security.

Data overload

Financial services organizations generate an enormous amount of data, so the speed of processing and transmitting it is of the utmost importance for both the financial institutions and their customers. Digital technology made the real-time transfer of data easy and inexpensive. Thanks to the internet, complex processes that would require the transfer of large amounts of complex data could now be conducted across the internet, enabling large documents to be rapidly downloaded and uploaded. This new capability made it possible for customers to receive and interact with large amounts of data: a prospective homeowner would be able to download their mortgage contracts at home or a small business could download a couple of years of transaction in moments and in a format that the comptroller could instantly upload into their accounting system. These new capabilities made it possible for banker and customer to transact remotely as effectively as if they were in branch – or even better.

The new higher data-sharing speeds also allowed the bank to improve their users' experience. By delivering new and improved banking interfaces to their customers' digital devices it became easier for a customer to bank online than in branch. Customers could now be offered the terms and conditions of a service and they could spend time reading them, away from a sometimes overly enthusiastic salesperson at the bank. More importantly they could now compare these products across different providers without spending time downloading from a slow interface or, worse, travelling (and probably queueing) from branch to branch.

This speed also enabled the banks to access different third-party data sources in real time to complement the interaction with their own customers. New customers could now be authenticated, validated and vetted online much more quickly and securely than in branch.

But higher data-transfer speeds did not come without a price. This transfer speed led to the need to not only transfer data but also to process it much more efficiently. Greater network speeds meant that customers and financial institutions engaged more frequently and demanded more data than ever before. This meant that the new digital banks needed to be able to process a good deal more information in real time than ever before.

As customers were enabled to perform basic banking transactions such as checking their balances and making payments with a few clicks on their device rather than having to walk down to their branch, they started to do this much more frequently than before. If, in the past, customers felt the need to go to their branch once a month, with digital interfaces it was not uncommon for customers to login to their bank online several times a week. As every access to data online would generate a similar demand from the core systems as a branch interaction, the success of online banking substantially increased demand from core banking systems.

In the early days of digital financial services, this more frequent interaction took most of the incumbents by surprise. When asked about how their platform evolved, technical leads at the Lloyds Banking Group (LBG) would tell stories about how, before the firm fully rebuilt their systems with their famed Galaxy platform, they would regularly have to limit internet access to certain services at peak times. The risk was the surge in online demand in specific areas at certain times of day – eg lunchtimes as people took breaks at their workstation – could disrupt the whole core banking platform that served not only digital but also branches and call centres.

Somewhat unbelievable to us today, there were times when online sales of personal loans for new accounts had to be suspended to make sure customers could still make payments in branch. That banks are still vulnerable to IT problems is evidenced most recently by the CEO of UK-based TSB Bank (part of Spain's Banco Sabadell) who resigned in the aftermath of a large IT and digital failure.

This just-in-time operating model meant that banks had to upgrade. Offering financial products and validating transactions remotely requires a much greater amount of core system data processing than doing the same in branch when a human being would take on at least part of the customer underwriting and authentication processes. These new data processing capabilities enabled banks to offer customers products and services online that were often better than those offered in branch. This combination of speed, quality and convenience is one of the drivers of the success of digital banking.

Banking APIs

Another dimension that has added complexity to the management of data by digital financial institutions is the emergence of banking APIs (application programming interfaces). Banks across the globe are being increasingly required by regulators or market pressures to open up their data to trusted third parties. In Europe, the European Commission's Payment Services Directive 2 (PSD2) requires all banks in the EU to open their data to trusted third parties enabling customers to share their bank data if they so choose to do so. Similarly, in China and the United States market demands are resulting in banks opening up their systems to partners and competitors. This data can now be used to not only authenticate but also to understand customers' needs better and to offer products and services that are much better targeted to their needs and circumstances. This has resulted in an increase in data management capabilities in speed, frequency and processing capability. We can expect that the demands from the data gurus of the banks and other financial institutions will only increase in the coming years.

The journey from PC to smartphone

Another important aspect is the evolution of hardware. In the early days of the internet, in order to 'log on' to the net, users had to use clunky hardware that required a substantial financial outlay and specialist know-how in order to access the web. The evolution of hardware slowly changed that. Devices like the DIY Altair in the 1970s, the IBM personal computer, the Apple II and Amstrad Commodore of the 1980s and the Compaq laptops of the 1990s were considered revolutionary for their time – today their processing capabilities are not even comparable to the processing power of a very basic smartphone. A mid-range smartphone of today would have been considered a supercomputer in the early days of personal computing days.

Migrating from desktop PC with a modem connection to an analogue phone line to a smartphone connected to a 5G network resulted in a huge upgrade of the digital banking experience. If in the past logging on to your bank system was a lengthy, noisy, touch-and-go situation (phone modems were not that reliable after all), mobile banking became all about a few taps on your phone and a smile for the face-ID function. These new capabilities made the smartphone one of the most important enablers of digital banking.

In many countries, the mobile phone has become the main channel for customers to engage with their bank. This has resulted in a real change of mindset in the customer – both retail and business. When the bank is in the customer's phone their relationship with the bank changes – they no longer think about going to the bank, the bank is always with them. This has several outcomes. Firstly, the frequency of interaction changes – mobile customers interact with the bank much more frequently than branch-only customers. Deloitte Consulting found that 33 per cent of mobile customers and only 5 per cent of branch customers engage with the bank more than six times a month (Deloitte, 2018).

Secondly, mobile customers started comparing the UX on their banking app with other online service providers and not with other banks. This substantially raised the bar on the UX expected by customers from their banks – it is hard to create a mobile UX that is comparable to Amazon and Facebook apps rather than to those of your local financial services competitors.

Another effect of the mobile phone is that some providers started designing propositions that took advantage of the fact that the customer was not at their desk or in branch. The likes of Monzo (a digital challenger bank) in the UK allowed customers to track their spending by where they were and when they made a purchase – helping them understand their spending patterns. Other banks have started offering foreign exchange deals if they detect the customer logging in from abroad.

Lastly, since the launch of the internet, the data processing capability of devices has grown logarithmically (we will not mention Moore's law here).

This means that the quality of data analytics done 'in device' rather than remotely has increased dramatically. A great example of the effect of this in financial services is facial authentication offered by many phone manufacturers. This technology allows the end-user to bank without having to remember account numbers and passwords; the customer is recognized and served simply by showing their face. This is not too dissimilar to what would have happened to Christopher Columbus when he met his banker at the Banco di San Giorgio in Genoa in the 15th century.

Cybersecurity

The ease of access to huge amounts of data needs to be matched by hugely improved security capabilities. As online is fast becoming the preferred way to engage with the banks in many markets, and customers have started to increasingly ask for products and services that require ever more complex data to be shared, the need for data security has never been greater.

The use of technology in banking has come with its own dark side. Hackers and cybercriminals have found fertile ground in digital financial services. Interestingly, even though banks' online systems are constantly attacked by fraudsters, bank breaches are relatively rare. What seems more common in banking is 'social engineering' where human psychology is used to get customers to share banking login details. The sustainable implementation of technology in banking requires that it be and is perceived as relatively safe. As hackers and cybercriminals see the rising stakes in hacking a financial institution, so too their attacks increase. In 2019, the FCA (the UK Financial Conduct Authority) acknowledged that in 2018 they were made aware of a five-fold year-on-year increase in attempted bank data breaches (Megaw, 2019). As the pressure from criminal groups increases so do the efforts of the banks to fight back. So far, the banks have kept one step ahead of their attackers, but this is an ongoing, unrelenting and costly pursuit in an exercise of vigilance and detection.

Both the incumbents and the challengers realized that the actual and perceived security of digital banking was a key component of their banking proposition. If customers felt that they were at risk online, they would not bank there. So, cybersecurity became a major focus of the banks. Every year banks spend an increasing amount to maintain the security of the digital bank. Today we are seeing substantial investment going into hardware and software cyber-defences. Across all industries, spending on cybersecurity will exceed $120 billion in 2019 (Gartner, 2019). But banks spend three times as much as non-financial institutions (Kaspersky.com, 2017).

Behaviour

Technology has clearly impacted the way we bank. However, it is likely that the general consensus would be that technology's most profound impact has been on the ways we interact with each other. We can be scathing about how technology is making most of us share intimate details of our lives with billions of complete strangers. Yet we thoughtlessly share data about ourselves to enable platforms to make money from us, by selling our data to third parties, but also by creating media channels through which parties that are willing to pay can manipulate us to do things we wouldn't normally do or sell us stuff we don't really need. This same technology allows us to get our daily dose of post-truth news, to buy most things we want when we want them and provides us with enough information so that, with every little effort, we can find out if what we are sold is good value for money.

This almost limitless connectivity fuelled the transformation of retail, travel, media, entertainment and now the financial services industry. As we said earlier, this evolution is driven by technology, but the real fuel of innovation is customer appetite. The fact that we are using the internet and digital devices to fulfil so many needs is in large part the result of the choices we make as end-users.

Customer acceptance

It follows that customer acceptance is the next factor driving digital change in banks. We established that the device with the greatest impact on banking is the mobile phone and most of us have some version of a mobile or smartphone. These addictive devices now govern the lives of most of humanity. According to the GSMA, the global mobile network operators trade body (GSMA, 2019), and the World Bank (World Bank, 2019), the world has 5.1 billion individual phone subscriptions (of which 2.7 billion are smartphones) and only 3.8 billion bank accounts. According to financial services technology firm Fiserv (Fiserv, 2019), mobile is the fastest growing engagement channel for banks.

As we stated previously, the reason for its success in financial services is that the mobile phone completely changes the relationship between the customer and the bank. For the first time since the creation of banking, the bank is no longer a place to go to; the bank is portable and always with the customer. Even with other previously remote channels, the customer either had to physically go somewhere (to the PC for online banking) or wait for the bank to be available (telephone banking). This new mode of interaction goes beyond simple convenience. The mobile banking experience puts the customer in control. Today, customers expect to interact with their bank at their convenience, not the bank's.

This 'paradigm shift' has had a profound impact on banks. This shift in customer expectation was initially seen as a simple redirection of the branch customer engagement to an interaction that took place online. This approach may have worked in the early years of digital banking, when banks merely overlaid a thin digital veneer on their existing products and processes. But this short-sighted approach had unexpected side effects – it exposed many of the flaws and inconsistencies of the banks' processes and products that were often resolved by branch staff when they were the primary customer interface. Complex onboarding processes or inconsistent product features became completely visible to customers on the digital channels. As a result, the move online became an almost endless quest to adapt a series of products and processes to a distribution model for which they were not designed.

The customer onboarding process was designed in the 1970s for branch customers. It has remained almost unaltered in subsequent decades and was frequently criticized by bank staff. It has finally had to be redesigned as the millions of digital customers voiced their disapproval, not by complaining, but by taking their custom elsewhere. This was just the first legacy issue highlighted by digital.

As customers were offered more and more banking products online, they started accepting that online banking was 'normal'. This perception led to increased expectations of service, higher quality and consistent reliability of the experience. Bank customers today base their perception of the quality of their interaction with their bank not by comparing it with other banks – they compare it to built-for-digital businesses. The expectations of speed, simplicity and comprehensive solutions are increasingly difficult for the banks to deliver.

This new set of expectations led a number of creative entrepreneurs to believe that they could deliver banking better than the current market leaders. The entry of these new actors (protagonists) led to the third factor behind the evolution of banking: the innovative fintech entrepreneur.

Innovation and capital

Entrepreneurs started targeting financial services at about the time of the dotcom boom in the late 1990s when industries like media, travel and retail were disrupted by startups collectively called 'dotcoms' by the press. These entrepreneurs set their sights on areas where their impact on the customer could be felt more immediately, such as payments, and then later on as challengers to incumbent banks.

The first financial service targeted by entrepreneurs was indeed payments as a P2P proposition and as support for e-commerce when PayPal was founded in 1998. We must not confuse these early arrivals with the first online banking providers: the existing banks started playing around with the internet as early as 1994 with the Stamford Credit Union (Rapport, 2004), and then later in 1997 Nationwide and Royal Bank of Scotland jumped on the bandwagon (Finextra, 2007). The first actual bank challengers started emerging at the end of the 2000s. These were often simple current account equivalents and not usually banks at their inception (ie they did not have a banking licence). Businesses like Fidor in Germany and Simple in the United States were amongst the pioneers in this category. These were often led by visionary individuals who made the fact that they were *not* a bank their unique selling proposition (USP).

Entrepreneurship

The success of digital technology in disrupting so many seemingly established industries pushed entrepreneurs to target financial services more aggressively, aiming to improve on the digital offerings of the incumbents. The perception that digital technology would not disrupt (but merely enhance) the financial services industry began to be challenged by entrepreneurs leaving traditional financial services businesses to create fintech startups. A great example of this is Eloan, established in the late 1990s by Janina Pawlowski and Chris Larsen. They were both working at a mortgage lender in Palo Alto when they realized that they could improve mortgage sales (University of Rochester, 2000). They left their jobs and raised $450,000 from friends and family to launch Eloan in 1997. Janina and Chris brought their knowledge of how the sector operated and used digital technology to create a new business that was better than the incumbent. After the sale of Eloan to Banco Popular de Puerto Rico (a large Caribbean bank), Janina moved away from fintech, while Chris went on to launch Prosper Marketplace and Ripple Labs (Eloan, 2019): two further disruptive businesses in wealth management and distributed ledger technology.

A similar story happened at fintech startups across the globe – companies like Zopa (a P2P lending platform), Fidor (now a bank, then a neobank),

LendingTree (a lending marketplace), Nutmeg (an investment marketplace) and many more were founded by people involved in and knowledgeable about the financial services industry.

Capital

Initially, financial services startups had a relatively hard time finding investors, as banking was not seen as a sector that could generate the returns expected by VCs. According to research firm CB Insights (CB Insights, 2018) and consulting firm Accenture(Accenture, 2015), VC investment in fintech remained quite flat until between 2013 and 2014 when it went from around $4 billion to over $12 billion. This period has been described as the time of FOMO (fear of missing out) and saw an almost frenzied level of investing activity as funds and firms attempted to get a foot in the door of what looked like a potentially lucrative pool of investees.

During the same period, another interesting phenomenon kicked in when corporate VCs (many bank-owned) started getting interested in startups alongside other investors. Between 2013 and 2018, the investment by corporate venture capital funds (CVCs) had a four-fold increase in absolute amounts invested (CB Insights, 2018).

Investment in financial services innovation is following a different pattern to what we saw in other industries where few incumbent players invested in digital technology. We are seeing large financial services organizations invest not only in fintechs, but also in building their own capabilities. The investment in this type of change dwarfs the investment in fintech. In 2019, the global spend on IT was estimated at $270 billion (Greer *et al*, 2019). If we use a ratio close to that stated by global bank JP Morgan in 2019, between 40 and 50 per cent of their IT spend went to finance change initiatives (JP Morgan, 2019). If this ratio is applied to global IT spending by banks, the spend on innovation is over $100 billion – and this does not include non-IT digital spend in areas such as marketing, sales, finance, product and risk. The banks see the need to become more digital and they are investing in it. The question is: are they investing in the right things? To use a metaphor erroneously attributed to Henry Ford: are the banks building cars or 'faster horses'? (Vlaskovits, 2014).

Regulation

Part of the reason for this growth in entrepreneurial creativity and VC investment in the fintech sector was the perception that key regulators across the globe were taking a step back and changing their position on digital innovation in financial services. Arguably, until the financial crisis of 2007–2008 the regulators saw themselves as the preservers of the status quo. The perception was that the established financial institutions may not be terribly innovative, but at least they know what to do to stay safe. Regulators believed that the big financial institutions were relatively trustworthy. In fact, the former UK Prime Minister and Chancellor of the Exchequer (the UK's most senior finance politician), Gordon Brown, was so confident about this that in a famous speech in 2002 he said:

> With Bank of England independence, tough decisions on inflation, new fiscal rules, and hard public spending controls, we today in our country have economic stability, not boom and bust...

SOURCE Summers, 2008

So, the government and regulators felt that they had things under control. They felt little or no need to push for competition from new entrants that were using a technology – the internet – that had caused the dotcom crash of the year 2000. Furthermore, the only real impact they had seen from the direct use of technology in financial markets was the Black Monday crash in 1987, where the use of automatic computer trading algorithms was largely blamed for the debacle. Then 2007 came and an industry that was thought of as safe experienced a systemic crash on a global scale.

Across the globe, financial markets collapsed under the weight of the complex web of interconnectivity that had been built between these trusted financial institutions. This web of connections seemed to be driven by one thing: short-term greed of key individuals and of the institutions that employed them. This unprecedented financial collapse resulted in the economic slowdown of many economies and even economic contractions in a few less fortunate countries. In a relatively short time, the public's long-standing trust in the existing financial system plummeted across the globe.

This was a tough moment for regulators, who were meant to provide solutions and safeguards against such situations, as public opinion, the press and politicians started accusing them of being part of the problem. Very quickly, regulators started realizing that their policies had enabled the existing banks to behave in ways that did not support the welfare of the markets they operated in. These financial institutions, who were under-capitalized, generated such large losses that they had to ask for governments and the national central banks to pump more capital in and bail them out.

These firms not only caused the economies of the countries they operated in to be badly hit; they were also asking their governments – and therefore the taxpayer – to pay to keep them from going bust. Governments reluctantly stepped up and paid for these losses as some of the financial institutions were on the brink of collapse. The fear was that these institutions were so large and interconnected with the rest of the economy, that if they were allowed to fail, the impact to the economy would be greater than paying for their losses. They were in fact too big to fail. This led to a push to not only regulate these firms more proactively but to also make them become smaller. In fact, Alan Greenspan, the former Federal Reserve Chairman, famously said: 'If they are too big to fail – they are too big' (Dealbook, 2009).

A new mindset

In response, regulators embarked on two concurrent strategies: the first was that of increasing scrutiny and controls over the work of financial institutions, and the second was that of increasing competition. The first signs of the regulators taking action were in expanding their scrutiny and the compliance burden for the banks; two good examples of this are the Dodd–Frank Act in the USA (CFTC, 2019) and MiFID II, the second Markets in Financial Instruments Directive in Europe (ESMA, 2019). In parallel, they began campaigning for the largest players in each market to become smaller. One of the initiatives in this space centred around the genesis of support for fintechs. This took a variety of forms, from Project Innovate in the UK and Smart Financial Centre in Singapore.

Project Innovate was created by the UK regulator, the Financial Conduct Authority, to provide support to fintech startups to test and refine their propositions (FCA, 2018). This included the FCA Sandbox, launched in 2016, which provides a monitored environment for fintechs and incumbents to work together on testing and developing innovative solutions for the financial services industry. As of 2019, 375 had applied to enter the Sandbox and 118 companies had been accepted to enter the programme (FCA, 2019a).

Similarly, in Singapore the Monetary Authority of Singapore (MAS) launched the Smart Financial Centre to provide a forum for fintech startups to explore and understand the regulatory environment and encourage competition in the sector, while safeguarding the rights of the public and professional bodies.

In 2018 MAS and the FCA joined forces with 11 other national regulators from countries including the United States, Canada, Australia, and Hong Kong, plus the World Bank, to create the Global Financial Innovation Network (GFIN), a global Sandbox with the explicit scope of understanding, supporting and regulating innovation in financial services. The goals of GFIN are to:

> Act as a network of regulators to collaborate, sharing experience and best practice, and communicate to firms; provide a forum for joint policy work; and provide firms with an environment in which to trial cross-border solutions (business to consumer (B2C) or business to business (B2B)).
>
> SOURCE FCA, 2019b

Not bad for regulators.

What is driving innovation?

The next chapter in the evolution of banking is being written now. As the incumbents and most fintechs battle it out for digital banking supremacy, a new type of contender is emerging. These are the agents of real disruptions, whose use of technologies such as robotic process automation, blockchain and DLT (distributed ledger technology), cryptocurrencies, AI (artificial intelligence) and many more will create a whole new wave of disruption in the financial services industry. This disruption will be further enhanced by the expected entry of a new type of contender: the Big Tech firm. The likes of GAFA (Google, Apple, Facebook and Amazon), their Chinese counterparts BAT (Baidu, Alibaba and Tencent) or even PayU in South Africa and Paytm in India, are either already financial services players or have announced that they will be soon. They have brand, customers, data and capital to spend.

All of these new contenders are there to help the customer engage with their finances better and they aim to make huge profits by doing this better than the banks. The incumbents and many fintechs believe that customers want to buy financial products. The reality is that customers do not see a financial product as an end – they see it as a means to an end. These new contenders will focus on addressing these needs. We will discuss these needs in Chapter 3.

References

Antioco, J (2014) How I did it: Blockbuster's former CEO on sparring with an activist shareholder, *Harvard Business Review*, 1 August, hbr.org/2011/04/how-i-did-it-blockbusters-former-ceo-on-sparring-with-an-activist-shareholder (archived at https://perma.cc/V5MY-KEVB)

Accenture (2015) *The Future of FinTech and Banking: Global fin tech investment triples in 2014*, CB Insights Research, 26 March, www.cbinsights.com/research/fintech-and-banking-accenture/ (archived at https://perma.cc/T8T2-HY4D)

Baringa (2016) UK current account market: the start of the revolution? www.baringa.com/en/insights-news/points-of-view/uk-current-account-market-start-revolution/ (archived at https://perma.cc/3SJ6-KDV3)

CB Insights (2018) *The 2018 Global Corporate Venture Capital Report*, CB Insights Research, www.cbinsights.com/research/report/corporate-venture-capital-trends-2018/ (archived at https://perma.cc/NWM2-P7X5)

CFTC (2019) Rulemaking Areas, US Commodity Futures Trading Commission, cftc.gov/LawRegulation/DoddFrankAct/Rulemakings/index.htm (archived at https://perma.cc/K6VY-GJVY)

Dealbook (2009) Greenspan calls to break up banks 'too big to fail', *The New York Times*, 15 October, dealbook.nytimes.com/2009/10/15/greenspan-break-up-banks-too-big-to-fail/ (archived at https://perma.cc/7AJ9-MLWG)

Deloitte (2018) Accelerating digital transformation in banking, *Deloitte Insights*, www2.deloitte.com/us/en/insights/industry/financial-services/digital-transformation-in-banking-global-customer-survey.html (archived at https://perma.cc/WK7K-QFJE)

Eloan (2019) Here's Why Eloan Was Founded, www.eloan.com/blog/personal-finance/heres-why-eloan-was-founded (archived at https://perma.cc/J884-4GDY)

ESMA (2019) MiFID II, www.esma.europa.eu/policy-rules/mifid-ii-and-mifir (archived at https://perma.cc/N8PV-TUN2)

FCA (2018) FCA Innovation: Fintech, regtech and innovative businesses, 20 December, www.fca.org.uk/firms/innovation (archived at https://perma.cc/EV2J-W7WU)

FCA (2019b) Global Financial Innovation Network Consultation, 31 January, www.fca.org.uk/publications/consultation-papers/global-financial-innovation-network (archived at https://perma.cc/4WEK-Y59P)

FCA (2019a) Regulatory Sandbox, 20 December, www.fca.org.uk/firms/innovation/regulatory-sandbox (archived at https://perma.cc/C3T8-CK9R)

Finextra (2007) *Who Launched the UK's First Internet Bank?* Finextra Research, 23 May, www.finextra.com/blogposting/237/who-launched-the-uks-first-internet-bank (archived at https://perma.cc/43U4-ZQMV)

Fiserv (2019) 2019 Expectations & Experiences: Consumer Payments, www.fiserv.com/en/about-fiserv/resource-center/consumer-research/2019-expectations-and-experiences-consumer-payments.html (archived at https://perma.cc/PL7E-ZLE2)

Gartner (2019) Gartner forecasts worldwide information security spending to exceed $124 billion in 2019, www.gartner.com/en/newsroom/press-releases/2018-08-15-gartner-forecasts-worldwide-information-security-spending-to-exceed-124-billion-in-2019 (archived at https://perma.cc/JK5V-G4TT)

Greer, S, Lodge, G, Mazzini, J and Yanagawa, E (2019) Global Tech Spending Forecast: Banking Edition, 2019, Celent, 28 March, www.celent.com/insights/964486482 (archived at https://perma.cc/22G3-H48Y)

GSMA (2019) The Mobile Economy 2019, www.gsma.com/r/mobileeconomy/ (archived at https://perma.cc/HN5M-4KF3)

JP Morgan (2019) Event Calendar, www.jpmorganchase.com/corporate/investor-relations/event-calendar.htm (archived at https://perma.cc/B8W6-VCJE)

Kaspersky.com (2017) www.kaspersky.com/about/press-releases/2017_banks-spends (archived at https://perma.cc/88UD-UUDC)

Local Data Company (2018) Retail and Leisure Analysis: 2017/18, *Market Research for the UK Retail Sector*, www.localdatacompany.com/download-ldcs-latest-retail-leisure-trends-report-2017/18 (archived at https://perma.cc/2N7S-ZUQX)

Megaw, N (2019) Cyber attacks on financial services sector rise fivefold in 2018, *Financial Times*, 25 February, www.ft.com/content/6a2d9d76-3692-11e9-bd3a-8b2a211d90d5 (archived at https://perma.cc/5EGH-YU5P)

NCTA (2016) A history of speed as the world wide web turns 25, The Internet and Television Association, 25 August, www.ncta.com/whats-new/a-history-of-speed-as-the-internet-turns-25 (archived at https://perma.cc/ZH6A-RJGF)

Rapport, M (2004) Stanford FCU set to mark 10-year anniversary as first financial to offer online banking, *Credit Union Times*, 3 February, www.cutimes.com/2004/02/03/stanford-fcu-set-to-mark-10-year-anniversary-as-first-financial-to-offer-online-banking/?slreturn=20190508064622 (archived at https://perma.cc/5VBQ-GBKF)

Satell, G (2018) How Blockbuster, Kodak and Xerox really failed (it's not what you think), *Inc.com*, 7 July 2018, www.inc.com/greg-satell/pundits-love-to-tell-these-three-famous-innovation-stories-none-of-them-are-true.html (archived at https://perma.cc/7CLX-6U4L)

Summers, D (2008) 'No return to boom and bust': What Brown said when he was chancellor, *The Guardian*, 11 September, www.theguardian.com/politics/2008/sep/11/gordonbrown.economy (archived at https://perma.cc/W3V5-D86L)

University of Rochester (2000) *Rochester Review*, www.rochester.edu/pr/Review/V62N3/feature6.html (archived at https://perma.cc/BDH3-4GYQ)

Vlaskovits, Patrick (2014) Henry Ford, Innovation, and That 'Faster Horse' Quote, *Harvard Business Review*, 23 July, hbr.org/2011/08/henry-ford-never-said-the-fast (archived at https://perma.cc/2KZU-6HD4)

W3.org (1989) Information Management: A Proposal, The Original Proposal of the WWW, HTMLized, www.w3.org/History/1989/proposal.html (archived at https://perma.cc/L2Q7-VLVP)

World Bank (2019) Account Ownership at a Financial Institution or with a Mobile-Money-Service Provider (% of Population Ages 15+), data.worldbank.org/indicator/FX.OWN.TOTL.ZS?end=2017&start=2011&view=chart&year_high_desc=true (archived at https://perma.cc/G353-YSV6)

03

The Shape of the Perfect Neobank

What does disruption look like?

When Russell Solomon opened the first Tower Records store in Sacramento in 1960 (McFadden, 2018), his aim was to sell vinyl records, not to start a retailing revolution. He wanted to fulfil a basic need of his customers: to listen to the music they liked when they liked. He therefore created a business that fulfilled the needs of the customer in the best way possible, considering what was possible technologically at the time. To achieve their goals, they would have to buy records. So Solomon created a great, and (at the time) successful, chain of stores that revolutionized the music purchasing process, and enabled customers to make the tedium of leaving home, travelling to a store, selecting and purchasing the record, taking it home, putting it on the turntable and finally listening to it, bearable.

He realized that he needed to make the process fun, so he transformed his stores into a destination for music-lovers. Tower Records stores were so good that even celebrities such as Bruce Springsteen, Bette Midler, Lou Reed and Michael Jackson were known to love going to his stores. But eventually his customers wanted something different.

Disruption starts

Russell adapted his business to new technology as well as he could. Tower started selling music Track-8 and cassettes in addition to vinyl records and eventually in the 1980s it started stocking the first digital music product: the CD. This was when the problems started.

Innovative individuals relaxed about music rights created the means to download this music from CDs and then distribute it illegally on platforms

FIGURE 3.1 Former entrance to Tower Records in London's Piccadilly Circus

like Napster. This had a real impact on the music industry and Tower was not immune. But the real trouble began in 2001 when technology firms like Apple and Zune created a proposition that made music downloading legal. These businesses enabled customers to buy music without going to a store. Tower Records could not challenge these without cannibalizing their core business. They responded as well as they could, but they eventually went bankrupt in 2004 (Figure 3.1). Disruption in the music industry did not stop there. Two years later, in 2006, Spotify was founded, giving access to much of the world's recorded music by paying a simple monthly fee.

Understanding the customer

One of the most important outcomes of the digital revolution is that it allows its users to fulfil basic needs. The purpose of giving money to the likes of Tower Records was not to buy a record – the purpose was to listen to music. The digital revolution enabled new business models to be created that deliver exactly that functionality. Businesses like iTunes and Spotify completely disintermediated the path from artist to fan. In the Spotify model the customer need is at the centre of their offering. Today, the whole music industry is centred around enabling the end-user to get to the music they want when they want. In the process, music streaming has revolutionized an industry. The profit pools have changed in size and location and established members of the music industry value chain have disappeared.

The impact of digital on the music industry has been profound. According to the International Federation of the Phonographic Industry (IFPI, 2018), music revenues from the sales of physical records and CDs between 1999 and 2018 went from $26 billion to less than $5 billion, and in the process of this decline, the music retailer has practically disappeared (goodbye to Tower Records and Virgin Music Stores). Sadly, we have also lost the club-like atmosphere of the mythical Tower Records stores including the ones in LA's Westwood, New York's 4th and Broadway, or London's Piccadilly Circus and the sheer chic scale of Virgin Music on the Champs-Élysées. These outlets have been replaced by a myriad of music and media blogs such as Pitchfork (pitchfork.com) and Hypebot (hypebot.com) – social platforms that are shared between friends and by the AI-based suggestive music streaming services such as Spotify's 'Discover Weekly' (Spotify, 2020) play-list suggestions, based on the music their member has listened to in the past. The era of the music store as a key link between artists and fans is over.

Similar tales of transformation can be found in other industries. The travel, retail and media industries – to name a few – are unrecognizable from what they were a few decades ago. A bit late to the party perhaps, this same industry re-think is now happening in financial services and banking.

The question is: if the incumbent banks are Tower Records and the challenger banks are iTunes, then who is Spotify?

Why customers need banking

Digital is allowing bank customers – both retail (individual) and business – to reconnect with the real reasons they seek banking and finance. Customers do not need or want financial products; they seek the outcomes these products enable them to obtain and achieve. As with the music industry, digital is disrupting business models in banking. The view is now much more customer-centric in both product and service design and delivery. The early relationship banks understood clearly that they were providing the means to an end. This changed slowly with the arrival of the industrial bank and the IT bank.

The first banks were clearly aware that they were selling outcomes and not products. The merchant talking to the Medici Bank in Florence did not want a loan – he wanted to be able to buy a shipment of silk in China to resell in Italy for a profit. People with surplus cash who gave their money to a bank did want to buy an investment product – they wanted their money to be safe and to be able to get a return for their trust in the bank. Both customers at some point wanted to send or receive money safely and cheaply.

Dealing with complexity

As societies became more complex, banking followed suit, creating an ever more complex set of products and services to offer their customers. In a similar way to the music retail industry, bankers often forget that, for their customers, banking is a means to an end and that few customers aspire to own a bank product. They want what the product enables them to do – just as Tower Records thought that their customers wanted to buy CDs and LPs when they simply wanted to listen to the music they loved. Today, many banks behave as if their customers want to buy personal loans, investment funds and international payments.

Banks should keep in mind that, fundamentally, people need a combination of only three things. As in the early days of money, customers' basic financial needs remain the same:

- they need to pay someone;
- they have a surplus of cash and they want to protect it;
- they want to do something they don't have enough money for.

What they want is for their bank to be a trusted friend and ally who will allow them to do these three things quickly, cheaply, safely and intelligently.

The perfect 'neobank' would be just that at its core.

The perfect neobank

Digital disruption and capabilities allow us to re-think banking and provide us with the biggest fintech innovation challenge of all; if we could completely redesign banking and make it new or 'neo', what would we do? What would the perfect neobank look like?

The best place to start would be with customers and how they see banking products – not as an end but as the means to achieve their goals.

As a first step let us go back to first principles. A redesigned bank ought to be truly customer-centric. It would not be concerned with selling products but with meeting customers' basic financial needs – keeping in mind that these are always means to an end. No one needs a financial product – customers need what the financial product enables them to do.

The perfect neobank would offer only three product groups designed around customer needs (Figure 3.2). These products would be coordinated by a layer of data and intelligence that would provide insight on how the customer could best manage their finances.

The three business products would be:

- a universal payments account;
- a capital protection tool;
- a master credit line.

FIGURE 3.2 Components of the perfect neobank

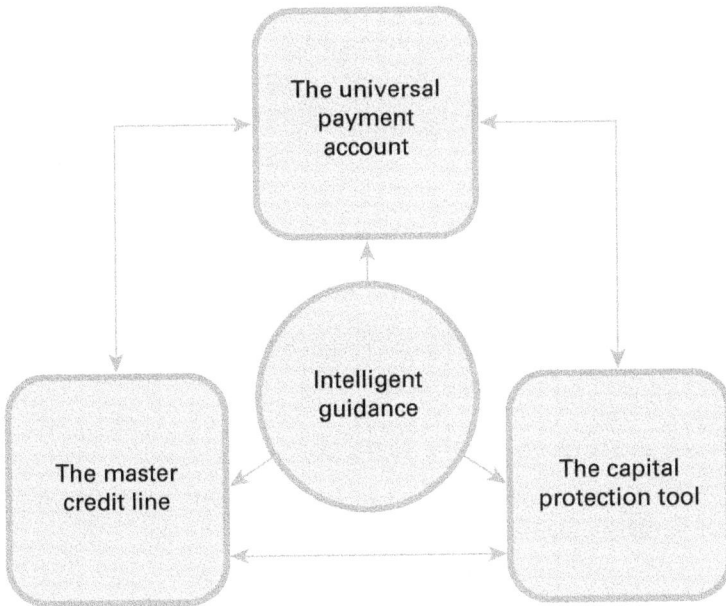

1. The universal payments account

As previously stated, one of the core features of banking – from its inception to today – is the ability to help the customer safely pay a third party. In general, customers have little interest in the mechanics of how the customer is paid. They simply want to be able to either see money leave or arrive in their account, as appropriate, and exactly as they expect the transaction to occur. The four components of a payment solution are: simplicity of use, cost effectiveness, transparency of requirements and speed.

EASE OF USE

This account should be straightforward and easy for customers to use. At its core it would hold a current or checking account equivalent where all the cash flows coming to and from the customer can be captured, analysed, visualized and managed.

COST EFFECTIVENESS

This account must make it easy for the customer to pay for things in the 'best' way possible. The word best is in quotations because the ideal bank should not bother the customers with choosing the means of payment; they should suggest the most appropriate way to pay to the customer. For example, if the customer is an individual who is travelling and needs to pay for their hotel bill, the bank should automatically route the customer to pay with their (for example) American Express card because in this instance that card offers a better exchange rate, points and settlement at the end of the month rather than using their own domestic bank cards with a terrible exchange rate. If the customer is an SME (small or medium-sized enterprise) that needs to pay a legal firm in a foreign country, the bank should direct the customer to the cheapest and fastest money transfer provider possible – even if this is not their own international payments service.

ONE-STOP-SHOP

Ideally a customer would be able to seamlessly use any payment device, channel, process and method they wish — including cheques and cash. Imagine a neobank account that when opened, automatically:

- provides you with the means to pay merchants that offer Visa, MasterCard, Amex, Discover, JCB and China Union Pay or any other scheme relevant in your market;

- opens you accounts on PayPal, Skrill, iTunes and any other relevant wallet;

- updates your phone so that Paym, Apple Pay, Google Wallet, Alipay, Paytm, PayU or whatever Amazon comes up with work;

- taps into a sleek, efficient, new instant bank-to-bank payments solution (think iDeal but better) that eventually may even make the card schemes obsolete;

- works with third parties that allow them to pay more efficiently in markets and segments they are not competitive in (TransferWise and Revolut are just two examples of these).

This solution would be seamless and easy to use, with no hidden fees. This does not mean no fees: the neobanks will clearly define and explain what they are charging for their services and why – no hidden transaction fees or penalties. It would be simple to manage so that the customer could have complete control in choosing how each payment is funded. If they don't want to choose themselves, they can count on the neobank to make the right choice on their behalf, knowing that it will always choose the lowest-cost option for them.

Today, we are seeing companies that are striving to build similar capabilities (Table 3.1). Good examples are PayPal, Apple Pay and the Curve card (an innovative London-based payments wallet). All three allow you to add multiple funding sources to their offering:

- PayPal's offering is predominantly online (with few exceptions on checkout you are redirected and offered to select your preferred funding source – that can be a card, bank account or stored value).

TABLE 3.1 Comparing innovative payments innovators

	APPLE PAY	PAYPAL	CURVE
Card Funding	Debit & Credit	Debit & Credit	Debit & Credit
Bank Funding	No	Yes	No
Stored Value	No	Yes	No
App Payments	Yes	No	No
Physical Card	No*	No	Yes
Payment Redirection	No	No	Yes

*Upcoming Apple card will offer a physical card
Reproduced with kind permission of Pacemakers Ltd

- Apple Pay (similar to Android Pay, Samsung Pay, etc) allows the customer to virtualize a number of payment cards, linked to the different bank accounts and to select the payment type they prefer when paying with their phone at a point-of-sale (POS) or online when using Apple devices.
- Curve (www.curve.app/en-gb) offers the features of Apple Pay delivered through a physical card. It allows customers to upload a number of cards onto their platform and then lets them select which card is billed when the Curve card is used at a POS or online. The distinctive feature of Curve is that if the user wants to redirect a transaction from one stored card to another they can do so. Curve allows customers to change funding source when the transaction has *already* happened.

These three examples offer a better UX than the incumbent banks are able or willing to do by simply focusing on customer outcome. That said, they could push the envelope further. All three of these providers have enough data at their disposal to provide information to their users on which funding source would be the best to use for every specific transaction in terms of speed, cost or many other perspectives. They are not doing so today.

These three and many more providers are offering customers information and insight on payments from another point of view – usage. Personal financial management (PFM) is offered by many payment providers. In its simplest form it provides a categorization of the spend based on the type or merchant. These services allow customers to get a better grip on their finances by understanding how they spend. From Lloyds Bank in the UK to N26 in Germany to DBS in Singapore, most banks – big and small – are providing some type of PFM.

Very few, however, take a further step forward. Those that do take this step prompt their customers on how to manage money better, predicting overdrawn accounts or highlighting funds that are not earning income, making it very easy for the customer to make the most from their funds. Simple Bank in the United States and Monzo in the UK have done some interesting work in this area. The neobank will make the financial wellbeing of their customers a fundamental objective.

These accounts also allow customers to instantly transfer currencies internationally directly to the end recipient. At the point of making a foreign exchange transaction the customer will know exactly how much it will cost her and she will feel confident that the bank will charge her a rate that is fair and competitive. Similar to what TransferWise does, only easier.

Of course, this system provides the latest fraud prevention techniques including high-speed data analysis and latest generation biometrics, without adding any complexity to the transaction.

A similar set of services should be offered to businesses. In most countries, domestic payments work relatively well for both small and large firms; cross-border payments are a different story. Whereas large businesses are able to dedicate time and resources to optimize payments, small businesses are not able to do so.

INTERNATIONAL PAYMENTS

The real money in payments is in the cross-border space. Consulting firm McKinsey and payment processor SWIFT estimate that banks earn margins of 6 per cent on consumer-to-consumer (C2C) payments compared to 0.1 per cent for B2B payments, so most smaller SMEs end up using the processes set up for consumers (McKinsey, 2018). Small businesses do not have the dedicated resources needed to minimize payment costs, so they are frequently using payment solutions that are not best suited to their needs. What they need is a bank that provides them with a service that allows them to choose the most appropriate payment option every time. Unsurprisingly, large firms would appreciate this also. If their bank always provided them with the best payment option, they could use the staff dedicated to payments somewhere else in the firm.

Overall, the universal payments account will offer its customers, consumers, SMEs and corporates a UX that is better than any other proposition out there. 'Good enough' doesn't get customers to switch – 'better' does. UX is the key to customer adoption. And if trends are to be believed it will be delivered almost exclusively on a mobile device.

When looked at holistically, the universal payment account could seem a counterintuitive proposition for a bank to offer. Why would a bank want to provide customers with access to the offering of its competitors? When seen from the perspective of the industrial bank or the IT bank this is absolutely true, but this is no longer the case with the digital bank. In a digital world where customers have much greater choice and much greater ease of movement, owning and retaining the relationship with the most desirable customers is a key objective.

Let us challenge the traditional banking paradigm further by taking a closer look at the second basic need of banking customers: to protect and grow their excess capital.

2. The capital protection tool

Customers with surplus capital want to protect it and, if possible, try to earn a reasonable return on it. The objective for this is not to protect the cash itself, but to safeguard the freedom of choice that it enables. As previously stated, having capital that exceeds immediate needs enables a consumer or a business to choose amongst a much wider range of purchase or investment options than would otherwise be available to them. As a consumer, I can choose to buy a bigger house, go to a better school or deal with an unexpected illness. As a business, capital gives owners the ability to choose strategic options that are more ambitious without necessarily putting the business at risk if the anticipated benefits do not materialize.

The 'protecting capital' needs of a banking customer can be grouped into four main objectives:

- protect enough to cover current needs;
- grow some capital with varying expectations of return and security;
- plan for less productive years;
- prepare for the unexpected.

These roughly equate to savings, investments, pensions and insurance (Figure 3.3).

FIGURE 3.3 Objectives of the capital protection tool in the perfect neobank

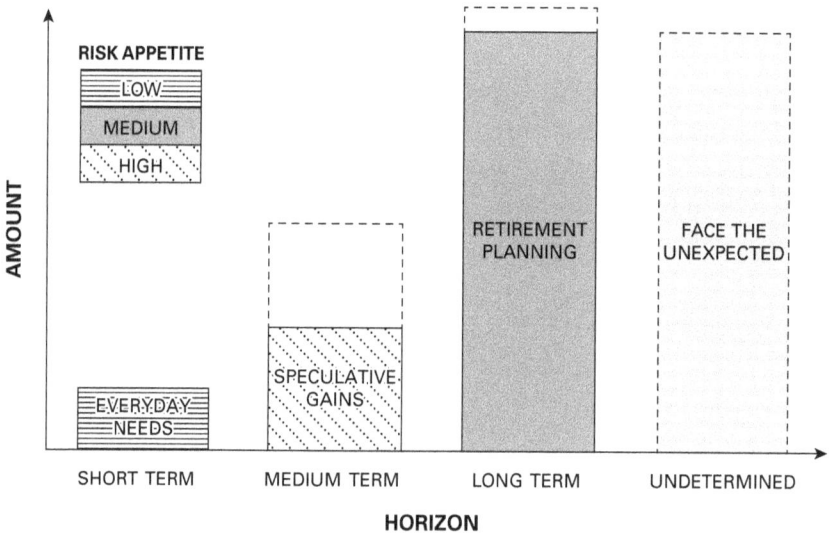

The traditional approach of banks when looking at these four areas is to provide advice and to direct customers to a set of products within the bank's portfolio that fits their needs. For most banks, when dealing with this basic need, what matters most is the selling of savings, investment and protection products that they manufacture.

WHOLE-OF-MARKET PERSPECTIVE

In a world where customers can get a whole-of-market view of any invest-ment, pension or insurance product with just a few clicks, only offering in-house products to customers is a risky decision. When customers see that their bank is not offering them a good proposition and/or making it hard for them to get a better product they will not appreciate it. Before digital bank-ing, customers had to work hard to get a whole-of-market perspective on products and pricing, and banks could get away with impunity in creating the impression that their offering was the same or better than other provid-ers. Today, this is no longer the case and institutions that do not realize this are not going to be left unchallenged.

Furthermore, the customer 'inertia' that many banks rely on is also fading. Historically, customers are more likely to change life partner than change bank account (Evans, 2013). Two things are changing this: first, digital banks make opening a new bank account very easy; secondly, regulation is making account switching easier than ever. New legislation such as the PSD2 has account portability at its core (European Commission, 2017). In the UK, CASS (or the Current Account Switching Service) (BACS, 2020) offers a seven-day account switching service, which is adding to the increasing numbers of customers voting with their feet. Without the customer inertia, disgruntled bank customers can easily ditch the banks that do not meet their expectations for those that do.

The capital protection tool offered by the neobanks would act as trusted adviser, using digital technology to help their customers create the best port-folio of savings, investment, pensions and insurance products to deliver on the customer's objectives. The tool would illustrate the likely outcomes of choices available to their customers through simple visualizations using the customer's actual data modelled on the different financial propositions available to them. These scenarios would enable customers to toggle between different options to create the end-result that best suited their needs. The tool would also be populated with the customer's actual transactional data and provide insight that is personalized to the clients' needs, providing customers with the means to make a better decision.

Customers will be provided with complete access to all savings and investment, pension and insurance products available to them in their market. This access would also include the ability to buy any product seamlessly through the tool. The neobank would manage authentication, verification and payment processing as required. The range of products will include P2P crowdfunded investments and, if available, the nascent P2P insurance offering.

The neobank's approach to savings, investments, protection and insurance is to act as the only place where the customer can get transparency, customized guidance and ease of execution. The tool would also provide a single aggregation point for the customer where they can get a complete overview of their holdings, the cost of these holdings and scenarios of different outcomes.

The capital protection tool would operate as a robo-adviser (an automated financial adviser), a marketplace, a broker and more, all wrapped into one. No business is attempting to do something similar. Some are doing it in the investments space – a few examples are new digital wealth management businesses like Betterment in the United States (www.betterment.com), Nutmeg in the UK (www.nutmeg.com) and Wacai in China (www.wacai.com), just to name a few.

This leads us to the last pillar of the neobank: the master credit line.

3. The master credit line

Unsurprisingly, customers can have different credit needs. These differ by things such as size, duration and urgency. The relationship bank understood this and the credit line that was provided by the early banks was not called an overdraft, personal loan, credit card, car loan, mortgage, growth capital or equipment financing – it was simply a line of credit.

The characteristics of the credit line were based on the banker understanding the customer's needs. This was a facility uniquely designed to meet the needs of the customer while meeting the return targets and risk appetite of the bank. At the discretion of the banker, this facility would have terms, conditions, costs and, if required, collateral. The product was custom-made to meet the lender's and the borrower's needs.

This relatively simplistic, but mutually beneficial arrangement all changed as banking evolved. The industrial and IT banks could not create bespoke products. So the credit line was broken up into a myriad of products that we call 'lending' today. Furthermore, flexibility in setting the terms of each of these products was taken away from the banker and transferred to product,

THE SHAPE OF THE PERFECT NEOBANK 49

operations and risk teams that did not directly engage with customers. These lending propositions were sold in branch as if they were physical products and customers were to choose – with some help by the branch staff – which product was right for them. In parallel, bankers started believing that an approach that was created to meet their own needs was what their customers wanted. Through a somewhat myopic lens, bankers started believing that customers craved loans and mortgages while they were actually craving fun holidays and cosy homes. In reality, customers just wanted some financial help to achieve their goals.

ALL BORROWING IN ONE PLACE

The master credit line would allow customers to manage all their needs with one master credit line serviced through one single periodic payment (daily, weekly, monthly) of whatever the bank and the customer agree on. Customers would start their line with the ability to spend a little more than their holdings (overdraft). As their needs grew customers would let their bank know and the bank would extend them a credit line, for example, to go on holiday. The bank could also require that this be paid back within a given number of months. The client would still pay one bill for this facility.

If the customer's needs grow, provided the bank felt they had the right means and behaviours (eg servicing a previous facility as agreed), they would be extended a larger credit line. Where appropriate, these facilities would be matched with conditions and potentially liens to items, goods and properties as required by the bank. This would apply to consumers' personal loans, car loans, mortgages or businesses' enterprise loans, equipment financing or property deals. The bank would of course also always reserve the right to say 'no' to the borrower if they felt that the product was not 'right' for the customer of the bank.

For customers this would be a game-changing proposition. They would get one monthly bill for all their borrowing on a facility that allows them to achieve all their objectives without all the complexity of understanding separate credit products: the bank is simply lending them the money they need.

From the customer's perspective, the bank is their ally, making it easier for them to achieve their goals. From the bank's perspective, they will have created an extremely satisfied customer with little appetite to move. Obviously, risk management and affordability parameters apply, and if the customer's circumstances change, costs or size of the facility may change. But in every case the customer will be informed with adequate notice with clear guidelines on how to address the problem.

With this proposition, customers would have an incentive to consolidate their credit needs in one place, so overall the neobank would own a greater share of the customer wallet. Product by product, the profitability of certain individual products may be lower but this would be counterbalanced by a deeper relationship and trust benefits.

The profitability of the master credit line is an interesting challenge for the neobank. The main driver would be, firstly, retention. After all, converting a master credit line into a portfolio of credit products would be something few customers would have an appetite for. Most customers would opt to remain rather than venture elsewhere.

The second driver is inevitability. As with the music industry and Spotify, the neobank must decide whether the master credit line is inevitable or not. If they decide that it is inevitable, then it would be better for them to offer it rather being disintermediated by a new firm or a big tech firm like Google, Apple, Facebook, Amazon, Baidu, Alibaba or Tencent.

The last element to bring everything together is guidance and advice (regulated or not). This can be called 'intelligent guidance'.

Intelligent guidance

What brings everything together is intelligent guidance: a smart layer that would provide the customer with a perspective through which he can make a smart decision about his money (Figure 3.4). This service would prompt the customer when a decision is urgent (for example, closing of the tax year), alert them when they are paying too much for something (for example, an overdraft is more expensive than a personal loan) and using the functionality made possible by open banking (thank you PSD2) to provide them with insight not only on the financial products they hold with the neobank but also those held at other banks and financial institutions.

Banks have access to unique data sets that are unparalleled in breadth, depth and complexity. This data has a number of different dimensions:

- **Personal financial data in-house:** This is the financial data generated by specific customers when using the bank's services. This is personalized data but limited to the products that the customer holds with the bank.

- **Personal financial data everywhere:** This is financial data created by customers when they use financial products provided by other banks. Competitive and regulatory pressures are forcing banks across the globe to share their customers' data if customers agree to it. The emerging wave

FIGURE 3.4 The data map of the neobank intelligent guidance tool

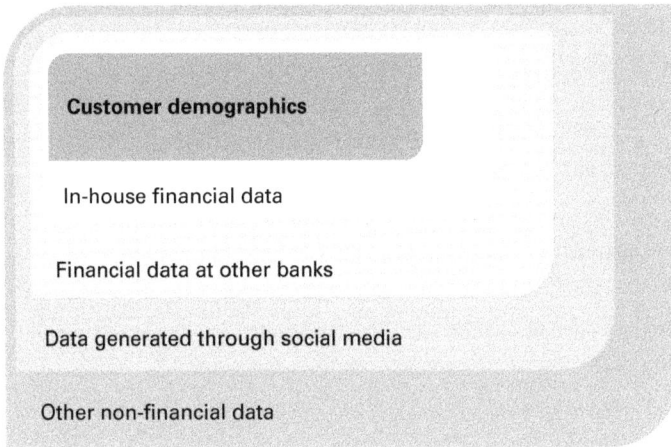

Customer demographics

In-house financial data

Financial data at other banks

Data generated through social media

Other non-financial data

of banking APIs (application programming interface – a software intermediary that allows two applications to talk to each other) will make it possible for a bank to access customer data on their competitors' platforms (Mulesoft, 2018).

- **Social-media-generated data:** By having access to the data generated by millions of customers while using social media, the banks can create predictive models that can be applied to each customer's hypothesizing needs, expectations and behaviours. This data can also be used to refine the way each customer is interacted with.

- **Other non-financial data:** A customer's financial decisions are driven by their lifestyle. Today, customers leave a huge trail of behavioural data that can be used (if permitted by the individual person or business) to better serve them. This data includes areas like educational information, professional experience, medical data, commuting patterns and much more. This data creates a vast array of information that is distributed across the web, and with modern technology and with the end-user's consent, it can be used to provide valuable insight.

THE CHALLENGE FOR REGULATORS

By using these data in conjunction with the emerging AI capabilities, banks can provide their customers with insight that is comparable to that provided by the banker in the early relationship banks, based on a deep understanding of the customer, their environment and their goals. This service would not simply advise a course of action – it would provide the data (and maybe simplify the execution) so that the customer can get the most out of their finances. The bank is no longer a seller of services – it becomes a partner for the long term.

The implications of this approach will have to be understood clearly on a case-by-case basis and the neobank will have to comply with all regulation associated with advised sales of financial products. Clearly, in order to deliver this service at its full potential, discussions need to be had with the different regulators. Today, regulation of financial advice is designed to protect the customer, but it is not making the most of the possibilities offered by well-designed robo-advice and AI. Ultimately, without a good automated advice solution in place, customers will be harmed.

A concept – not a product

The concept of the neobank is intended to be simplistic and sketchy – we don't have all the answers on how it could be delivered. Challenges are numerous: IT and operational delivery will be complex, the product-centric organization of most modern banks would have to be replaced, the path to profitability is not obvious, and, last but not least, support from the regulator is not a foregone conclusion.

All that considered, banks are slowly appreciating (we would hope) that to really meet their customers' needs they need to start thinking of themselves as enablers rather than as retailers. To do so they will need to profoundly alter their business model to one based on the guiding principles of transparency, openness, fairness, affordability and ease of use. Cosmetic tweaks are not enough. A better-designed app will not cut it in the long term.

Done right, however, this new model will deliver growth, customer satisfaction and... sustainable profitability.

References

BACS (2020) Banks and building societies signed-up to the current account switch service, www.currentaccountswitch.co.uk/banksandbuildingsocieties/Pages/banks.aspx (archived at https://perma.cc/Q9SV-XHH4)

Evans, R (2013) Why are we so afraid to switch banks? *The Telegraph*, 16 September, www.telegraph.co.uk/finance/personalfinance/10313019/Why-are-we-so-afraid-to-switch-banks.html (archived at https://perma.cc/UK9Z-Q6SD)

European Commission (2017) Payment Services Directive (PSD2): Regulatory technical standards (RTS) enabling consumers to benefit from safer and more innovative electronic payments, European Commission Press Release, europa. eu/rapid/press-release_MEMO-17-4961_en.htm (archived at https://perma.cc/ UQZ2-THSA)

IFPI (2018) Representing the recording industry worldwide, IFPI Global Music Report, www.ifpi.org/downloads/GMR2018.pdf (archived at https://perma.cc/ GTT4-SGV9)

McFadden, R (2018) Russ Solomon, founder of Tower Records, dies at 92, *The New York Times,* 5 March, www.nytimes.com/2018/03/05/obituaries/russell-solomon-founder-of-tower-records-dies-at-92.html (archived at https://perma.cc/ UA2L-M8HJ)

McKinsey (2018) A Vision for the Future of Cross-Border Payments, McKinsey & Company, www.mckinsey.com/industries/financial-services/our-insights/a-vision-for-the-future-of-cross-border-payments (archived at https://perma.cc/J4W9-Y8UZ)

Mulesoft (2018) What Is an API? (Application Programming Interface), MuleSoft, 14 February, www.mulesoft.com/resources/api/what-is-an-api (archived at https://perma.cc/DQL8-YDAZ)

Spotify (2020) *Discover Weekly,* www.spotify.com/discoverweekly/ (archived at https://perma.cc/9PD5-B8UP)

04

The Journey from Bricks and Mortar to Digital

The consensus in the industry is that digital innovation will change banking beyond recognition. Like retailers, travel agents and record companies before them, banks will soon be transformed. In fact, it is surprising it has taken almost 20 years from the dotcom boom for digital innovation to disrupt financial services, as banking is the ultimate digital product:

- it does not require physical delivery – loans, savings accounts and current accounts are inherently non-physical;
- it can be configured based on customer needs and circumstances offering a perfectly personalized offering for each customer;
- it benefits from being delivered at the point of need – you do not need to be in a bank branch to enjoy an overdraft or benefit from travel insurance.

As digital technology becomes more widely adopted by end-users, better understood by regulators and – most importantly – more secure, banks and financial institutions are slowly reinventing themselves.

In the next few years we can expect to see the financial services market dominated by two types of entities: the new entrants that have made it and the incumbents that have adapted. What will be missing in the future marketplace are the new entrants that were not able to gain traction and incumbents that were not able to adapt to the new reality.

The surviving incumbents will have gone through a transformation process that will have pushed them to challenge some of their most fundamental core strengths: consistency, reliability, repeatability and standardization – all traits that made the industrial bank and the IT bank successful. Unfortunately, these characteristics are not what comes to mind as core skills for a business that needs to adapt to an evolving industry.

Phases of digital transformation

With digital transformation, some of these characteristics are proving to be liabilities for banks that want to evolve. The incumbents' challenge is how to reconcile the need to change with behaviours and characteristics that support a well-established business-as-usual (BAU) operating model. Incumbent banks realize that changing operating model without disrupting BAU is far from easy. As it becomes clear that the benefits of change are greater than those of stability, most incumbents are approaching digital innovation in some form. A study by global strategy consulting firm McKinsey (Broeders and Khanna, 2015) reports that banks can expect two outcomes from digital transformation. On average the incumbents can expect a fall in margins equal to 35 per cent of net profits due to competitive pressures, margin compression and increased operational risk. They can also expect a growth in margins of 45 per cent of net profits due to new products, new channels and new servicing capabilities. So, adopting digital change can yield an upside of 10 per cent of net profits. Banks increasingly see digital innovation as both an opportunity and a risk – with the 'do-nothing' option as the worst possible strategic option. So, most incumbent banks are developing their own digital capabilities.

FIGURE 4.1 Three phases of digital evolution

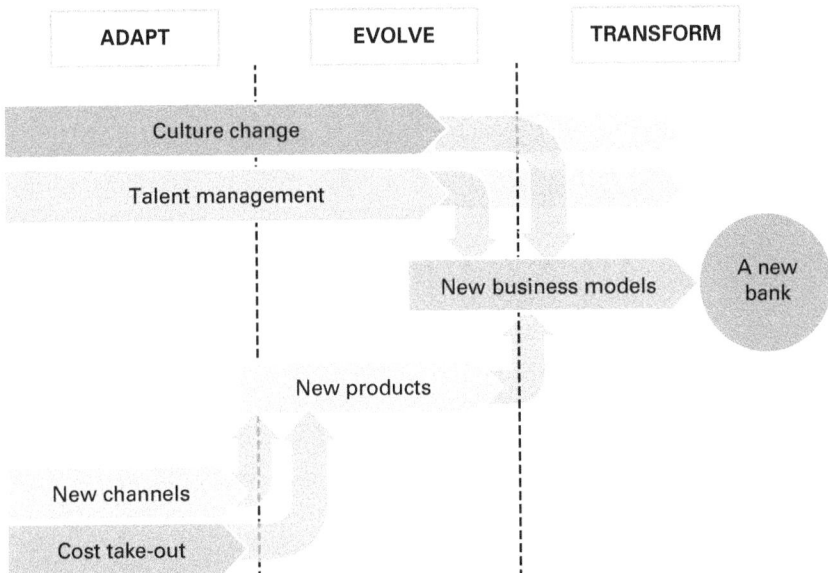

In doing this they usually follow a well-tested path. They go through three stages: Adapt, Evolve and Transform (see Figure 4.1).

Phase One: Adapt

This is where banks look at digital technology to improve their offering without altering the way products are currently designed, manufactured and delivered. In this phase the bank identifies business areas that would benefit from change, aiming to generate measurable upside with relatively little disruption of BAU. This phase is built around strengthening the core business by extending the offering using digital channels.

In the Adapt phase, change usually focuses on two areas: cost reduction and sales improvement.

COST TAKE-OUT

Most businesses that have not yet adopted digital technology will have business functions that can be relatively easily improved without a complete overhaul of existing internal and back-end processes. Using digital to simplify the way things are done is often the fastest way to gain tangible benefits from digital change. The first areas that banks start digitizing are usually simple account servicing capabilities as there is little upside for a bank to have customers come into a branch to check their bank balances. According to Broeders and Khanna, (2015), in an average bank, cost take-outs can account for an upside equivalent to 30 per cent of net profits. Incumbent banks can retain this saving or they can push it to their customers. So, customers will receive better service at a lower cost. First-mover incumbents can (at least initially) make digital innovation a competitive advantage vis-à-vis their peers. Process re-engineering from physical to digital can take time but offers a real upside.

SALES IMPROVEMENT

The other half of the Adapt phase is to enable the sale of bank products online. Without the need to change the way products are manufactured on the core systems, digital distribution can be a quick and effective way to monetize digital change. The scope here is to enable products currently sold by the business to be marketed and sold online. The estimate made by McKinsey of the potential upside of new channels and new products is approximately 15 per cent of net profits.

Delivering compelling new channels and products using new digital technology is not trivial from the design, commercial, marketing, regulatory, security and technology standpoints. But on the whole, its potential is relatively easily understood and accepted by the rest of the firm. Most people understand the potential of enabling customers to open new current accounts or apply for personal loans online or on their mobile.

The impact of digital sales on the bank is in many ways similar to cost take-outs. Digital sales create access points for cybercriminals, overload the systems, potentially encounter internal cultural hostility and face lack of skills.

However, the benefits from new sales and cost take-outs can come with a sting. By digitizing, banks are creating direct access points to their core platform that can create a much better UX for their customers. But this can also create a dangerous backdoor for ill-intentioned individuals to attack the bank and its customers. According to Accenture the sector most targeted by cybercrime is banking. The cost of cybercrime in banking grew by close to 10 per cent between 2017 and 2018 (Bissell *et al*, 2019).

Legacy IT platforms are also a challenge. Many banks have systems at their core that were not designed for today. Most of these platforms were designed to retrieve information at the pace of customers coming into the branches. In the past, customers would check their bank balance once a week by going into the branch; today some check them several times a week using their mobile phones. This new engagement model can cause severe processing capacity issues for systems designed for much less data-intensive environments. Efficiency in one area can cause overload in another part of the bank with repercussions across the business.

Also, we cannot underestimate the people impact of digital innovation. A digitized process also means that different employees are necessary to carry it out. This often means closing of branches, shuttering of call centres and reduction of IT teams servicing the legacy platforms – with all the potential PR, morale and cultural impacts that closures can bring.

There is also the less discussed impact of staff reductions due to digital. Banks are environments where power and remuneration of key individuals is often directly proportional to team size, spend, and budgets. When digital innovation cuts these, even the most well-intentioned executive may become hostile to change if they see their scope, budgets and potentially bonuses curtailed. There have been instances in banks where conservatism and the protection of home turf have become formidable barriers to change. If we also add the societal impact of lay-offs due to branch closures and call-centre decommissioning and the subsequent PR fallout, digital efficiency improvements can bring about real challenges beyond mere implementation.

A significant outcome of the Adapt stage is that it enables the bank to cautiously enter the world of digital change. As the stage progresses, more and more products and services are digitized. As these propositions deliver value and employees are adequately rewarded for delivering them, the bank starts becoming increasingly accepting and even supportive of digital change. This slowly leads to the next phase of digital innovation.

That said, this functionality will also find some resistance, as it will lead to a reduced need for branch sales staff, leading to staff lay-offs and branch closures. The latter is in fact often blamed as a key contributor to the decline of the high street in many smaller towns and city centres across the globe.

Phase Two: Evolve

This is when things start to become interesting. Having optimized back-end processes and created new digital channels, a business on its path to evolution finds itself with new capabilities that can be used to create new products and services.

These new products and services are the first generation of propositions created for the web designed to be delivered primarily through digital channels. The way these products are configured, priced and sold is geared on capabilities and service levels made possible by the Adapt phase. These products pose an interesting set of challenges for incumbent banks.

CHANNEL CONFLICT

The first challenge is omnichannel delivery. This is the commitment by most incumbent banks to enable their customers to access their services through any channel they see fit; be it in branch, by telephone or digitally, and via any other device of their choosing. This is supposed to ensure that no customer is disadvantaged by not having access to a specific channel. With the onset of digital banking in the Adapt phase, the banks modified products and services designed for the physical channels to be delivered on digital channels. As the digital channels were at first considered secondary, the fact that some of the capabilities offered by the bank were not available online was not seen as a major issue. After all, if something could not be done, online customers could be directed to branches. The branch was the default channel and the digital channels were complementary, so if fewer products and services were available online than in branch this was not considered a problem by the bank, its customers or the regulators.

The reverse is not true. Most incumbent banks find it problematic to offer 'digital-only' financial products. Very simply, if digital customers want a product not available online, they can be directed to a branch. But the reverse is often not considered acceptable: banks do not want to send branch customers online if a specific product is not available in branch. The branch is supposed to be 'the bank' while online is often treated as a limited subsidiary of the branch. The perception is that all customers have 'branch skills' while only some customers have 'digital skills'.

This issue can pose a real challenge when competing with most challenger banks that have a clear understanding with their customers that their products are only available through digital channels. They are built from the top down and the bottom up to be purely digital offerings, and are, as a result, freed from the shackles of the physical–digital hybrid. Crucially, this gives many challengers a clear cost advantage as they do not have to manage expensive (and unproductive) physical channels. Globally, a number of incumbent banks are addressing this by creating digital-only sub-brands. With these sub-brands the banks can offer products that are not available in branch without fear of customer or regulator backlash.

THE INCUMBENTS START BUILDING CHALLENGERS

Table 4.1 presents some examples of incumbent challenger banks across the globe.

Interestingly, account servicing poses fewer problems than product sales. Incumbent banks have no problem in taking up the competitive baton, and offering mobile payments, alerts when customers are overdrawn or personal financial management tools that analyse and create graphs of customer spend. All of these servicing capabilities are not easily delivered in branch.

In the Adapt phase, the incumbent banks often attempt to replicate the offering of many of the challenger banks. They are able to offer an end-user experience that is comparable to the fintechs, but they are able to complement them with the ability to address in branch (at least conceptually) issues that the digital interface cannot resolve. Plus, they have a stronger brand recognition and the perception that they are more reliable. So, the Adapt phase should be the stage at which the incumbent banks beat the challengers.

Sadly, for the incumbents, this is not always the case. The main reason for this is legacy. In the past, banks have achieved a lot by relying on a series of tried and tested processes, platforms and behaviours. In the Digital Age many of these legacy features are no longer fit for purpose and some are even becoming a liability.

TABLE 4.1 Digital banks launched by incumbent banks

Select Digital Banks Launched by Incumbent Banks		
Region	Bank	eBank
Americas	Wells Fargo	Greenhouse
	Green Dot Bank	GoBank
	Goldman Sachs	Marcus
	CIBC	Simplii Financial
	Capital One	Capital 360
	Scotiabank	Tangerine
Asia Pacific	Bendigo and Adelaide Bank	Up
	NAB	Ubank
	DBS	Digibank
	State Bank of India	Yono
	Kotak Bank	Kotak 811
	CITIC Bank and Baidu	aiBank
	Halyk Bank	Altyn-i
	Standard Chartered Bank.	SC Virtual Bank
Europe	BNP Paribas	Hello bank!
	Unicredit	buddybank
	Banco Santander	Openbank
	CYBG	B
	ABN Amro	Moneyou
	CaixaBank	imaginBank
	OTP Group	Touch Bank
Middle East & Africa	WEMA Bank	ALAT
	Mashreq Bank	Mashreq Neo
	Emirates NBD	Liv
	Bank Leumi	Pepper
	Gulf International Bank	meem
	Commercial Bank of Dubai	CBD Now

The platforms on which many of the IT banks run their banking services were created many years ago to serve a market that is different from today and using a technology that is now often obsolete. Many incumbent banks have a siloed architecture that was originally built to run on rooms full of mainframe computers using programming languages like COBOL, which debuted in 1959. However, updating technology is the least complex aspect of this permeating and overarching legacy. Across the globe, banks are over-hauling their IT platforms, redesigning processes and replacing hardware. In the last decade huge amounts of capital have been spent on addressing the IT legacy issue. This is reflected in the huge proportion of the banks' IT spend dedicated to maintenance. According to IT research firm Celent the average bank spends over 70 per cent of its IT budget on maintenance (Braithwaite, 2015).

In fact, this point was recently highlighted by Anne Boden, the founder and CEO of Starling, a UK challenger bank. Boden says that banks 'will copy everything we do', but two years later. But the big battle, she says, will be on cost. 'The big banks are increasing their cost base all the time, and they won't be able to compete because our cost of delivery here is very low' (Browne, 2017).

THE LEGACY CHALLENGE

But when you dig deeper and lift the bonnet of an incumbent's banking engine, you see that legacy goes beyond IT. The way an incumbent bank's processes are designed is often a greater issue. Incumbent banks not only designed many of their processes before modern technology was available – they also designed these to meet data, risk, fraud and regulatory requirements that are sometimes obsolete. A great illustration of this is the way new small business customers are onboarded.

Simply doing a quick survey of providers of banking accounts to small businesses reveals that the documentation required by the different providers varies. Some require paper documentation to be brought into the branch (mostly the incumbent banks), others simply ask for information that can be collected and verified online (mostly the challengers). All the providers oper-ate within the same cost, regulation and customer appetite constraints. Yet some have decided that a low-cost digital-only onboarding poses acceptable risks and is compliant with regulation, while others have decided that digital onboarding is not adequate. This group has chosen to onboard online prospects through a version of their traditional process, requiring digital customers to go to the branch – with all the costs, inefficiency and inconven-ience that that option entails. This is an indication of a cultural legacy that is much harder to address than changing the banking IT platform. The 'this is how we do things here' approach is the real challenge to change. But this mindset is slowly but surely changing.

Phase Three: Transform

This more evolved phase of innovation kicks off when the bank has digitized most of its in-branch capabilities and has extended the offering to new digital-only products and services. At this stage the bank can count on more engaged customers, who are more willing to accept new ways of banking and with a richer understanding of their expectations. Using the more advanced product delivery capabilities it has built in the Transform phase, the bank can finally 're-think' itself into something new and ideally better. When a bank reaches this stage, it will often have gone through major changes in its internal culture and talent pool.

At the Transform stage, the bank will be able to design and implement new products and services that go beyond extending core capabilities to re-thinking the relationship with customers to create completely new business models that complement and even potentially disrupt the legacy business.

RE-THINKING THE BUSINESS

Banks that get to this stage will be better able to withstand the challenges brought about not only by the fintechs (digital financial services challengers) but also by big tech giants. In China, tech giants like Baidu, Tencent and Alibaba dominate the financial services industry. The likes of Google, Apple, Facebook and Amazon all have real interest in adapting financial services to their own needs, posing a real threat to the way incumbent banks operate today.

The Transform stage is when evolving challenger banks start exploring areas such as AI, robotic process automation, distributed ledgers, cryptocurrencies and the like. These are innovations where the teams in the incumbent banks – no matter how innovative – have little expertise. The result is that the incumbent starts to look outside its organization, and a collaboration between the incumbent and innovators becomes the smartest course of action.

The experiments that some of the more innovative banks are making with AI, robo-advice, the blockchain and cryptocurrencies are good examples of these new disruptive propositions. Perhaps surprisingly, the partner or the collaborator in this new relationship is not always the new kid on the block, aka the fintech, but interestingly, this is also when banks start exploring collaboration with big tech firms. The JPMorgan Chase current account for Amazon customers announced in 2018 (now on hold) and the Apple card launched in collaboration with the Goldman Sachs retail bank Marcus in 2019 are some of the most recent examples.

The most important outcome of this gradual digitalization is that it will change the banks from the inside, one step at a time. This gradual approach results in real change at the centre of the banks – complementing their highly-valued core assets of reliability, consistency and trustworthiness with customer-centricity and creativity. A powerful combination.

Innovation strategies

What is clear is that all three phases of digital evolution require the incumbent banks to do things differently. Digital innovation requires big, established (and often still successful) businesses to change their ways. In practice, most large firms are well able to answer the 'why', 'when' or 'what' when defining innovation. Often what many banks struggle with is the 'how' question: because ideation is often easier, but implementation with genuine intent almost never is.

When it comes to innovating, firms have three fundamental routes for implementing new digital change. They can either *build* the innovation in-house, they can *acquire* a business or organization with the right capabilities, or lastly, they could *collaborate* in innovation with a partner. Each choice comes with its own set of implications and challenges. Let us take a closer look at 'how'.

1. Build

Building in-house capabilities is almost always the first option explored by a business, large or small. In theory, if done well, it can deliver a proposition that fits exactly with the needs of the organization, it can also be cheaper and delivered more quickly than other choices. Most importantly, it can provide a competitive advantage as (in principle, at least) no competitor will have an identical proposition. But, especially if what needs to be built is challenging or unfamiliar to the bank, building in-house can also see costs and delays ramp up quickly.

Build is relatively straightforward in the Adapt phase. This phase often consists of simply enabling the engagement of customers and colleagues with the existing business through digital channels. It usually does not require changes to the core business core delivery capabilities.

The major drivers of success in the Build phase are:

- **Goals:** Does the business know what it needs to do and is this aligned with the overall strategic goals of the organization? This may seem obvious, but many times incumbent players embark on 'digital innovation' without a clear understanding of the outcome or of a blueprint in mind of how to build it. As a first step it is much better to aim to build a simple but well-defined capability (such as to enable online account opening) rather than aim to embark on an ambitious but vague change project (for example, 'we want to digitize the bank').

- **Talent:** Are the right skills available in the business? Lack of digital talent is a real problem in financial services. Attracting and retaining knowledgeable individuals can be even harder for a large business, as the more qualified individuals often do not want to work for established 'traditional' corporates. Making sure that the right talent is at hand is a first step and being unrealistic about what skills are needed is a common reason for failure of Build projects. As businesses across all industries – not just financial services – realize the potential of digital change, individuals with the right skills have become increasingly scarce. This competitive talent environment has repercussions on compensation as the most talented individuals are in demand everywhere. So, a big barrier to build digital change is not having access to people who can actually deliver it.

- **Timing:** Unless the business is building something it knows well, it is unlikely that Build will prove to be the fastest option. So, when choosing the right approach, choosing to build when time is tight is probably the riskier choice.

- **Culture:** Many established firms are proud of their strong cultures. These cultures are consistently at the core of what has made a firm successful in the past. Will the business culture allow the development of something new internally without corporate 'antibodies' slowly breaking it apart? In a recent survey the consulting firm PwC (PwC, 2014) found that most businesses see that having the right culture to support innovation is a key factor in successful innovation.

- **Costs:** By definition, innovation is something new and any business may find it challenging to predict the costs of something it has not done before. This often results in innovation projects overshooting budgets and timelines. Cost creep is a real risk in Build projects. Building innovation in-house can be expensive when compared to the end-to-end costs of working with a specialist firm.

- **Optionality:** If the business decides to change direction, how hard will it be to disband or repurpose the new division and its team? How much will it cost to do so? Internal innovation can be expensive to unwind without impact that goes beyond the financial. Shutting down projects that have required substantial financial, reputational, intellectual and emotional investment can be painful and traumatic for any business. Building a new proposition that can easily pivot or change direction is very difficult.

Being able to build innovation in-house can have its benefits, but it requires a set of considerations that should not be underestimated. After all, if a business is looking to innovate – and therefore do things differently – how realistic is it that it can do so with internal resources only, without outside input?

2. Buy

The other popular route to digital innovation is to Buy or invest in a firm with the right capabilities to deliver what is required. The most common outcomes of Buy normally sit somewhere in between two models: the merger and the satellite.

THE MERGER

In its most extreme version, the merger sees the absorption of the acquired business into the acquiring entity. The acquired business is integrated into the acquirer's business. A transaction takes place with a clear understanding that the fintech will be integrated and rebranded within the bank. This gives the bank the benefit of delivering innovation under its own brand, increasing customer goodwill and stickiness.

An example of this has been the acquisition of Final, a California-based digital credit card, by Goldman Sachs' consumer bank Marcus. The Final brand is gone, and the team and customer portfolio have moved over to Marcus. Marcus has in fact accelerated building an internal team by acquiring and integrating a startup into its challenger banks.

THE SATELLITE

The other acquisition model is the satellite. In this case, the bank decides to acquire a fintech but then leaves it to operate relatively independently. The fintech receives an injection of capital, implicit validation of their business model through the investment of the bank and possibly access to the bank's customers. The bank can see this investment as the means to experiment in a specific business area without impacting their existing operations. With this approach, the bank gets good market intelligence and also ensures exclusivity and control of a new proposition.

By leaving the fintech separate the bank also shields it from any detrimental impact from a mismatch between the way the bank is run and the needs of an earlier-stage business. Also, this approach – done right – makes it easier to retain talent. Many talented employees of fintechs may not want to be part of a big, structured legacy organization like a bank but will work in a fintech owned by a bank. This approach also shields the innovative business from cultural and operational legacy issues of the acquiring bank.

A good example of this is the acquisition of Simple Bank by BBVA. Simple has been left relatively untouched operationally and a customer would have to look hard to realize they are in fact a BBVA company. More recently, the acquisition of Nickel by BNP Paribas is another example of 'one owner, two brands'.

As with Build, Buy requires caution and careful consideration of several factors:

- **Speed:** Acquisitions can be very fast. A business can end up with a fully functional innovative division very quickly. Choosing the right acquisition is by far the fastest way to bring innovation into a firm.

- **Costs:** The upfront capital outlay to acquire another business is often larger than that required for an in-house build or partnering alternative, often requiring a substantial upfront capital outlay. This can cause complexity and executive management anxiety that is often unwelcome when attempting to innovate a well-established business. That said, buying a successful going concern may actually be cost effective in the long term.

- **Fit:** The integration of a business that is already relatively well formed with its own culture and ways of doing things into another business is not an easy endeavour. Smaller firms are often less complex, have fewer layers and legacy issues. Large corporates, especially successful ones, have multi-layered organizations, with complex governance structures and well-established operating models aimed at stability, predictability and control. Both businesses believe that their approach is best and trying to reconcile the two mindsets requires real effort. Often in an acquisition scenario the acquired firm is in a vulnerable position – so the acquiring entity should focus on protecting the characteristics of what made the smaller firm an attractive target in the first place. Big businesses are known for slowly neutering acquired businesses from within – conscious effort by the incumbent leadership is required to make sure this does not happen.

- **People:** As previously stated, talent in a smaller, innovative firm usually does not like working for a bigger, more structured organization. When buying a new firm, provisions are often put in place to retain talent at the executive level; retaining people at lower levels is much harder and is often neglected. Making sure that the needs of the staff within the acquired business are met is fundamental. Employees in a smaller firm often value different things from those in an established corporate. Often compensation and a clear career path are less of an incentive than working on an interesting project or acquiring new skills. Furthermore, a differentiated treatment of the team in the new acquisition could have a backlash within the acquiring firm and existing employees could resent a different set of conditions and opportunities being offered to the new colleagues and not to them. Managing people issues is one of the most important aspects in an acquisition; it is often a people problem that lies at the centre of many unsuccessful acquisitions.

- **Optionality:** Even though acquiring a business can be quick, divesting from an acquisition that has gone bad can be very difficult and expensive. Furthermore, the fact that the acquisition has not worked inevitably has an impact on valuation. Sometimes a flawed acquisition leads to a write-off of the asset acquired and possibly lay-offs. An acquisition can be a fast (and even cost effective) way of injecting innovation in an established business but undoing a flawed acquisition can be costly, difficult and even painful.

3. Partner

One of the most far-reaching outcomes of the Digital Age is fragmentation. Increasingly, smart individuals are willing and able to set up small firms that provide products and services that are equivalent or superior to those provided by their much larger competitors. These firms, based on the creative coupling of the entrepreneurial skills of their founders and an intelligent use of technology, can be great partners for larger businesses seeking digital innovation.

Partnering is a very effective way of getting an injection of digital innovation, enabling large firms to benefit from the fragmentation (or 'uberization') of their digital offering into discrete, on-demand services. There are two fundamental modes of partnering, and most actual partnering situations are a hybrid of these two modes.

THE DISTRIBUTION CHANNEL

The first mode is a distribution channel relationship, where the bank helps the fintech to sells its products to the bank's customers. The benefit to the bank is to offer a new product or service to its customers, spending relatively little time, effort and capital in creating it. The bank also gets good insight on whether customers like the proposition so that it can decide what to do next: walk away, build in-house or deepen the relationship with the fintech.

The fintech benefits from access to new customers and new sales, improvement to their brand through association with the (ideally) well-respected bank and market insight to refine their products. Customers get a new offering from their bank that they may find interesting. They also get reassurance from the bank that the fintechs can be trusted with their money.

Ideally, the bank could learn from the way the fintech operates, but if not managed carefully, it risks potentially nurturing a competitor in exchange for market intelligence. It is also worth asking: Who is responsible if the customer is somehow negatively impacted by the fintech? Even if the bank can legally insulate itself from things going wrong at the fintech, the PR and even regulatory pressures may force it to take on the liabilities. Examples of this model of collaboration include the collaboration between The Royal Bank of Scotland and Funding Circle to deliver SME loans and the partnership between JPMorgan Chase and OnDeck.

THE SUPPLIER

In the supplier model the bank engages with the fintech as if it were third-party service provider. A new proposition is created by integrating the capabilities of the fintech within the bank's offering. To the customer the offering looks like the bank is providing the service, even if there may be some statement on the contribution of the fintech in the offering's terms and condition fine print.

To the bank, this is a good way to explore new propositions with customers. If successful it will improve the relationship with customers and provide insight on the most desirable next steps. For the fintech there is little brand erosion as a result of collaborating with a third party. It also provides a certain flexibility as the bank can pull the plug with relatively low cost. We can also see the bank making a minority investment in the fintech. One caveat is that this model often does not provide exclusivity, as the fintech could collaborate with other banks.

A few examples of this partnership model are the collaboration between two personal financial management fintechs in Europe: Bud and First Direct (part of HSBC Bank) where they are the engine behind the First Direct Artha app, and the partnerships Swedish firm Tink has created with banks such as SEB, ABN AMRO and Paribas Fortis.

In all, when partnering, a business should consider the following:

- **Speed**: It can be very fast. By partnering with the right organizations a business can deliver a new digital proposition faster than with most other options. Jointly developing a solution, be it through a joint venture, a collaboration or a client–supplier relationship, is usually the fastest way of getting a new proposition into the market or of developing a new capability.

- **Costs**: Compared with Build and Buy, Partner often demands a smaller capital outlay to deliver the same impact.

- **Optionality**: One of the possible outcomes of a good partnership is that it can be a stepping stone. A successful partnership can be the first step in building a successful innovative business in-house – or it can be the safest way to identify the right acquisition target. Furthermore, dealing with failure is less difficult with partnering. Large organizations will find that a proposition delivered with third parties can be unwound much more quickly and cheaply than with the other innovation models. It is easier to replace a supplier or a partner than it is to divest an acquisition or dismantle an internal team.

- **Contracts**: Compared to building in-house or an acquisition, the contractual requirements can be more complex. Some of the key things to look for are ensuring that everyone's objectives are aligned, ownership of intellectual property is clearly defined and that the process to follow in case of failure is clearly defined.

FIGURE 4.2 Digital change strategies and partnering models

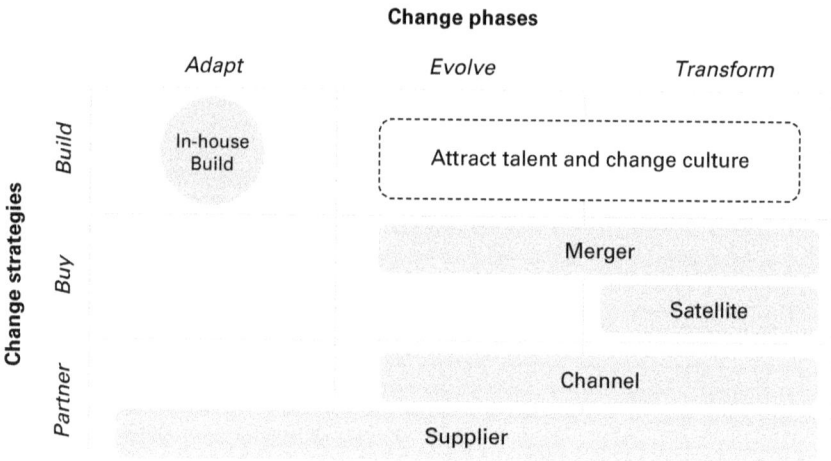

Change phases

	Adapt	*Evolve*	*Transform*
Build	In-house Build	Attract talent and change culture	
Buy		Merger	
			Satellite
Partner		Channel	
		Supplier	

(Change strategies)

It is becoming clear that in the coming months and years we will see an increasing number of banks collaborating with fintechs. Choosing the best way forward is going to be a determining factor in ensuring the success or even the survival of both the incumbents and the challengers, especially as big tech is about to enter the fray.

The big tech challenge

GAFA (Google, Apple, Facebook and Amazon) are all taking steps in financial services. Apple first launched Apple Pay, which was recently followed by the Apple card – great products but with niche appeal for now as they are not yet widely embraced by customers. Google still supports Google and Android Pay but its efforts are not worrying the banks. Facebook is experimenting with P2P payments with limited success, but it has recently announced the ambitious Libra project – the global cryptocurrency aimed at replacing all global currencies. It is still early days for Libra, but this is the big tech project to watch. Amazon's upcoming US current account (supported by JPMorgan Chase) is a sign of things to come. If they follow the example set by Baidu, Alibaba and Tencent in China the real battle for the future of financial services has not yet started.

Today, it seems inevitable that something analogous to what happened to retail, travel and entertainment is now happening to banking. As customers we will all benefit from it, but bankers will need to accept that business-as-usual is no longer an option. Since the beginning of the 21st century, many banks have successfully begun adapting to the demands of the Digital Age, developing the skills, operating models, technical platforms and business cultures needed to transform. The Digital Age is transforming our society like the other 'Ages' of humanity have done. The Stone Age, the Classical Age or the Age of Steam are all examples where technical change accelerated and transformed the way we engage and interact. Each one of these ages required people to change and adapt to a new reality. In the past, most people could retool and retrain to be able to move, survive and even thrive from one age to another. The Digital Age is not dissimilar to its predecessors in that it requires us to adapt; the difference is that the time people and organizations are given to 'retrain and retool' is now so short that people and organizations will inevitably be left behind

Playing by the rules of tech

The difference with the revolutions of the past is speed. The digital revolution of today is forcing change at an unprecedented rate. If we look at the other stages of the evolution of banking, the relationship bank lasted roughly 400 years, the industrial bank lasted for under 150 years, the IT banks lasted about 60 years. All indications are that the pace of change of the digital bank will be much faster than its predecessors (see Figure 4.3).

It is a fool's errand to try to describe the future in an ecosystem where the key inputs are in constant flux. We can only take in insight from industries that are ahead in their journey of digital disruption. Using this approach, we can probably make some educated guesses on the shape of banking and financial services in the coming years.

First and foremost, we know that the successful financial services providers will be more customer-focused, and that the term 'customer-centric' will need to be more than a PR tag. For future banks, true customer focus will mean defining themselves on the basis of metrics that drive real customer needs and outcomes.

FIGURE 4.3 Banking evolution curve

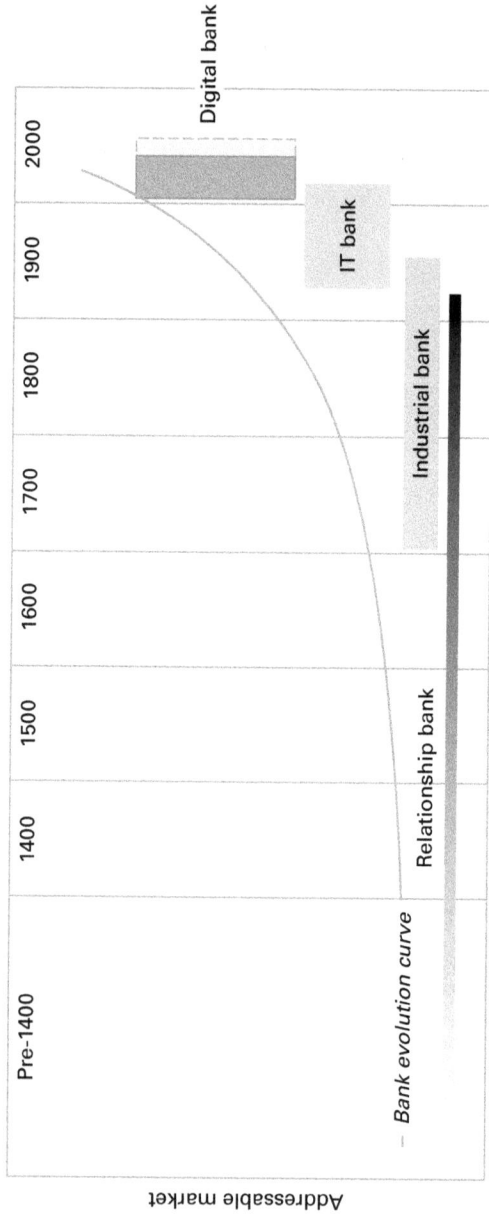

GAFA and customer need

Most incumbent banks today are still run along product-related profit and loss silos. As we said, customers do not need financial products, they need support in achieving their goals. If an institution measures success on the basis of how many loans or credit cards it sells, they are not focusing on the customer needs and outcomes. Organizations need to define metrics and performance targets that maximize customer welfare, while being compliant and profitable. In today's market, technology enables a customer to easily quantify and compare the offering of any institution and to easily move from a less favourable provider to one that is a better fit with their needs. In future, retaining customers while remaining profitable will be much more difficult than it is today.

Disintermediation will be an increasingly serious problem for financial institutions. Many of the challenger banks are already describing themselves as 'platforms', where they provide the means for their customers to access a wide range of financial propositions, not all 'manufactured' by their bank. Furthermore, we are seeing an increasing push from big tech firms in creating platforms.

A good example is again Apple Pay and the Apple card where several cards (and bank accounts) offered by multiple banks can be accessed through the Apple interface. If Apple is the way customers authorize payments and check their spend on all their cards and bank accounts, are the providers of these accounts not already disintermediated? When a customer uses their Citi card on Apple, are they banking with Citi or Apple? If disintermediation is the future what will the 'Re-think' phase bring about? Some banks will try to deepen the relationship with their customers, making it impossible for a platform to replicate the richness of their customers' engagement. Some will embrace disintermediation and elect the platforms as their customer interface.

Regulation will become a much more complex beast. Regulators will realize that digital technology has made the banks more complicated than before. In addition to the traditional metrics driven by financial stability and fair customer treatment the regulators will increasingly start focusing on areas that they do not directly regulate today. Financial regulators will certainly become more hands-on in regulating data management, technical resilience and possibly even areas such as sustainability and ethics.

The future is an unknown but one thing is certain. Incumbent banks will have to fight hard to remain relevant.

References

Bissell, K, Lasalle, RM and Dal Cin, P (2019) Ninth Annual Cost of Cybercrime
  Study, Accenture, 6 March, www.accenture.com/us-en/insights/security/
  cost-cybercrime-study (archived at https://perma.cc/7FCY-YFF8)

Braithwaite, T (2015) Banks' ageing IT systems buckle under strain, *Financial
  Times*, 18 June, www.ft.com/content/90360dbe-15cb-11e5-a58d-00144feabdc0
  (archived at https://perma.cc/FG5V-XUTQ)

Broeders, H and Khanna, S (2015) *Strategic Choices for Banks in the Digital Age*,
  McKinsey & Company, www.mckinsey.com/industries/financial-services/
  our-insights/strategic-choices-for-banks-in-the-digital-age (archived at
  https://perma.cc/YG8X-AFBG)

Browne, R (2017) You don't just build a bank overnight: Banking start-up Starling
  is taking financial services by storm, *CNBC*, 2 December, www.cnbc.com/
  2017/08/21/starling-bank-ceo-anne-boden-big-banks-will-copy-us.html
  (archived at https://perma.cc/M9LM-GB6M)

PwC (2014) Unleashing the Power of Innovation, PricewaterhouseCoopers,
  www.pwc.com/im/en/assets/document/unleashing_the_power_of_innovation.pdf
  (archived at https://perma.cc/WV57-LF2E)

05

The Fintech Hubs

Even though the internet is, by definition, global, fintech startups are, at least at the outset, very local. Fintechs are shaped and defined by the markets they serve. The best fintechs take advantage of local conditions to build solid businesses that at some point realize that they are able to scale and expand outside their home market. Firms like PayPal, Alibaba, Klarna and N26 were all created to address a local market need. Once they were able to make the most of local conditions, they expanded to other markets.

Local conditions in each market have created their own fintech ecosystems or hubs. Looking closer at these drivers can help us understand the evolution of global fintech better.

The fintech hubs emerge through the interaction of four fundamental drivers:

- people;
- money/capital;
- innovation;
- regulation.

Let us take a closer look at each one.

FIGURE 5.1   The forces shaping fintech hubs

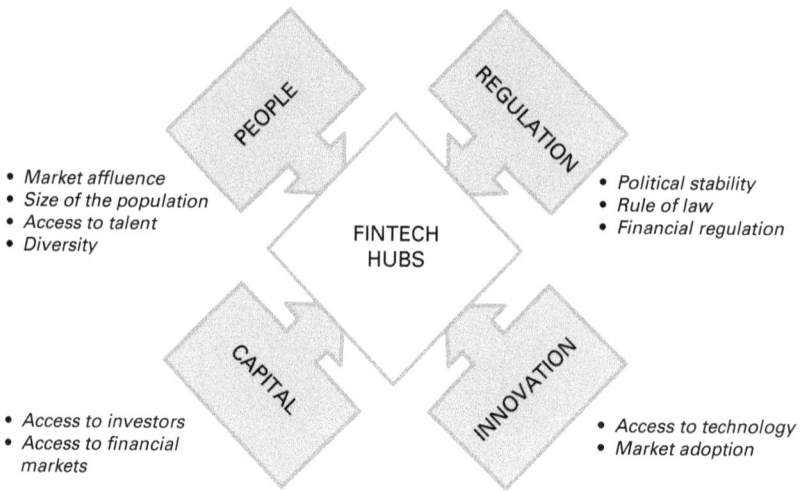

- Market affluence
- Size of the population
- Access to talent
- Diversity

FINTECH HUBS

- Political stability
- Rule of law
- Financial regulation

- Access to investors
- Access to financial markets

- Access to technology
- Market adoption

People

The size of a market is a fundamental measure of the potential opportunity offered by a fintech hub. There are two main dimensions to size. The first is affluence or the monetary value of the market. The other is the number of potential customers. Any new business's primary goal is survival. Launching a proposition that is able to show growth and generate profits relatively fast increases the chances of its success. Succeeding in a sizeable geography makes it easier to attract capital, visibility, talent and all that is necessary to thrive. Fintechs can become viable either by offering a high-margin product to a small wealthy market or by offering a product with very little margin to a very large number of people.

Market affluence

Addressing an affluent target market means that the provider of a new service can expect margins that are superior to those of less-rich markets. Most of the early markets for developed challenger banking propositions have been affluent. The first challenger banks in fact appeared in Western Europe (Klarna and Zopa were both founded in 2005) and North America (Simple was founded in 2007). The affluence of the market they served enabled them to generate revenues from the outset, arguably because their customers' affluence made them less risk averse.

When leading UK P2P lender (now a bank) Zopa launched in the UK in 2005, its objective was to earn an upside from the spread between the savings rates and borrowing rates. As the CEO of Zopa, Giles Andrews says (Skinner, 2015), the idea was to provide better value to consumers by being a more efficient connection between people who have money and people who wanted money. Fundamentally, Zopa wanted to provide a better experience to their customers by incentivizing 'people who have money' to move their business to Zopa by offering better rates than the banks were able to. And then to offer lower interest rates to 'people who want money'. They could afford to do so because their cost base was considerably lower than that of the banks. At the core of the success of their offering was access to an affluent customer base with individuals who felt that they could afford the risk of giving their money for a higher return. The fact that the UK had a substantial number of such individuals was a key driver of Zopa's success. The ability to create a proposition that was competitive with the banks' offering was not enough to ensure their success. They also needed a market with a sufficiently large population of affluent individuals that could afford to hand over hard-earned cash to what at the time was a startup, for the promise of higher returns – a key factor in their success.

Similarly, BankSimple (now just Simple) was a solution that addressed rich-country problems. BankSimple was famously created to be a bank that 'doesn't suck' (Fernholz, 2012). When Joel Reich and Shamir Karkal decided to launch Simple, their driver was dissatisfaction with their existing banking offering. They aimed to serve a customer base that already had access to bank accounts and finance. They were creating a better interface to an existing very well-established industry: the US banking system. From their offices in Brooklyn they were not aiming to help the unbanked; they wanted to help the banked be 'banked better'. Their offering gathered support across the affluent millennial customers segment. When, in 2013, Simple was sold to BBVA (Spain's Banco Bilbao Vizcaya Argentaria, one of Europe's largest banks), it had close to 100,000 customers.

Klarna (the Swedish fintech, now a bank) was created to help consumers buy more online by offering customers an innovative solution that gave them interest-free credit at the web checkout. They set out to simplify the sales finance process by making the checkout process smoother, separating the buying from the paying of an item. They created a solution aimed at a market with customers who are online, have an appetite to buy and have the credit rating to allow them to borrow. Klarna addresses the needs of the top of the global financial pyramid. This approach made Klarna the most valuable fintech in Europe in August 2019.

Size of the population

The fact that many successful fintech firms were created in wealthy countries to serve relatively well-off customers does not mean that less affluent countries did not create their own fintechs. While companies like Zopa, Klarna and Simple were addressing the needs of wealthy nations, entrepreneurs in developing countries were looking for ways to use technology to help the unbanked. This is another definition of market size. In this case the size is not measured in financial terms but in terms of number of potential customers. By addressing the problems of a very large population, a fintech can become very successful even if in absolute terms its margins are very small.

A wonderful example of the use of technology to shake up the banking industry happened in Kenya and Tanzania and the agent of change was not a startup but a telco. We are of course talking about M-Pesa. In many ways, M-Pesa both is and is not a fintech. Its origins lie in unbanked customers. With few options available to them, these customers started using what was intended as a way to share mobile phone minutes as a means of transferring money – a purpose not initially intended by the Kenyan and Tanzanian subsidiaries of telco Vodafone. In the beginning, a number of customers in the big cities started to send 'airtime' – minutes of mobile phone talk – to their friends and relatives in the countryside. They then sold this airtime for cash locally. De facto, the city dweller had sent cash without cost except for the very limited processing cost of buying airtime. This was so successful that M-Pesa revenues in 2015–16 accounted for about 10 per cent of the total revenues of the commercial banks in Kenya, and over the period 2011–16 M-Pesa revenues have been growing at 29 per cent per annum, faster than the commercial banks. Between 2008 and 2016, 'Access to the Kenyan mobile money system M-PESA increased per capita consumption levels and lifted 194,000 households, or 2 per cent of Kenyan households, out of poverty' (Suri and Jack, 2016).

A similar story occurred in Afghanistan where Roshan, a local telco, implemented a programme to replace cash with m-Paisa (the local version of M-Pesa) to pay the salaries of the policemen. Before m-Paisa, cash was handed to the police commanders who would in turn pay the officers. On receiving their salaries directly for the first time, many Afghan policemen assumed that they had been given a salary increase: in fact they had simply received their full pay for the first time. In an interview, Karim Khoja, CEO of Afghanistan operator Roshan said that when they implemented the service:

> 250 policemen came and kissed me on both cheeks and I wondered why and they said 'thanks for giving us a pay rise'. In five years, they had never got their full salary because money was being eroded down the food chain.

SOURCE Mobile World Live, 2015

As Chinese society is becoming increasingly cashless, beggars are having a hard time raising money. But this is changing. Visitors to high-traffic areas such as train stations and tourist spots in China are increasingly noticing that some beggars have added Quick Response (QR) codes to their begging bowls. (A QR code is an image or pattern of black and white squares that can be read by a smartphone, allowing the phone user to get more information about something. It is often used to provide payment details.). Any individual with a mobile phone can make a small payment using the beggar's QR code (via the Chinese digital payment wallets Tencent or Alibaba apps). As most beggars do not have smartphones, their payments are cashed in by helpful local merchants (Lim, 2019).

These three examples illustrate the huge impact that fintech can have in countries with large, relatively poor populations. The impact of fintech in the developing world can be truly profound. In richer countries fintech helps customers to manage their finances better. In poorer countries fintech can change people's lives.

Access to talent

Fintech ecosystems are also shaped by other people-related factors. A very important one is access to talent. Fintechs need employees who are skilled, capable and open. Access to high-quality education, attractive living places and cultural openness creates such a workforce.

By looking at the centres of fintech hubs across the globe we can clearly see that access to quality education is an important metric. If we take a quick look at the top centres of fintech across the globe, Greater London, Northern California, the US East Coast and India, for example, all have access to some of the greatest centres of higher learning in the world. Be it Cambridge, Stanford University, MIT, INSEAD or IIT, access to highly educated individuals has a strong correlation with the success of fintech. From the founders' team to most recent hires, fintechs' access to educated talented individuals is a key advantage.

Very successful educational institutions do not simply happen. They are the tip of the iceberg of an established system that creates educated individuals. These systems are underpinned by communities that support students from pre-school to PhD level, providing the means for talented individuals to get access to the right institutions to grow academically. According to the OECD three leading global fintech hubs (United States, UK and Sweden) are in the top five countries worldwide ranked by spend on education per student (OECD, 2019).

But formal education is not the only kind of education that contributes to the success of fintech. Global fintech hubs are often co-located with major business hubs. In these business hubs large corporates, multinationals, consulting firms and many smaller firms serving them operate as magnets in attracting talented individuals. Cities like London, Hong Kong, Singapore and New York are global financial hubs and the home of numerous fintech startups. Many of these fintechs are run by talented individuals who were attracted to these hubs by well-paying jobs in large corporates before taking a leap to set up their own startup business. For example, Simon Loong, founder of Chinese lender WeLab, Rishi Khosla, co-founder of UK challenger bank OakNorth, and Eli Broverman, co-founder of US investment hub Betterment, all had corporate roles in Hong Kong, London and New York before establishing their successful fintechs. A review of the rank and file of these successful fintechs will inevitably reveal even more former corporate professionals that have pivoted their careers.

Similarly, hubs like Boston and Silicon Valley also operate as 'work experience' centres for successful fintechs. Skills learnt at firms based on the West Coast have fed some of the most successful fintechs in the United States. In fact, several founders of West Coast fintechs are veterans of firms such as PayPal, Amazon, Google and Facebook. For example, Jack Dorsey, the founder of Square was also the founder of Twitter; Max Levchin, founder of US lender Affirm, was also co-founder of PayPal.

Diversity

A side effect of a society that is affluent, large and educated is that it becomes diverse. Affluence makes a society desirable for talented people from across the globe. The most productive, educated and capable people are attracted to environments where their talents can be rewarded – financially and otherwise.

When talent is the only metric in measuring an individual's merit, the best people, regardless of sex, race, religion, sexual orientation or social background, are attracted to such a market, making it not only increasingly more affluent, large and talented, but also more diverse. Such a community is the ideal market for the introduction of innovative business propositions.

This diversity leads to an open mindset, with customers demonstrating an affinity to experiment with something new. All the major fintech hubs are home to diverse, educated, large affluent societies. Markets with these characteristics are often the best places to launch new propositions as their populations tend to be more accepting of innovation. Historically, wealth, size, education and diversity are great indicators of propensity to innovate. From the acceptance of the first banknote in Imperial China to the mobile phone adoption in the United States and Western Europe, the ability of a society to adopt the new is defined by these characteristics.

Capital

The economic structure of a market is another fundamental force behind the success of a fintech hub.

Access to investors

Access to capital is another important element behind the success of fintech. This goes beyond the presence of a small group of smart ex-investment bankers and ex-consultants getting institutional money to invest in early-stage growth companies in appealing sectors. It demands the presence of individuals with enough vision and courage to invest in a small team of smart, talented and motivated individuals with a dream. The first (and maybe most important) driver behind an innovation is access to early-stage investors to support entrepreneurship. Markets like London, New York, Hong Kong, Singapore and Silicon Valley are hubs for innovation because some of their residents have the courage to invest in startups.

The profile of such investors is remarkably similar across the globe. They are usually individuals who have been able to amass a certain amount of capital from work they did somewhere else. In the case of New York and London, this work done elsewhere was usually banking. In the case of Silicon Valley, the capital was more often than not the result of profits generated in the first wave of digital disruption in the 1980s and 1990s. Often the first investor in many of the leading fintechs is a courageous angel investor. And courageous is the right word. In fact, according to research firm CB Insights, about 70 per cent of startups will fail in their first year (CB Insights, 2019). Not great odds for any investor.

Once the business scales, finding later-stage investment becomes the focus of fintechs. Across the globe, successful fintech hubs are often also home for later-stage investors, from VC to private equity (PE) to floatation. Providing the fintech with access to investment across the different stages of its evolution – from inception to IPO (initial public offering) or sale – is a key element in the hub's success.

The physical co-existence of startups and investors in the same geographical space is a fundamental contributor to the success of this collaboration. This physical co-location enables investor and investee to create informal touchpoints before any deal is discussed. Informal connections are often an efficient way for entrepreneurs to find and assess the fit of a potential investor. And on the other side, investors can use social connections to source deals and vet the venture (validating aspects such as the value of the proposition, the quality of the team and more).

Access to financial markets

As fintechs establish themselves, they often need to engage and interact with the incumbents. A P2P lender needs to have access to a banking network to enable the flow of funds from lenders to borrowers. Cross-border payment platforms need access to existing payment networks connected and run by the incumbents to serve their customers. Also, challenger banks and fintechs often need access to additional liquidity to fuel their lending activities.

Being co-located within or close to a traditional financial hub goes a long way in reducing friction in the interaction between the fintech, the incumbent and the customers of both. This collaboration is often a source of income for the incumbent and the means of accelerating growth for the fintech. When Taavet Hinrikus moved to London as part of the digital telecom Skype team, he was frustrated by the inefficiency of the money transfer possibilities between the UK and his home country of Estonia (Li, 2014). So he used some of the P2P principles he had picked up as the first employee of Skype to build a money transfer system that used the incumbent banking system to create a solution that was cheaper, quicker and better honed to customer needs than the banks were able to provide. To deliver competitive international money transfers his company, TransferWise, had to engage with the incumbent banks in all the markets in which it operates. This collaboration is at the core of his company's success.

Being located within an existing financial hub also enhances competitiveness. A competitive market where many firms are fighting for customers and capital has two effects: firstly, it raises customer expectations; and secondly it makes it easier for customers to consider switching to a better supplier. If a startup is able to survive (or even thrive) in a competitive market it is more likely to do well in less competitive markets as it expands internationally. And customers in non-competitive markets, where the supply of the financial product they require is limited and concentrated in a small number of players, may feel less comfortable about moving their custom to a newcomer. In competitive markets customers are used to switching to a better provider.

Innovation

We all know digital technology innovation has made it possible for customers to access their banks, get to the data they need and safely control their finances. The perception is that once a new technology breakthrough happens and it is made available to businesses and consumers, its adoption may take a little time but will eventually happen everywhere. This is not always the case. The success of fintech hubs across the globe is very much dictated by the availability and adoption of technology.

Access to technology

First and foremost it is about access to supporting infrastructure. There is little upside for a startup in building a wonderful new fintech proposition that makes the most of the latest smartphone features for a market where mobile data access is patchy or where only a small percentage of the population can use smartphones for banking.

Global fintech hubs are all based in countries where there are few barriers to the use of technology. Most fintechs need to interact with their customers, technology providers and financial players. If a geographical area is unable to connect to technology, it will be unable to develop. For example, cross-border payments providers need to have access to their customers, their customers' bank accounts and to technology providers (smartphones, 4G networks, cloud-computing, etc) through technology. It is no surprise that TransferWise was created to enable money to change hands between two technologically advanced markets (the UK and Estonia). Similarly, businesses like US payments processor Stripe, German fintech N26 and SoFi rely on widespread access to technology by their customers, their suppliers, their partners and their competitors.

A good – and possibly surprising – example of how access impacts fintech is Iran. According to the World Bank (World Bank, 2016), 95 per cent of the population has access to a mobile service, 70 per cent regularly uses the internet and 90 per cent of the population has a payment card and can use them to make transactions. The Central Bank of Iran has created a national payment scheme as an alternative to Visa and Mastercard who do not fully operate in Iran (Central Bank of Iran, 2019). The Central Bank has recently launched mobile payments and according to the World Economic Forum (WEF) Iran is about to launch the e-Rial – a state-sponsored cryptocurrency (WEF, 2019). But Iran is affected by a number of global sanctions that impact its access to technology (this is further compounded by global financing sanctions on Iranian financial products). Sanctions have closed Iran off from the global fintech ecosystem (Ilia, 2019).

With all of this creativity, tech penetration and a population of over 70 million people, Iran could potentially be a fintech hub. But it is not, because Iran cannot openly connect to global technology platforms, and its institutions are barred from accessing other partners and financial institutions worldwide. Lack of access has prevented it from developing as a fintech hub, as nearby Dubai has done with a fraction of the population and a similar size economy, making a real impact on the people of Iran.

Market adoption

The other factor determining the effect of the technology is adoption. Using the economic principles of supply and demand, if access defines the supply of technology, adoption defines its demand. As we said, few fintechs would consider launching a business in a market that is technologically underdeveloped. If customers are not able to adopt technology the market is unable to develop its fintech potential. The most common and insidious barrier to adoption is cost. Many developing countries would benefit from fintech, but if customers cannot afford to access the internet, they cannot use these services. In a few instances the creativity of the local market has trumped this barrier. The M-Pesa story, where mobile payment with ordinary mobile phones created one of the largest global payment success stories, is one such example. Unfortunately, human ingenuity does not always succeed in beating lack of means.

Lack of adoption also has one other negative effect: it results in the market's workforce not being able to develop technical capabilities. Markets with small pools of tech users are also by default unable to develop the technical servicing capabilities in their workforce. This reduces access for fintechs to a technologically savvy workforce. Interestingly, cross-border outsourcing has mitigated this trend. In the early 2000s, many multinational organizations began outsourcing customer service to less expensive markets.

India is a great example of this. As local staff were trained to service European and US customers, they were trained to answer questions relating to servicing products that were sometimes developed online or on mobile. One of the reasons why India has become a global fintech hub is presence of skilled individuals who have been trained to service financial products not available in the home country.

Regulation

The last building block of a successful fintech hub is the effectiveness of the laws and regulations within which the market operates. This goes beyond financial regulation; it touches all aspects that define how the different members of the market engage with each other. Most fintech hubs have rules and regulations that are clear, strong and enforced that result in three outcomes: political stability, clearly defined rule of law, and financial regulation.

1. Political stability

The first need for a successful fintech hub is the relative stability of the market in which it operates. The ability of a market to offer consumers and businesses a modicum of certainty that their livelihood is safe and protected is a key attribute of any financial hub and therefore a requirement of any fintech hub. At the core of this stability is a clear set of laws and regulations that are enforced fairly by the state. These often go beyond the financial and extend to the social and political.

Areas such as freedom of speech, freedom of the press and political plurality are often part of this equation. The effectiveness of a legal system is obviously also linked to the effectiveness of the enforcement of the laws – so many of the hubs are governed by a hands-on type of government where engagement goes hand-in-hand with fairness. The fate of the Iranian fintech industry is a clear indication of the importance of political stability in a hub.

2. Rule of law

The knowledge in the minds of all actors in a fintech hub that breaking a country's rules and regulations will result in clearly defined sanctions is a key source of trust and compliance. The fact the rules are clearly defined and sanctions for diversion are fairly levied on those who break the rules are fundamental requirements for a successful fintech hub. The first global fintech hubs were in the United States and the UK. Both of these markets have a reputation for defining and enforcing their own laws very energetically.

As an example, a key requirement for a fintech hub is to provide confidence that it is a relatively secure environment (no market is 100 per cent secure). A great example of the effect of this confidence is the introduction of the PSD2 by the EU (European Commission, 2012). This is a legislation that impacts close to 500 million people and mandates that all EU banks provide secure access points for customers to allow third parties to access their bank data. PSD2 has been hailed by customers and fintechs as a great way of levelling the playing field and improving competition in the EU. This new Open Banking regulation is gradually enabling fintechs to provide services that they would otherwise have been unable to offer.

As this new legislation will generate thousands of new entry points to the core banking systems of EU banks, it renders them vulnerable to malicious attacks. The EU regulators are well aware that this creates the potential for the banks to be hacked. The bet that the EU is taking is that the benefits generated by opening up access to customers' data will greatly outdo the damage done by any cybercrime. This confidence comes from the European Commission's and the Member States' belief that their laws and enforcement institutions are up to the challenge. Many EU citizens are hoping that they are right.

3. Financial regulation

The rules set out by a government to address financial transactions directly impact a fintech hub's potential for success. All financial regulators have a main objective in mind – to protect consumers (people or businesses) of financial products from potential abuses by financial services institutions. Traditionally, regulators felt that the best way to protect customers was to make sure that things stayed as they were: maintaining status quo delivered stability in the past and will do so in the future. The problem is that 'keeping things as they are' led to some major financial crises in the recent past, leading many regulators to change their approach. Across the globe, financial regulators have become more hands-on, substantially increasing their scrutiny. According to the financial journal *The Economist*, larger financial institutions dedicate over 10 per cent of their workforce to compliance (*The Economist*, 2019). This is almost double the percentage they allocated in the mid-2000s.

Certain regulators, though, have started to believe that – at least in part – the problem with financial mis-behaviour is lack of competition. The promise of a fintech challenge to the incumbent banks, providing better outcomes, speed and transparency, seemed a great alternative to the existing situation. So, some regulators started to cautiously support financial innovation. For example, the UK financial regulator the Financial Conduct Authority (FCA) began proactively interacting with fintechs in the early 2010s. A review of the UK retail financial services market led them to see increased competition as a viable antidote to market domination by a small number of very big institutions. This led them to begin engaging proactively with startups and in 2016 to the launch of a Sandbox for financial innovation. Twice a year, around 25 firms are allowed to sign up customers for a new product or operational approach, with full disclosure and an FCA guarantee that they will not lose out if things go wrong. Firms must comply with all the usual prudential measures and checks for money laundering, fraud and so on, but are granted permission to innovate within the spirit of the rules. This is a formula that was copied in several markets across the globe including the US Bureau of Consumer Financial Protection, the Monetary Authority of Singapore and the Hong Kong Monetary Authority. Today, an increasing number of governments are using smart regulation to make their markets become more attractive as fintech hubs, serving their market better and attracting both investors and talented individuals.

The hubs and the tribes

The financial services market is seeing new players entering, old players changing and big tech firms entering the fray. We are seeing new products, better services and greater options emerging across the globe. In a few years, the financial services, banking and payments industries will be unrecognizable.

The interaction of people, capital, innovation and regulation has helped define the different fintech hubs across the globe. Each of these hubs is inhabited with creative entrepreneurial business that exist to seize an opportunity, address a problem or even follow a calling. These businesses are firmly based in the hubs but the scope of what they want to achieve transcends where they are located. Fintechs can therefore also be grouped according to their vision, which can range from trying to be better than the banks to disrupting the way finance is run worldwide. These groupings are sometimes called 'fintech tribes'.

In the coming chapters we will explore in more depth a number of fintech hubs to provide a fuller picture of how the world is changing the financial services industry.

References

CB Insights (2019) The Venture Capital Funnel, *CB Insights Research*, 5 June, www.cbinsights.com/research/venture-capital-funnel-2/ (archived at https://perma.cc/RT94-GBRE)

Central Bank of Iran (2019) Shetab, Central Bank of The Islamic Republic of Iran, www.cbi.ir/page/16090.aspx (archived at https://perma.cc/6ZJY-3P5P)

European Commission (2012) Payment Services (PSD 2): Directive (EU) 2015/2366.,27 August, ec.europa.eu/info/law/payment-services-psd-2-directive-eu-2015-2366_en (archived at https://perma.cc/TGG8-7GSG)

Fernholz, T (2012) BankSimple: A bank that doesn't suck, *Fast Company*, 30 July, www.fastcompany.com/1757032/banksimple-bank-doesnt-suck (archived at https://perma.cc/LMB7-MKJB)

Ilia Corporation (2019) Iran Central Bank, ILIA Corporation, www.ilia-corporation.com/insights/white-papers/iran-central-bank/ (archived at https://perma.cc/CM6T-S58Z)

Li, C (2014) Bye Banks? A Q&A with TransferWise co-founder Taavet Hinrikus, *Tech.eu*, 12 March, tech.eu/features/764/transferwise-taavet-hinrikus-interview/ (archived at https://perma.cc/M272-4PAC)

Lim, J (2019) No Cash? No problem because this beggar from China accepts donations via WeChat, *Mashable SEA*, 29 November, sea.mashable.com/culture/7720/no-cash-no-problem-because-this-beggar-from-china-accepts-donations-via-wechat (archived at https://perma.cc/8688-7TF8)

Mobile World Live (2015) Afghanistan's Roshan aims to keep the cash out of police pockets', 12 March, www.mobileworldlive.com/money/news-money/afghanistans-roshan-aims-keep-cash-policemens-pockets/ (archived at https://perma.cc/ZT8F-F6Y4)

OECD (2019) Education Resources – Public Spending on Education – OECD Data, OECD, data.oecd.org/eduresource/public-spending-on-education.htm (archived at https://perma.cc/HP5A-UJ2X)

Skinner, CM (2015) The Finanser Interviews: Giles Andrews, co-founder and CEO, Zopa, Blog, 1 December, thefinanser.com/2015/07/the-finanser-interviews-giles-andrews-co-founder-and-ceo-zopa.html/ (archived at https://perma.cc/EFV8-H3RT)

Suri, T and Jack, W (2016) The long-run poverty and gender impacts of mobile money, *Science*, **354**, no. 6317, pp 1288–292, https://science.sciencemag.org/content/354/6317/1288 (archived at https://perma.cc/3JWL-6VW3)

The Economist (2019) The past decade has brought a compliance boom in banking, 2 May, www.economist.com/finance-and-economics/2019/05/02/the-past-decade-has-brought-a-compliance-boom-in-banking (archived at https://perma.cc/448Z-394S)

WEF (World Economic Forum) (2019) Central banks and distributed ledger technology: How are central banks exploring blockchain today? www.weforum.org/whitepapers/central-banks-and-distributed-ledger-technology-how-are-central-banks-exploring-blockchain-today (archived at https://perma.cc/ZXE7-BRVX)

World Bank (2016) World Development Report 2016: Digital dividends, World Bank, www.worldbank.org/en/publication/wdr2016 (archived at https://perma.cc/3E2P-R93S)

06

The Fintech Tribes

In Chapter 5 we defined how local conditions define the development of fintech in different markets. Another approach that is useful in understanding the global fintech ecosystem is to look at their mission or objectives. Notwithstanding local conditions (but nevertheless influenced by them), fintechs can also be grouped along the lines of what they want to achieve and why they were created.

This outcome-focused perspective allows us to see how some of these fintechs transcend geography and location to face complex problems. They address issues like poverty, financial exclusion, facing up to oligopolies and responding to cybercrime.

These fintechs come together to operate as global communities across different geographic hubs. These are some of the most important and effective fintech tribes (see Figure 6.1):

- **The bank challengers:** Fintechs aiming to replace the banking infrastructure in their market;
- **The payments innovators:** Fintechs addressing how financial services are lagging behind the needs of the rest of the digital economy;
- **The champions of the unbanked:** Fintechs using technology to reduce the huge number of unbanked people across the globe;
- **The social banks:** Fintechs using social media to redesign the way we bank;
- **The infrastructure builders:** Fintechs aiming to use technology to change banking from the inside.

Let us take a closer look.

FIGURE 6.1 Global fintech tribes by region

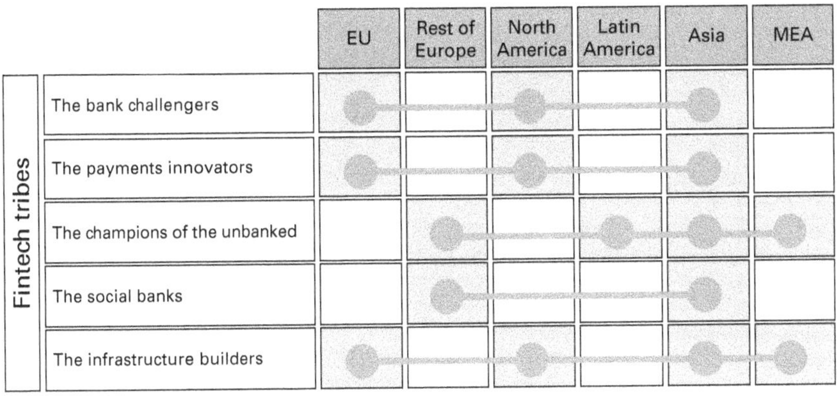

Fintech tribes	EU	Rest of Europe	North America	Latin America	Asia	MEA
The bank challengers	●		●		●	
The payments innovators	●		●		●	
The champions of the unbanked		●		●	●	●
The social banks		●			●	
The infrastructure builders	●		●		●	●

The bank challengers

The fintechs in this tribe address the frustration with their market's lack of banking innovation. These bank challengers are often located in more developed markets. They were not created because their market did not have access to banking; they were created because the founders felt that banking could be done better.

Motives

The founders of the bank challengers are often not new to the banking world. Many founders are former bankers, management consultants or accountants and therefore very familiar with the industry. Anne Boden, CEO of the UK bank Starling, Matthias Kroner former CEO of German digital bank Fidor and Chris Britt at the US bank Chime were all working in the financial services industry prior to launching their bank challenger. These founders saw an opportunity to disrupt an industry by leveraging two main factors: their own understanding of how financial institutions operate and their belief that they could do better by using capabilities that were already available in the market.

These insiders saw that the markets they were familiar with were dominated by players that were unashamedly offering banking services that were not aligned with the times. They were painfully conscious of the fact that the incumbent banks' offerings were not reflective of the possibilities offered by new regulatory, social and technological changes in their markets. They clearly realized that the incumbents were, by and large, obsolete.

The bank challengers saw that banking in their markets was controlled by a small number of large banks with very little new blood. For example, at the start of the 2010s Metro Bank was the first new high-street bank to open in the UK for over 150 years. There was a perception that banking, and a lack of innovation were treated as almost a requirement in order to deliver on the promise of reliability and trustworthiness of the sector (*The Economist*, 2010). When the 2008 banking crisis hit, all of this was put in doubt. Importantly, the public started doubting that the innovation inertia of the banks was aimed at protecting customers. This is when a group of enterprising individuals across the globe took advantage of the zeitgeist to launch the first propositions to challenge the banks.

Approach

From N26, to Monzo, to Simple – what unites all of these players is their desire to be better that the incumbents. They compete with the banks in very subtle ways. Most bank challengers started competing with the big banks by providing a specific niche product better than the banks did. When N26 was launched in Berlin in 2013 it wasn't a bank. It created an app that offered users a simple current account that had features and functionalities that were superior to a bank by using what is called an e-money licence. This was a simple prepaid card that offered a better current account than that offered by German banks. Interestingly, N26's customers did not care that their 'bank' was not really a bank. Like Bill Gates said in the mid-1990s (Long, 2000), customers felt that banking was necessary, but banks were not. N26 eventually became a bank in 2016 and is now expanding in 'better banking' services beyond Germany.

A similar path was taken by Nickel in France and Monzo in the UK. Nickel was launched in 2014 by a technology firm as a payment card. Its USP was that it could enable the opening of an account in minutes without having to go to a branch. This account was not the equivalent of a full-service bank, but it was good enough for the 630,000 customers that opened an account with Nickel, before it was acquired by BNP Paribas, one of the largest banks in France (BNP, 2017).

Monzo is one of the poster children of the UK fintech sector. Launched in 2015 as a prepaid card, it became a bank in 2017 – and in September 2019 it announced it had reached 3 million customers (Monzo, 2019). Monzo's original name, Mondo ('world' in Italian), betrays its ambitions to be a global player. It has recently announced the imminent launch of its proposition in the United States – something it is well-funded to do after raising in excess of $300 million in several funding rounds. It is also one of the UK's fintech 'unicorns' (a privately held startup company valued at over $1 billion).

Results

The effect on the markets in which the bank challengers operate has been profound. The UK, Germany, Scandinavia and the United States today have a much more competitive banking sector. In all these markets we have seen challengers become mainstream. We have seen banks investing in the sector – often de facto funding their future competitors – and several challenger banks have been acquired by incumbents to accelerate their own evolution. Several have done very well in attracting investment to grow and become sizeable players in their own markets. Most importantly, customers have learnt to expect more from their banks.

The payments innovators

The West Coast of the United States was the cradle of the dotcom revolution in the late 1990s, with small technology-based businesses disrupting entire sectors. Industries such as travel, music, retail were upended and sacred cows like bookstores, music retailers and the friendly local travel agent were wiped out in a few short years. One thing that all these businesses had in common was the need for payments.

As the payments industry was not able to offer these new businesses the payment solutions they needed, entrepreneurs got busy and took matters into their own hands. A number of markets became hotbeds of payments companies to help the emerging fast-growing dotcoms get paid for their services. These companies gathered individuals who understood tech and felt that finance needed to change.

The founding member of the payments innovators tribe is digital payments pioneer PayPal.

First came PayPal

PayPal, one of the authors' alma mater, was set up by (amongst others) Elon Musk and Peter Thiel, two of the godfathers of tech in the Silicon Valley, founders and/or early investors in firms including Tesla, SpaceX, Facebook and startup accelerator Ycombinator to name just a few. They set up PayPal because they realized that the payments infrastructure available at the time was not able to serve the fast-growing dotcom economy. The payments providers of the time allowed online transactions but becoming a 'merchant' (an entity allowed to accept card payments) was a painful experience. More importantly, at the time P2P payments were a practical impossibility online. This was a real issue for platforms such as eBay.

eBay was launched by tech entrepreneur Pierre Omidyar. AuctionWeb was just one of four sites housed under Omidyar's umbrella company, eBay Internet. The other three included a site about the Ebola virus. The first item on sale on the site was a broken laser printer – the story of the PEZ dispensers being the first items on sale is a piece of marketing spin. From the outset, receiving payments on eBay was an issue. PayPal realized this and through a very aggressive marketing strategy was able to gain a big enough slice of eBay's transactions to convince eBay to acquire them and to replace the previous payments platform, Billpoint.

PayPal was able to grow quickly inside eBay. Eventually, this success led to a number of businesses starting to use it outside of eBay. Its focus on making payments simple was the key to its success. PayPal's creative use of technology made it possible to create a payments solution that was easy to sign up to, easy to install on a retail website and easy to make a payment on. This customer focus made it the leading alternative payments platform online.

PayPal then went on to seed its own fintech ecosystem, creating the rest of the payment innovators tribe. They did this in several ways.

1. SETTING THE STANDARD

First, by acting like a role model, PayPal's success proved something that was disputed until then: finance and the internet can successfully work together. Both corporates and startups were inspired to find new ways of bringing digital technology and finance together.

Great examples of these are the propositions created by the payment schemes Visa and Mastercard. They realized that they had missed an opportunity with online payments. A large percentage of transactions on PayPal are not processed by the card schemes and therefore do not earn them any income. Had they been more proactive at the right time, they could have stemmed this loss. Propositions such as VPay and eMaestro, conceived by Visa and Mastercard respectively, would probably have been a lot more successful if they had appeared 10 years earlier.

It wasn't long until the tech giants saw the potential of PayPal's approach. Google's launch of Checkout and Wallet, both now merged into Google Pay were both arguably inspired by PayPal's express checkout. Subsequently (and more successfully), Amazon and Apple both launched payments propositions – Amazon Pay and Apple Pay – that are serving them well. Payments processors like Stripe and Square always had PayPal in focus when developing their solutions. Digital payment wallets such as Moneybookers and Neteller that emerged across the globe were competing with PayPal, targeting markets that were largely not well served by it, eg gaming and gambling. And more recently payments platforms like Stripe and Adyen took the PayPal legacy to a new level of ease of integration.

But the most important PayPal 'followers' are actually in China. Alipay, part of Chinese tech giant Alibaba group, was created to serve its global trading platform as an alternative to PayPal. Alipay in fact resulted in PayPal never becoming a leading solution in China. It launched in 2004 and became the largest mobile payment platform in the world, beating PayPal in 2013.

2. INVESTING IN INNOVATION
Secondly, by investing in the sector, PayPal often added new capabilities by acquiring promising businesses. Through the years, PayPal has acquired companies such as Billmelater, iZettle and Braintree to enhance its core by offering POS financing, physical payment acceptance and better merchant servicing respectively.

In parallel, PayPal also made minority investments in fintech through its investment arm PayPal Ventures (PayPal, 2019). This invested in a number of exciting fintechs across the globe, building a portfolio that includes firms such as Raisin, Ellevest, Tink, Acorns and Tala. Interestingly, PayPal alumni also seeded a number of visionary VC funds. For example, Founders Forum (the Silicon Valley VC) founded by several PayPal alumni is an investor in big successful tech firms including Facebook, Airbnb and Spotify but it has also invested in fintech firms such as Stripe, Affirm, Credit Karma and Nubank.

3. DISSEMINATING TALENT
The third way that PayPal has contributed to the growth of the sector is through what is jokingly called the 'PayPal Mafia'. These are individuals with a deep understanding of digital finance that have left the firm and gone out to help drive the growth of other fintech players. We mentioned Elon Musk earlier, but we can also cite several other instances of this talent migration. For example: Steve Chen, Chad Hurley and Jawed Karim, co-founders of

YouTube; Max Levchin, founder of digital consumer credit Affirm; Osama Bedier, founder of payment processor Poynt; Dave McLure, founder of business accelerator 500 Startups; Joe Lonsdale, co-founder of data analytics firm Palantir; Premal Shah, co-founder of non-profit micro-lender Kiva.org; Laurent LeMoal, CEO of global digital payments and credit firm PayU; and Richard Ambrose, CEO of online remittance company Azimo. Plus scores of senior executives in roles at big banks, big tech firms and startups across the globe who are leaving their mark on fintech and banking innovation.

PayPal was a forerunner of what became fintech. It used its success and its understanding of the potential of technology to change financial services in order to revolutionize the payments system. It is the 'fintech academy'.

The champions of the unbanked

Big countries such as Brazil and India or regions such as East or Southern Africa have huge populations. These populations are young, relatively technologically savvy and terribly badly served by the incumbent banks. These banks were created to serve a very small part of the population and were not able (or willing) to tweak their business model to serve the rest of their society.

These champions of the unbanked have often relied on the principles of social media to attract and serve their customers. Some started by using technology that was not conceived for financial services to address the financial needs of the customers, adopting creative solutions that enabled them to use less 'advanced' technology than that used by their US and European peers to create their solutions.

These fintechs had a clear mission: millions of people across the globe are unbanked and therefore harmed because they are excluded from the benefits finance can bring to their lives. This tribe realized that even though these millions did have access to banks, they had access to something else: mobile phones. So, the champions of the unbanked set out to build their banking businesses using this technology.

M-Pesa

We previously mentioned M-Pesa's success in Kenya, Tanzania and (to a lesser extent) South Africa. M-Pesa was created almost organically out of an innovative use of mobile technology by the customers of Safaricom (part of Vodafone).

In the early 2000s, customers in the big cities realized that they were able to send 'minutes' to the phones of friends and relatives in the rural interior where banks were not present. The recipients of these minutes would then convert them to currency by offering them to willing buyers locally. Mobile phones were being used as wallets. Safaricom noticed these spikes in minutes transfers and decided to address this opportunity: in 2007 they launched M-Pesa, allowing customers to store actual currency on their phones. They had de facto bypassed the banking system, giving unbanked customers across the country a banking solution (Monks, 2017). Slowly new competitors such as Airtel Money, Equitel, MobiKash also started offering mobile wallets. In 2018, Kenyans processed the equivalent of half of the country's GDP through mobile wallets like M-Pesa and its competitors (Businesswire, 2019).

Nubank

Nubank in Brazil went for the same target market, but took a completely different route. Nubank launched in 2013 to offer a fee-free credit card that could be ordered and managed by an app – a first for Brazil's branch-centric banking market. This proved extremely successful, leading Nubank to target Brazil's 60 million unbanked citizens (Mari, 2017). The Nuconto ('nu' means naked in Portuguese) was a simple current-account equivalent that was easy to open and allowed people with no access to finance to access banking services. Nubank today is one of the largest challenger banks in the world with over 14 million customers.

Paytm

Paytm in India is a leading bank challenger converting mobile phones into e-wallets, with a customer base that includes both banked and unbanked customers. The banked customers use Paytm for the convenience it offers in paying for simple everyday transactions such as transport. 'Our approach is to identify the pain points for customers and then solve them really, really well – better than anybody else can,' said Harinder Takhar, former CEO of Paytm in India (KPMG, 2019).

The unbanked use Paytm as an alternative to a bank account to safely store and disburse cash. Paytm has over 400 million active accounts in India and is accepted as payment at over 7 million merchants across India (Habiby *et al*, 2019).

Alibaba Group and SoftBank have both made significant investments into Paytm over the past 10 years. So have financial investors such as Sapphire Ventures and Berkshire Hathaway. As of the start of 2018, the company was valued at more than $10 billion.

Mobile technology in the hands of the champions of the unbanked is becoming a formidable force in the democratization of finance.

The social bank challengers

Using social networks to reach new banking customers has proven to be a smart approach in several markets, where we see large social networks developing a successful fintech business on top of their platform. In many instances, the first step is to develop payments capability, then quickly morph this into a variety of products.

The path taken by Alipay in China and Kakao in Korea are good examples of this, where social networking organizations (ie networking between individuals in the case of WeChat and Kakao and between companies in the case of Alibaba) developed very large, successful financial organizations. Large social institutions in the West are following the same path with both Amazon and Apple investing in financial services propositions.

In all instances, the social bank has one thing in mind – the welfare (actual or perceived) of its members. Social networks are platforms where like-minded individuals or companies meet to exchange 'things'. These platforms operate as infrastructure that enables its member to manufacture, exchange and consume ideas, services or products. These 'things' are not manufactured by the platforms. The platforms provide the infrastructure that its members can use to upload descriptions of their goods according to a clear taxonomy. This taxonomy and a series of related tools provided by the social platform renders these goods discoverable by other members of the platform, making the exchange of content, services and goods possible. These platforms thrive from this exchange of 'things'.

One of the factors that supports this exchange is finance. Platform members who interact with each other often want to send or receive payments from each other in order to drive these and future exchanges. The ability of a social platform to integrate financial services as closely as possible to its core proposition is a factor in its success. The integration of PayPal into eBay was key to the success of both.

WeChat

When Tencent, the Shenzhen-based tech giant, launched WeChat in 2010, the objective was to create an 'app for everything'. Customers could run a huge part of their lives on the app from messaging to gaming. Things moved up to a different level with the very successful introduction of a digital version of the *Hongbao* – the red envelope where, in the Chinese tradition, people make monetary gifts during the Chinese New Year and other holidays (Pasternack, 2017). This led to WeChat Pay and changed everything. Users were able to spend the whole day on WeChat, talking to friends and colleagues, hailing taxis, paying for meals (this normally requires cash as credit cards are still rare in China), and shopping in online and physical stores. And for most of them, the gateway to it all was an ancient custom made digital.

Today, businesses across the globe accept WeChat payments. WeChat operates as a platform offering a wide range of financial products to its users – in part delivered by its own financial arm WeBank but also in partnership with other fintechs. Tencent's WeChat is one of the largest retail banks in China providing banking services to over 100 million customers and 16 million SMEs (including sole traders) (Skinner, 2019). They do this with a cost base that is a fraction of that of the traditional banks, having focused on building a technical capability that is superior to its competition.

Ant Financial

A similar story applies to Alibaba, a major conglomerate that includes Alibaba.com, a B2B marketplace that benefited hugely from the economic growth of China. Alibaba became the gateway through which the world could access the formidable Chinese manufacturing engine. Western businesses could search through hundreds of Chinese manufacturers to find the goods they needed, but they then had to pay for them, and in the beginning that was painful. So Alipay was launched, to enable buyers to easily and safely pay for the goods they wanted to buy. Since its launch in 2004, and its subsequent renaming as Ant Financial 10 years later, it has become one of the world's largest fintechs, offering a range of products that as well as payment processing include loans, investments and insurance. With the launch of Taobao it also entered the C2C space in direct competition with eBay and giving it a broad retail customer base. In 2019, Alibaba announced the creation of an investment fund of $1 billion to invest in Asian fintech (McMorrow, 2019).

Kakao Bank

In South Korea, messaging service Kakao launched Kakao Bank in 2017 and grew to approximately 8 million users within 18 months, and overtaking the 10 million mark in 2019. The Kakao Bank portfolio is targeting the younger segment of the population. Close to 50 per cent of its users are under 30 but over 40 per cent are in their 30s (*The Korea Herald*, 2019). This age group is very desirable for banks as they are usually gainfully employed, and as their lives become more complex they start requiring valuable banking products such as savings, investments, credit cards and mortgages. Traditional banks in Korea are losing valuable customers to Kakao Bank.

WeChat, Kakao and Alibaba are social platforms that have successfully built fintech businesses to support their core. They are the shape of things to come in banking.

In the West, the social bank challengers are being developed by four major contenders: Google, Apple, Facebook and Amazon. We have already discussed the financial aspirations of some of them, but it would be worthwhile to take a closer look at the motivations of each of them (see Figure 6.2).

Google

Google's main incentive in entering financial services is access to data. By entering the financial services arena, they will gain access to financial information, a completely new set of data that they can use to make their cost-per-click (CPC) advertising model more profitable. Much of Google's

FIGURE 6.2   GAFA and financial services: Key motivations

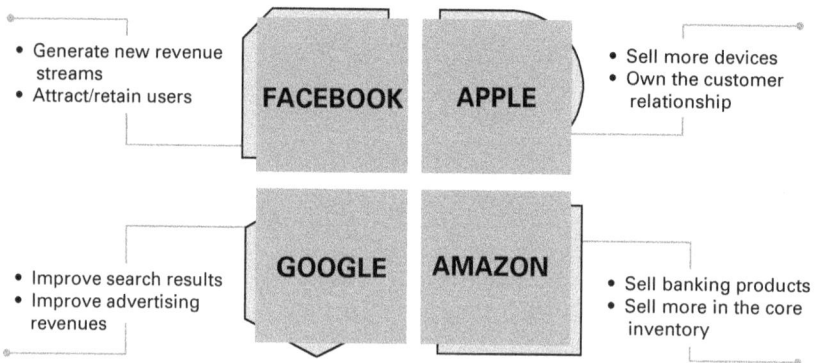

- Generate new revenue streams
- Attract/retain users

FACEBOOK   **APPLE**

- Sell more devices
- Own the customer relationship

GOOGLE   **AMAZON**

- Improve search results
- Improve advertising revenues

- Sell banking products
- Sell more in the core inventory

revenues comes from placing ads next to customer searches. By having access to financial data they can prove to the advertiser that a search has resulted in a sale. Google could charge more for a cost-per-action (CPA) model than it can charge for a CPC. For example, instead of charging $0.05 for a click sending a customer to a retailer's webstore, Google could charge $5 for a click that sends a customer into a webstore *and* then generates a sale of $100.

Apple

Apple is first and foremost a hardware manufacturer. Adding financial services to the suite of services it provides allows them to connect to yet another aspect of their customers' lives, eventually becoming the digital gateway through which their customers can manage their lives — as Steve Jobs proposed in his famous 'Digital Hub' speech in 2002 (Tam, 2001). All the services it provides are aimed at making sure that their customers' next digital device is an Apple device.

Apple, therefore, is extending its offering to finance and banking. To succeed, it will need to make its customers' engagement with their bank through Apple a more efficient and enjoyable experience than going direct (either physically or digitally). The first step in entering the financial services market, as we saw with WeChat and Alibaba, is payments. Apple is rolling out Apple Pay across the globe and vigorously challenging protective moves from incumbent banks. It has also taken a cautious first step towards banking, recently announcing the launch of the Apple card in the United States and UK in collaboration with Marcus, the retail bank arm of Goldman Sachs (Dilts, 2019).

Facebook

Facebook makes most of its revenues from ad sales. These are presented to customers on the back of analysing their preferences when they engage with ads on one of its platforms (Facebook, Instagram or Messenger). The data privacy challenges that it has been exposed to recently suggest that Facebook needs to diversify its revenue streams. As its customer profiling is being seen as increasingly intrusive, it needs to find better ways of monetizing its customer interactions. Enabling in-platform financial transactions could pave the way – as the WeChat and Kakao models suggest.

The first steps in this direction are being taken by providing P2P payments. WhatsApp Pay (another Facebook company) was launched as a pilot in

India in 2018 (Murgia, 2019). Global rollout is probably imminent. In the meantime, Instagram is slowly moving into e-commerce with the launch of 'Checkout with Instagram' earlier this year. The eMoney licenses Facebook was recently granted in Spain and Ireland and the recent hires of senior experienced payments professionals in the sector suggest more is to come.

Amazon

Amazon already resells financial products like the Amazon Card (a consumer credit card), Amazon Lending (limited working capital finance for their merchants) and Amazon Pay (enabling buyers to use their Amazon account to pay away from the Amazon webstore). Most of Amazon's financial products are provided through partners. Amazon Pay, headed by several ex-PayPal people, is managed in-house.

Recently, Amazon announced the launch of a current account in partnership with JPMorgan Chase (JPMC). This project has now been put on hold but it is a very likely indication of things to come (Anand and Dugan, 2019).

As a retailer, Amazon wants to sell more products. By providing a current account, they can get a much better understanding of their customers' financial characteristics and score them accordingly. The obvious opportunity here is to offer POS financing, increasing the sales of their core products.

The real prize is to authenticate and rate their customers so that they can buy relevant financial products (loans, mortgages, savings accounts, pensions, etc) at the click of a button – as they would buy any other product on Amazon. Amazon would display only products for which the customer is pre-approved by third-party financial services businesses and banks. This would provide customers unprecedented range and ease in buying the financial products they need.

The launch of the current account with JPMC could be the first step in creating a platform through which Amazon can sell other financial products. In this scenario, Amazon, and not the banks, could become the first port of call when customers look for a new financial product.

The infrastructure builders

Certain fintechs see the opportunity to engineer the future. These infrastructure builders are looking at how an intelligent use of digital technology can re-engineer banking from the inside. They are using innovation such as AI to automate complex processes such as advice and risk management. The infrastructure builders are looking at how the trading IPO and fixed income trading could be replaced by initial token offerings, how the blockchain can revolutionize payments or how fintechs can keep one step ahead of cyber-criminals.

The infrastructure builders tribe is a heterogeneous group of companies with one shared characteristic: the desire to re-think banking. They are rebels with a cause.

The banking platforms

One of the most frequently quoted issues with innovation within large incumbent financial institutions is legacy. The simpler legacy issues to address are technology. It is relatively easy to get an overhaul of an outdated technical platform. All that it takes (apologies if you've suffered while implementing a similar project) is to map existing processes and re-implant them onto a new platform. You end up with a new platform that allows the bank to do what it was doing before, faster and more efficiently. The harder legacy to address is with processes. The redesign of these, if done right, should lead to a complete re-think of the engagement with the customer.

As we mentioned before, this would mean becoming truly customer-centric on a huge scale, developing the capability to create products and services designed to meet the needs of each specific customer. Very few platforms are able to deliver a solution that enables each customer to receive a bank offering that is created specifically for them. A number of banking platforms are emerging worldwide that allow the banks to design an offering that is perfectly tailored to their customer's needs. A few examples of these are Thought Machine in the UK and Mambu in Germany.

The P2P platforms

One of the more interesting models in fintech is P2P finance. These are propositions that re-think the bank as a convergence point where supply and demand of financial services meet and are fulfilled. In theory this is not a new model. When the first bankers decided to use funds deposited by their clients to make loans to other clients, they were in fact operating a P2P platform.

The difference was that the bank treated the deposits as a pool and for most depositors and investors it guaranteed the rate of return. So, in the traditional model customers usually have no visibility of the performance of the loan portfolios that funds their returns. The bank charges a fee for its ability to source borrowers, assess the riskiness of the borrower, determine the right price to take on their risk and, most importantly, to pool the risks and guarantee a return to the lender. To the lender the bank was offering a return and to the borrower a loan. There was no obvious link between the two types of bank clients.

The P2P models proposed to change that by making the lender directly share some of the risks of default by the borrower in exchange for a higher return. These models leverage modern technology to transform the bank–lender relationship. In the traditional model the bank sells a return; in the P2P model the 'bank' is a broker of risk. Technology makes it viable to broker this risk at scale.

The P2P model has evolved into many products. We are seeing lenders of all sizes enter the market from consumers to large corporates and everyone in between. On the borrowing side the range of products offered is broadening, going from personal loans kicked off by the doyen of P2P (Zopa) to mortgages with SoFi and also to insurance with innovative platforms like Friendsurance in Germany.

The crowdfunders

At the core of the crowdfunding proposition is the desire to simplify the fundraising and investing process. The concept is simple: to create a platform where businesses and investors can come together, bypassing intermediaries like investment banks and brokers. The challenge here is to be able to replace the middlemen without detriment to the businesses and to the investors. The intermediaries are responsible for compliance, liquidity, pricing and security of a funding transaction. A popular type of crowdfunding is for equity – good examples are Seedrs in the UK, Indiegogo in the United States and OurCrowd in Israel.

This model also allows an interesting twist to the basic funding model: reward-based crowdfunding, where an investor provides capital for a benefit that is not necessarily financial. This can be a donation for a cause or early access to a new product. Examples of this model are Kickstarter and Kiva.org, both in the United States.

The distributed ledger champions

There is a grouping of infrastructure builders focused around the concept of distributed ledgers. These companies believe that the community is the best guarantor of the accuracy of data. A ledger that is distributed across millions of nodes is a lot more difficult to corrupt. The distributed ledger champions believe that they can offer greater security, speed and efficiency to the financial world's infrastructure. There are many players operating in this sector, though none have truly broken through.

An emerging trend is for different stakeholders to come together as consortia (CB Insights, 2019). These groupings usually have three components: a distributed ledger business to provide the innovation; a big technology partner to help integrate the innovation with the legacy systems; and several incumbent banks that would be greatly impacted by the successful implementation of the technology. A few examples of these consortia are: Votron, using R3 technology to address the letters of credit market (Finextra, 2019); we.trade, using Hyperledger Fabric technology, targeting trade finance (Finextra, 2018a); and Komgo, using Ethereum to address trade finance (Finextra, 2018b).

The global currencies

The dream of Bitcoin was to create a currency that was stable, that could be traced, that would make paying easy and that could not be stolen. It is safe to say that its success in achieving these goals has been mixed at best. Bitcoin has been a ridiculously unstable currency, making it useless for anything beyond speculative trading and illicit transactions. The fact that it is unstable and perceived as untraceable has made it very hard for it to be adopted by mainstream merchants and payments platforms, making the intended ease of use for customers impossible. And lastly, the fact that very few trustworthy and safe wallets are available for Bitcoin has resulted in making it a payment option that is less than flawlessly safe.

So, as a mainstream global currency Bitcoin has largely failed. But that does not mean that the concept is wrong. Several interesting solutions are being proposed that could address the shortcomings of Bitcoin in order to deliver a global currency that will make global payments simpler. The leading example of this is Libra, the global currency proposed by Facebook. The solutions in the market today may not be the future global currency – but something that looks a lot like them will be.

Making banking better

These are just some of the fintech tribes. New ones are surely being developed in garages and dorm rooms across the globe. In the following chapters we will explore the different geographic homes of these tribes and attempt to compare and contrast them.

The different fintech hubs have evolved in different ways, affected by different influences and market conditions. However, one thing unites all of these hubs (and all the tribes): the desire to use digital technology to change banking into something that is better.

References

Anand, P and Dugan, K (2019) Amazon quietly scrapped checking account plans, *The Information*, www.theinformation.com/articles/amazon-quietly-scrapped-checking-account-plans (archived at https://perma.cc/2EF3-9FSD)

BNP Paribas (2017) BNP Paribas completes the acquisition of Compte-Nickel, BNP Paribas, group.bnpparibas/en/press-release/bnp-paribas-completes-acquisition-compte-nickel (archived at https://perma.cc/E9G7-E74V)

Business Wire (2019) Kenya mobile wallet and payment market opportunities databook 2019: ResearchAndMarkets.com, 11 July, www.businesswire.com/news/home/20190711005461/en/Kenya-Mobile-Wallet-Payment-Market-Opportunities-Databook (archived at https://perma.cc/AB5A-FNW3)

CB Insights (2019) 80 corporations working on blockchain and distributed ledgers, CB Insights Research, 3 January, www.cbinsights.com/research/organizations-corporates-test-blockchains-distributed-ledgers/ (archived at https://perma.cc/CS9D-794E)

Dilts, E (2019) Apple to launch a new credit card with Goldman. Are the perks worth it? *Reuters*, 25 March, uk.reuters.com/article/uk-apple-television-creditcard/apple-launches-credit-card-with-goldman-sachs-idUKKCN1R6271 (archived at https://perma.cc/RK9D-3J75)

Finextra (2018a) We.Trade on Blockchain: Yes We Can! Finextra Research, 3 July, www.finextra.com/blogposting/15519/wetrade-on-blockchain-yes-we-can (archived at https://perma.cc/V2C8-ADYE)

Finextra (2018b) Komgo: Dutch banks going blockchain for commodities trade finance, *Finextra*, 25 September, www.finextra.com/blogposting/16030/komgo-dutch-banks-going-blockchain-for-commodities-trade-finance (archived at https://perma.cc/PE6G-NNVD)

Finextra (2019) Voltron Consortium Grows to over 50 Banks and Corporates, *Finextra Research*, 8 May, www.finextra.com/newsarticle/33785/voltron-consortium-grows-to-over-50-banks-and-corporates (archived at https://perma.cc/JKZ9-7NMR)

Habiby, M (2019) India's Paytm gets $1 billion investment, plans expansion in a boost to underserved payment services, *Karma*, 25 November, karmaimpact. com/indias-paytm-gets-1-billion-investment-plans-expansion-in-a-boost-to-underserved-payment-services/ (archived at https://perma.cc/V8UB-L2E6)

KPMG (2019) Paytm: Solving problems to create opportunity, KPMG, home. kpmg/xx/en/home/insights/2019/09/paytm-solving-problems-to-create-opportunity-fs.html (archived at https://perma.cc/Q8J9-3L44)

Mari, A (2017) Brazilian fintech Nubank aims for the country's unbanked, *ZDNet*, 25 October, www.zdnet.com/article/brazilian-fintech-nubank-aims-for-the-countrys-unbanked/ (archived at https://perma.cc/C54E-BWVE)

Monzo (2019) 3,000,000 people are now using Monzo! [blog] monzo.com/ blog/2019/09/16/three-million (archived at https://perma.cc/F7XP-6WU7)

Murgia, M (2019) WhatsApp's push into mobile payments, *Financial Times*, 2 January, www.ft.com/content/e045cdd2-0503-11e9-99df-6183d3002ee1 (archived at https://perma.cc/4QXY-GZPQ)

Long, S (2000) The virtual threat, *The Economist*, www.economist.com/special-report/2000/05/18/the-virtual-threat (archived at https://perma.cc/WLY7-FCE6)

McMorrow, R (2019) Ant Financial builds $1bn start-up investment fund, *Financial Times*, 27 November, www.ft.com/content/234c3472-10f7-11ea-a7e6-62bf4f9e548a (archived at https://perma.cc/3XNN-QEQ2)

Monks, K (2017) M-Pesa: Kenya's mobile success story turns 10, *CNN*, 24 February, www.cnn.com/2017/02/21/africa/mpesa-10th-anniversary/index.html (archived at https://perma.cc/ZR2F-4H7C)

Pasternack, A (2017) How WeChat became China's app for everything, Fast Company, 29 June, www.fastcompany.com/3065255/china-wechat-tencent-red-envelopes-and-social-money (archived at https://perma.cc/7AD6-H9NG)

PayPal (2019) PayPal Ventures, www.paypal.com/us/webapps/mpp/paypal-ventures (archived at https://perma.cc/6GE5-X93Y)

Skinner, CM (2019) A bank that runs accounts for just 50 cents a year [blog] 14 August, thefinanser.com/2019/08/accounts-that-cost-a-bank-just-50-cents-a-year-to-administer.html/ (archived at https://perma.cc/RW67-GBNH)

Tam, P (2001) Apple's CEO Steve Jobs Describes vision of new products as center of digital hub, *The Wall Street Journal*, 10 January, https://www.wsj.com/articles/ SB97906597854441661 (archived at https://perma.cc/B3MY-6LCN)

The Economist (2010) Computer Says No, *The Economist*, 22 July, www.economist. com/finance-and-economics/2010/07/22/computer-says-no?story_id=16646044 (archived at https://perma.cc/F9WT-7YXE)

The Korea Herald (2019) Kakao Bank accounts top 10 million, 12 July, www.koreaherald.com/view.php?ud=20190712000432 (archived at https://perma.cc/Y4EM-7DUW)

07

London

Background

History

As the capital of Britain and the United Kingdom, London has been a leading financial hub for centuries. Starting with the Roman invasion, leading into the Elizabethan colonies and the Victorian Age of Empire, the UK and its capital have been at the forefront of globalization. In part as a consequence of the Industrial Revolution and increased trade with the colonies, the country became a point of convergence for trade and finance flows from across the globe. To service this growing trade, merchant banks and trading houses were created across the country, but slowly converged into the City of London. By the 1960s and 1970s, the 'Square Mile' was seen as a global financial hub. With the entry of the UK into the European Community (EC) in 1973, London gradually became the preferred access point not only to the UK and its former colonies but also to the markets of the Member States.

While London has always hosted a substantial number of banking institutions from across the global, it has been a leading hub of choice for the United States. This was driven in part by a common language, but also by the similarities between the US and UK legal systems. This made London's financial hub – also known as The City – a cosy club where merchant bankers convened to make money in a slow-paced, heavily regulated fashion.

BIG BANG

For decades, this club-like status quo carried on uninterrupted. Then, in the 1980s, the UK political climate changed dramatically under Margaret Thatcher, with a knock-on effect on financial services. The then Prime Minister initiated the deregulation of the UK financial services and the London Stock Exchange

(LSE) in what came to be known as the 'Big Bang'. It resulted in a huge increase of trades being cleared by the LSE, making London a much larger financial market that it had been in the past. This deregulation attracted a large number of financial institutions to the City from across the globe. These new City residents attracted a large number of specialist consultants, accountants, IT firms and the like to the City, dramatically increasing the size of the economy. Increased activity and population created a huge number of very challenging and well-paid jobs that attracted a large number of talented individuals, making London a magnet for talent from the UK and across the globe.

In the meantime, the countries in the EC continued integration, morphing into the EU with the signing of the Maastricht treaty in 1992. This implemented the Freedom of Movement regulation that resulted in EU citizens being hired in large numbers by institutions in the City. Today, the UK Office of National Statistics (ONS) estimates that over 3.5 million EU citizens live in the UK and the City of London Corporation estimates that 18 per cent of the employees in the City were born in the EU (City of London, 2018).

THE DIGITAL REVOLUTION

Then in the late 1990s and early 2000s, the spread of the internet, technological evolution and societal changes triggered the digital revolution. In the United States, dotcoms such as Yahoo, Amazon and eBay become giants, valued at many millions of dollars. The first wave of the digital revolution hit the UK in the late 1990s. A poster child of this wave was auction site QXL. Created in 1997 and floated on the LSE, it briefly reached a valuation of £2 billion. This success, however, was short-lived as QXL was hit by the dotcom crash of 2000: in March 2000, the Nasdaq (the US stock exchange on which most new digital firms were traded) crashed, resulting in nearly a trillion dollars' worth of stock value to evaporate in less than a month. Markets rapidly moved away from the dotcom world, and the once-envied QXL ended up as a member of the 99 per cent club – businesses that had lost 99 per cent of their value.

At the same time, Freeserve – a large UK internet service provider – floated on Nasdaq and on the LSE, reaching a valuation of close to £2 billion and was subsequently acquired for a similar sum by what is today called Orange, the global French telecom.

The story of these firms – and of others across the globe – created a yearning in some Londoners. Ambitious entrepreneurs were inspired by the success of the likes of QXL and Freeserve and could envisage a business worth millions becoming a reality. Many thought, 'If they could do it, why not me?'

By the mid-2000s, future fintech entrepreneurs began to realize that the next frontier in the digital revolution was in finance. Talented individuals began using the skills and contacts they had built and acquired during the dotcom era to start new firms in finance, igniting the spark that would eventually fuel the flames of the London fintech scene. To contain costs, these firms decamped from their increasingly expensive City, Mayfair, Soho and Farringdon offices to cheaper, grittier neighbourhoods such as Shoreditch – laying the foundations of what became known as the Silicon Roundabout.

Soon, new startups would be launched to challenge the established banks. In 2010, Metro Bank was issued the first new banking licence in 100 years (Wallop, 2010). Since then over 21 new banking licences have been issued by the Bank of England.

Key strengths

London has also had a long and illustrious history when it comes to innovation, talent and capital. These factors make great foundations for a fintech hub, but there are also a number of other significant drivers that make London unique. These drivers include:

- talent;
- capital;
- legal framework and regulation;
- academia;
- language and geography.

Together these factors combined to make London the fintech hub of Europe. Talented individuals created ventures that were backed by local institutions and wealthy individuals with the aim of building the future of banking under the benevolent gaze of the local regulators. Let us explore each of these drivers in more detail.

Talent

Post-Big Bang, London had become a multinational microcosm of talented, highly educated, ambitious individuals. At this stage London attracted not only banks; it also attracted a huge number of businesses that came to serve the finance houses. These included consulting firms that developed individuals able to define complex strategies; accounting firms populated by people that could put together business plans and knew how to talk to investors; marketing agencies whose staff understood how to speak to customers; and, most importantly, technology firms with employees that understood tech.

Most of these people were also young, relatively affluent, and with a positive attitude towards risk. This often meant that they were usually equipped with the latest technology, understood the potential of the web and were well informed about trends and innovation across the globe. Many of these individuals would become future tech entrepreneurs.

The London talent pool is distinctive on several levels.

EXPERIENCED PROFESSIONALS

By being the preferred location for many global multinationals, London had (and still has) access to a great pool of talented, experienced professionals. These professionals are often entrepreneurs and fintech founders. Taking a close look at the founders of some of the most successful London fintechs, one is struck by what can only be described as almost an alumni list of large corporates. For example, Anne Boden, CEO of Starling is an alumna of RBS, AON and ABN Amro; Kristo Käärmann of TransferWise is an alumnus of PwC and Deloitte; and Nik Storonsky, CEO of Revolut, is an alumnus of Lehman and Credit Suisse.

Such professionals find startups more attractive workplaces than large corporates, because of the nature of the work, the company culture, an upside beyond salary, and because they value the startup's mission. As Ricky Knox, ex-consultant and founder of Azimo (an international payments provider) and challenger bank Tandem, said during an interview:

> The banking sector felt broken: for an industry that plays a central role in someone's daily life, it wasn't thinking about customer problems. I felt there was a place for a bank that genuinely wanted the best for its customers and, with this in mind, I co-founded Tandem.
>
> SOURCE Specialist Banking, 2019

But the experienced professionals are not only founders. Many others are brought into the fintechs to help the founders scale the business. One of the most delicate stages of a fintech is when it graduates from being a Startup into a Scaleup. This is when the business has proven its value and is being adopted by many. The business's complexity skyrockets. Millions of customers create issues in customer service, risk management, compliance, fraud, servicing and much more. These challenges are very similar to those found in large successful traditional businesses. As a result, when successful fintechs reach this stage they often reach out to talented professionals who have encountered similar issues before. The founders take this decision either to compensate for a lack of expertise in-house or because running a growing business is not what drives them. A few recent examples of this type of hire are Richard Davies joining Revolut as COO from TSB Bank, and HSBC and Jaidev Janardana joining Zopa as CEO from Capital One.

The hire of this type of person is a big step in the life cycle of a fintech. Attracting this type of talent can be difficult and expensive. The fintechs are asking professionals who have well-paying prospects in the traditional economy to take a chance on a new business that, by definition, has a limited track record and a risky outlook. Offering an attractive package that includes not only compensation but also equity, leadership clout and personal growth potential, is not a trivial matter.

TALENTED BUT LESS EXPERIENCED

London provides two sources for this type of talent. The first, as with the experienced professionals, is the corporate world whose employees often join accelerators and other programmes in the role of mentor to startups in order to 'scratch an entrepreneurial itch'. London is a powerful target for talented individuals from across the globe. Eager, well-educated professionals come to London to secure roles at some of the large corporates based there. But not all enjoy their chosen corporate roles. The silver lining in this potential employment cloud is that this pool of talented individuals is a great source of talent for fintech.

The other source of talent is the impressive concentration of higher education institutions in London and its environs. London universities, together with select others in Cambridge, Oxford and the rest of the UK, create a formidable higher education hub. These produce a steady stream of talented individuals in both fintech founders and also essential data scientists, computer engineers, quants and other critical skill areas. As an example, a number of the founders of Zopa, OakNorth, Monzo and Funding Circle have degrees earned in the educational ecosystem centred in London.

NON-BRITS

One of the great resources of London is the fact that it has always been welcoming to foreigners. The City has always been a place where people were valued for their contribution not their background. This made London an attractive place for talented non-UK professionals. Many of the UK's fintechs were founded by non-UK professionals. For example, Curve, Revolut and TransferWise – three prominent London-based fintech startups – were founded by non-UK individuals.

In the last couple of decades, this attractiveness has been further enhanced by the open-borders policy of the EU. European citizens with the right skills could easily come to London to look for the right job or to set up their business. It is unclear how this openness will be affected when the UK leaves the EU.

To mitigate this potential curtailment to the UK's talent pool, the UK government has promised to set up a streamlined process to enhance today's work visa schemes to enable talented foreigners to work in the UK. One innovation that was brought forward to address this issue is the proposed Tech Visa scheme, delivered under the auspices of Tech Nation in London. The details of these new processes are still not clear and there are anecdotal indications that the supply of talented EU professionals is slowing down (Gentleman, *et al*, 2019).

Capital

As we have seen in other fintech hubs, while there are varying levels of capital being invested in fintech, London is leading the European charge for investing in innovation in financial services. For years, London was seen as a great place to start a fintech with favourable seed and early-stage tax schemes (for some investors and categories of fintech), plenty of money looking for a better return than it would get in a savings account, access to talent from all four corners of the Earth and a thriving accelerator scene providing opportunity for vetted and curated early-stage deal flow to a grateful investor community.

According to consultants KPMG (Blackman, 2019), European fintech investment for 2018 increased sharply to $34.2 billion from $12.2 billion in 2017 – the UK and London accounted for $20.4 billion in 2018 up from $5.6 billion the previous year. Most of this increase was fuelled by massive M&A (merger and acquisition) and buyout deals like the WorldPay acquisition at $12.8 billion.

The City has generated a large number of wealthy individuals who are less risk averse and therefore liked to make early-stage business angel investments in what were perceived as higher risk startup ventures. These are often professionals, who in large part came from corporates and financial services institutions and who benefited from the wealth created by the Big Bang (Howard, 2016). These individuals are keen investors in the early-stage ventures proposed by the ex-corporate types turned entrepreneurs. As many of these investors are finance people, they are less wary of investing in fintech than many of their counterparts in the Silicon Valley. London early-stage investors understand the potential and complexity of finance and are not wary of investing in ventures that are complex and regulated. Also, the UK tax treatment of venture investing, which until recently was fairly unique in Europe, has a real impact on angel (very early-stage) investing in the UK.

The City also has its fair share of venture capitalists and PE firms, investing in post-seed and later-stage fintechs. Many of the decision-makers in these firms are also former corporate employees who were attracted by the potential financial upside associated with choosing the right startup.

Different types of support for ventures is required at the various stages of evolution of a start-up. Let us take a closer look at the major sources of capital.

ANGELS

Seed and angel investors are significant contributors to London's fintech leadership. One of the side effects of London's status as a global commercial hub is the fact that it is home to high-earners. These individuals often have disposable income that they are willing to invest in promising new ventures. Many fintech startups were funded by the well-established 'friends and family' pool of investors. One aspect of the London-based fintech founders is that they often have well-established pools of wealthy contacts that they developed while working at the corporates or at a top university – similar to New York and the Silicon Valley. These investors prove to be a great source of seed capital.

When it comes to investing, one of the factors that sets London (and the UK) apart is the tax treatment that investment in startups can provide. Benefiting both investor and ventures, the Seed Enterprise Investment Scheme (SEIS)and the Enterprise Investment Scheme (EIS) provide tax relief for VC investors. EIS was launched by Chancellor Ken Clarke in 1994, while SEIS was launched in 2012 under the then Chancellor George Osborne. Both schemes have created real incentives for individual investors to support early-stage firms. Since 1994, 27,905 companies have received investment of over £18 billion via the EIS (Glencross, 2019).

London is the hub of several angel and seed investor associations that provide valuable advice and support to investors and entrepreneurs. Some of the leading angel funds investing in fintech are Angel Investors Network, Local Globe, Archangels and Anthemis.

CROWDFUNDING

Startups in the UK and London are also supported by active crowdfunding platforms, who are mostly fintechs themselves. These organizations have dramatically cut the cost of fundraising, thus enabling individual investors to invest amounts that can be very small compared to traditional angel and VC channels. This democratization of VC has enabled individual investors with limited financial means to enter the market. According to market intelligence firm Beauhurst (Rewal, 2019), between 2017 and the first half of 2019 in excess of 900 crowdfunding deals were secured in the UK, raising in excess of £500 million. Some of the highest-profile fintech fundraises via these platforms include Revolut and Monzo, who have raised multiple or partial rounds on crowdfunders Crowdcube and Seedrs.

The UK Crowdfunding Association (UKCFA) brings together the leading UK crowdfunding organizations, which include Crowdcube, Seedrs, CodeInvest and Syndicate Room.

GRANTS

A number of grants are available in the UK for startups (Lewis, 2019), and for those with genuine intellectual property or genuine disruptive technology, research and development (R&D) or innovation grants (Innovate UK) they are particularly attractive opportunities. These are capital injections that are offered to entrepreneurs with certain conditions. These grants can often be treated as gifts and do not result in transfer of equity to the provider. One of the most prolific sources of such grants is Innovate UK (previously known as the Technology Strategy Board), part of the UK government's Research and Innovation office (UKRI) (UKRI, 2019).

Other noteworthy providers are associated with the EU, including Horizon 2020, the EU's Research and Innovation programme. However, once the UK exits the EU, it is unlikely that UK firms will be eligible to benefit from these in the future.

VENTURE CAPITAL

London has been a hub for VC for a long time. For example, the British Venture Capital Association (BVCA), which brings together investors, venture capitalists and PE firms, was established in 1983. London has the largest number of VCs in Europe.

According to Venture Pulse Q4 2018, a quarterly report on global trends published by KPMG (KPMG, 2019), enterprise VC investment in Europe reached $24.4 billion (£18.9 billion) in 2018, surpassing 2017's record numbers. In January 2019, they found that $7.7 billion (£5.96 billion), or 31.5 per cent, was invested in UK startups over the course of 2018. This was more than 1.5 times the level invested in fast-growth businesses in Germany, and 2.6 times the level of investment seen by the startup ecosystem in France (Capgemini, 2019).

Most London VCs investing in fintech are primarily tech investors, looking at digital financial services. The list of London-based VCs investing in fintech is very long and as a result the UK capital leads in Europe and is in the top three largest investment hubs globally.

Some of the most active VCs in fintech that have big London offices are Index Ventures, Seedcamp, Passion Capital, Balderton, Illuminate, MMC and Accel Capital.

CORPORATE VENTURE CAPITAL (CVC)

One of the distinctive factors in fintech is that it is increasingly attracting investment from corporates in the financial services industry. UK banks have consistently played an active role as minority shareholders investing in fintechs, whether it is strategic investment or investing to deploy the solutions internally.

CVCs in the UK have largely three aims: the first is to create preferential or even exclusive engagement with fintechs they rate; the second is to acquire and integrate technology they consider strategic; and the third is to invest into a promising fintech and to benefit from a possible upside from the growth trajectory the firm could create. In many cases, in addition to the financial and strategic upside, CVCs also hope to provide their corporate sponsors with better insight into the market and potential access to a broader talent pool.

Some of the most active CVCs in the UK are Barclays, Lloyds Banking Group (LBG), RBS and Santander. London also attracts investment from non-UK CVCs. For example, Spanish global bank BBVA recently acquired a substantial stake in UK challenger bank Atom.

Legal framework and regulation

One of the greatest assets of London in becoming a global hub for financial innovation and fintech is the effectiveness of English law and the financial regulation that underpins it.

LEGAL FRAMEWORK

As business becomes truly global, companies have increasingly seen the British legal framework as one of the world's most transparent, flexible and reliable systems to engage with. This has made English law, its courts and London the preferred choice for cross-border deals:

- **English law**
  The UK is the international law of choice because it is predictable, transparent and flexible. Its governing principles are based on freedom of contract and supporting commerce.

- **English courts**
  English courts are often seen as the international forum of choice. This is due to factors such as its judges being experienced in international disputes, its thorough but proportionate procedures, and last but not least the availability of world-class legal advisers.

- **Legal London**
  The City is the internationally preferred seat of arbitration. This is the natural confluence of the previous points. London courts benefit from a clear legislative framework and excellent judicial support for arbitration. They are a neutral forum for international disputes with world-class arbitrators, legal advisers and arbitration organizations.

The UK and London are therefore seen as the international forum of choice for innovative organizations with global aspirations – the ideal home for a fintech.

REGULATION

The other factor that sets London apart from other financial hubs is regulation. For many years, UK regulators felt that the best way to support the welfare of the market was to make sure oligopolies were challenged and that the City remained innovative and competitive. The Financial Services Authority (FSA) and its successors the FCA and the Prudential Regulatory Authority (PRA) have proven to be much more pro-innovation than their counterparts in Europe and the United States. From their availability to engage with fintechs early and the creation of sandboxes (where startups can create and test new financial propositions while being monitored), UK regulators have been emulated across the globe. By promoting innovation in their domestic market, UK regulators have pushed their European counterparts to innovate. It will be interesting to see how the separation from the EU will shape the future of financial innovation in both the UK and Europe.

Banking regulation in the UK is centred around three organizations: the FSA, the Bank of England and the Treasury. Following the financial crisis, the scope of regulation was realigned along two major objectives: micro-prudential and macro-prudential regulation.

The first deals with risks relating to specific businesses while the second looks at the industry as a whole. This realignment was driven in large part by the EBA. Post-Brexit the UK is not expected to diverge too much from this approach.

This realignment makes UK regulation more hands-on than in the past, where it was sometimes described as light-touch, with regulators preferring to intervene only when necessary, and only in limited ways.

MICRO-PRUDENTIAL REGULATION

This regulation refers to the regulation and supervision of individual firms in the financial sector, to ensure that they remain solvent and operate in the interests of consumers. In effect, this means ensuring that each bank has a balance sheet which can withstand economic and financial shocks.

Prior to 2013, the FSA was the main banking regulator. In that year, micro-prudential regulation was handed over to a new regulatory authority – the PRA. Furthermore, the FCA was created to maintain high levels of competition in the financial sector:

- **The PRA**

  The role of the PRA (part of the Bank of England) is to create and maintain a stable financial system. To ensure this, the PRA was given responsibility for the day-to-day regulation of around 1,700 financial institutions, including banks, building societies and credit unions, insurers, large investment firms and fintechs.

- **The FCA**

  The FCA is not part of the Bank of England and has the responsibility for ensuring that financial markets work effectively, ensuring that firms in financial markets have a code of conduct that is acceptable and meets the legislative standards. The FCA acts like a watchdog to make sure competition is maintained and that financial institutions do not abuse their dominant positions.

- **Project Innovate**

  One of the most noticeable aspects of both these regulators – especially when compared to regulators in other markets – is their interest and support for innovation in the sector (FCA, 2017). This is reflected in initiatives such as the FCA's Project Innovate: a series of initiatives aimed at providing support for innovators to design, validate and test their innovative financial services propositions directly with the regulator. Through Project Innovate, firms are helped to tackle regulatory barriers to innovation by clarifying regulatory expectations, examining their own rules or even by initiating policy changes – all to make sure innovation delivers changes that are in the interest of consumers. This initiative includes the FCA Sandbox where the regulators are working more deeply with innovative firms to trial and bring innovative propositions to market. Since its launch in 2016, 29 companies had been admitted into the Sandbox by mid-2019.

- **Global Financial Innovation Network (GFIN)**
  The FCA is also working with a number of regulators in other countries to drive innovation abroad (HM Treasury, 2019). The GFIN was formally launched in January 2019 by an international group of financial regulators and related organizations, including the FCA (FCA, 2019). The GFIN is a network of 50 organizations across the globe committed to supporting financial innovation in the interests of consumers. It seeks to provide a more efficient way for innovative firms to interact with regulators, helping them navigate between countries as they look to scale new ideas.

- **New Bank Startup Unit**
  Another initiative in support of innovation is the joint PRA and FCA New Bank Startup Unit launched in 2016. This is a joint initiative giving information and support to newly authorized banks and those thinking of becoming a new bank in the UK (FCA, 2018). This unit – staffed from both the PRA and the FCA – assists new banks entering the market and through the early days of authorization by providing information, materials and a focused supervisory resource. The unit assigns case officers to the entities going through the authorization process to provide such support. Given that there have been dozens of new bank applications and licences issued since Metro Bank received the first new licence in 150 years in 2010, the unit has been kept very busy and is vital in shaping the UK's future banking landscape. New banks benefit from access to a helpline, supervisors at both agencies and regular capital and liquidity reviews.

MACRO-PRUDENTIAL REGULATION

Macro-prudential regulation looks at the financial system as a whole in order to avoid the risk of losses by limiting the build-up of system-wide financial risk. This is led by the Financial Policy Committee (FPC), a specialized committee at the Bank of England.

This committee's role is to address 'systemic risk', to make recommendations and to give instructions to the other regulators on actions to be undertaken to eliminate or mitigate that risk. That said, the FPC has no direct regulatory enforcement capability over individual businesses.

One way of doing this is through periodic 'stress tests' to determine how the financial system as a whole would respond to an economic and financial crisis, such as a stock market crash or a long-lasting recession.

The UK's regulatory processes and policies have been the secret behind the success of fintech in London.

Academia

London is home to some of the most highly rated academic institutions in the world. Under the umbrella of the University of London, some of the world's top academic institutions provide London with a pipeline of high-quality graduates. Universities such as University College London (UCL), King's College and the London School of Economics (LSE) are all based in the UK capital. World-renowned universities at Oxford and Cambridge are a short train journey away, making London a global hub for academic excellence.

The cross-fertilization between academia and business is at the core of London's success. Let us take a closer look at the leading academic institutions in London that are involved in fintech.

RESEARCH UNIVERSITIES

These are large universities with global standing, highly rated curricula, large student bases and highly qualified instructors. London is home to a large number of these institutions. The following are just a few of those institutions with an active involvement in the London fintech ecosystem:

- **Imperial College London**
  Imperial College London is a world top 10 university with an international reputation for excellence in teaching and research. It is a multidisciplinary science and innovation space for education, research and commercialization. It runs several courses on finance and technology including a course specifically on fintech (Imperial College Business School, 2019).

- **King's College London**
  One of the oldest universities in the UK and a leading research university with five campuses in the heart of London, King's College offers a

Master's degree in Computational Finance and Fintech and hosts a research centre on 'FinWork', researching the impact of technology on the financial services sector (King's College London, 2019). King's is also home to the Entrepreneurship Institute (kcl.ac.uk/entrepreneurship/) which supports entrepreneurial thinking, skills and experiences amongst King's students, staff and alumni.

- **University College London**
  UCL is one of the largest universities in the UK, with faculties that range from liberal arts to the sciences, and whose academics have been awarded 29 Nobel prizes. It houses the Institute of Finance and Technology (IFT) to provide leadership and training for future financial and business leaders with a focus on inclusion and fairness in finance, and offers fintech modules on two of its Masters' courses.

SPECIALIST UNIVERSITIES

These are independent institutions often linked to the research universities. They were usually created to fulfil a specific mandate or to focus on niche academic areas. Some of the institutions most involved in fintech are:

- **London School of Economics and Political Science (LSE)**
  LSE is one of the foremost social science universities in the world. It offers a number of courses that touch on fintech including a short course on the blockchain and cryptocurrencies (London School of Economics, 2019).

- **School of Oriental and African Studies (SOAS)**
  SOAS at the University of London is the leading higher education institution in Europe specializing in the study of Asia, Africa and the Near and Middle East. It focuses on informing and shaping current thinking about global economic, political, cultural, security and religious challenges. In collaboration with leading universities across the developing world it runs seminars and courses on the impact of fintech and technology in emerging economies.

- **London Business School (LBS)**
  LBS is also part of the University of London federation, and was established in 1964 to offer postgraduate degrees focused on business. It is an active player in the London fintech scene, offering several fintech courses for students and corporate executives.

- **Cass Business School**
  Cass is part of the City University of London and was also created in the 1960s to provide postgraduate business education. Partly due to its

proximity to the City, Cass has always had a close link to London's financial institutions. It is an active player in the London fintech ecosystem.

OUTSIDE LONDON

London is the destination for many graduates from other prestigious schools across the UK. These include universities in Oxford, Cambridge, Bristol, Manchester and Edinburgh. All have educated entrepreneurs that have contributed to making London a global fintech hub. Two of the most distinctive of the non-London institutions involved in financial services innovation are:

- **Judge Business School**
  The Cambridge Centre for Alternative Finance, part of the University of Cambridge's Judge Business School, is an international interdisciplinary academic research institute dedicated to the study of alternative finance, including financial channels and instruments that emerge outside of the traditional financial system, ie regulated banks and capital markets (jbs. cam.ac.uk/faculty-research/centres/alternative-finance/). It is proactively looking at the impact of the most innovative developments in fintech and is also heavily engaged with academic institutions outside the UK – with a particular focus on China.

- **Saïd Business School**
  Säid is the business school of the University of Oxford. It is part of Oxford's Social Sciences Division with both undergraduate and postgraduate degrees in business, management and finance. They have a number of courses on fintech including the intensive Oxford Fintech Programme and the MBA Executive Education Programme.

Language and geography

Two of London's greatest assets are language and geography. The English language is the first language of 20 per cent of the world's population and the lingua franca of technology and finance, as many of the leading finance and tech firms were started or have large operations in the United States.

The ubiquity of the English language combined with a benevolent geography and time zone have given London a unique upside. Sharing a language leads to sharing similar legal and cultural frameworks. Historically, this has led to US firms who are expanding into Europe to often choose London as their first outpost in the region, enhancing the financial and commercial importance of the City. Also, conducting business on a global scale makes London's time zone, or GMT, more favourable from Silicon Valley to Sydney, giving the City an edge over other contenders for the crown of 'global fintech hub'.

Key institutions

London is also home to a number of organizations created to encourage and support the development of innovation in financial services. They include:

- incubators;
- accelerators;
- networks;
- programmes and institutions.

Incubators

London is home to several incubators, designed to help promising entrepreneurs and very early-stage businesses thrive. They provide advice, support and seed capital. Some of the best-known organizations in London include the following.

- **Aviva Ventures Garage**
  A collaborative working space, which includes Aviva partnership advice focused on 'insurtech'.
- **CyLon**
  An incubator focused on cybersecurity across several industries including financial services.
- **Founders Factory**
  A multi-sector global accelerator and incubator with its base in London. Backed by 11 top global corporates including L'Oréal, easyJet, Guardian Media Group, Aviva, Holtzbrinck, CSC and Marks & Spencer. It provides execution support to top entrepreneurs and leverages their network to build new technology businesses.
- **Seedcamp**
  A tech-focused VC fund, which provides funding and mentoring support for early-stage startups, focused on proven capital-efficient businesses. Great portfolio including Revolut, TransferWise, Monese and Curve.

Accelerators

These are organizations that help early-stage businesses scale by providing support, advice and sometimes investment. Some of the leading London accelerators include the following:

- **Accenture Innovation FinTech Lab**
  An accelerator run by global consulting firm Accenture, it provides an angel network and mentoring, with frequent corporate showcases.

- **Barclays Accelerator**
  A programme powered by Techstars (the global accelerator programme) and backed by Barclays Bank. It offers a 13-week programme where the bank invests a small minority equity stake in the startup, providing mentoring and access to their customer data and knowledge.

Networks

London is also home to a number of organizations, professional bodies and events focused on helping individuals and organizations realize the opportunities and threats related to digital innovation in financial services. They are aimed at supporting the growth of new businesses, and provide networking, some advice and access to finance. Some of the more prominent fintech networks in London and the UK include the following:

- **ELITE programme**
  A programme run and delivered by the London Stock Exchange in collaboration with Imperial College Business School and which provides high-growth companies with education, business support, mentorship and increased funding access. It is supported by, amongst others, the Confederation of British Industry (CBI), the British Venture Capital Association (BVCA) and Tech Nation (the Association of Startups formerly called Tech City).

- **Alan Turing Institute**
  This government-funded non-profit organization was created to attract leading data scientists and mathematicians globally and to form partnerships with industry players to help position the UK as a world leader in the analysis and application of big data and algorithmic research.

- **London Institute of Banking and Finance (LIBF)**
  LIBF is one of the oldest training and professional bodies for banking and financial services in London. It works with partners across the globe to

establish sector-wide professional standards around the world. Its Centre for Digital Banking and Finance provides a number of qualifications around digital innovation in banking with a distinctive focus on regulation (LIBF, 2019).

- **Level 39**
Level 39 is considered one of Europe's largest fintech communities. It provides startups (and some scale-ups) with office space, mentoring, networking and the ability to join and host events. Its location in Canary Wharf (London's second financial hub outside the City) provides fintechs with unique opportunities to engage with some of the world's largest financial institutions.

Programmes and institutions

These organizations are aimed at supporting and facilitating the engagement of investors, experts and entrepreneurs. They are sometimes sponsored by the government, and include:

- **British Business Bank (BBB) and BBB Investments**
This is a state-owned economic development bank supporting SME access to finance. The UK government allocates capital to the BBB to be lent via funds and other financial intermediaries to companies (including fintechs) focused on SME lending.

- **Innovate UK**
The UK innovation agency, responsible for driving science and technology innovation by funding projects, determining key focus sectors and connecting innovators with partners and supporting their growth.

- **Innovate Finance (IF)**
The independent industry body that represents and advances the global fintech community in the UK with a mission to accelerate the UK's leading role in the financial services sector by directly supporting the next generation of innovators. IF is a key force behind many initiatives undertaken by the UK government and businesses in supporting innovation in financial services and fintech.

- **Financial Services Trade and Investment Board**
This government and industry collaboration identifies growth opportunities in the financial services industry to support foreign trade and investment in the UK fintech sector.

- **Tech Nation UK**

  A non-profit organization launched in 2011 as Tech City UK to support digital technology businesses and entrepreneurs in London. In 2017, it merged with Tech North to serve all of the UK through entrepreneurship programmes and policy work. Amongst its programmes it offers The Founder's Network supporting startups, Upscale aimed at growing firms and Future Fifty focusing on later-stage firms. It also includes targeted industry programmes on fintech, cyber and AI. Notable fintech alumni include fintech successes Monzo, Revolut, Starling and TransferWise.

Key events

London hosts large fintech events on a regular basis. In fact, scarcely a week passes without an event targeting innovation in financial services. The following list outlines some of the most popular ones.

- **MoneyLIVE**

  This organization holds a number of events during the year at different locations across the globe. They bring together senior leaders and innovators across banking, payments and fintech to meet, network and share ideas. Two of the events hosted by them, the flagship MoneyLIVE Summit and the Digital Banking summit, are both held in London.

- **LendIt Fintech**

  LendIt Fintech is a well-structured event focused on financial services innovation. It hosts three conferences per year in the United States, Europe and China (lendit.com/Europe/2019). The European summit is hosted in London, bringing together major fintechs, digital banking companies and established players from around the world. Well attended by professionals in the financial services industry.

- **FinTech World Forum**

  The FinTech World Congress and Banking Summit Forum (FinTech Conference, fintechconferences.com) is targeted at professionals in the global financial services and banking technology industry. In the past, speakers have included Mastercard, ING Bank, Microsoft, IBM, Citibank, Oracle and Credit Suisse.

- **UK FinTech Week**

  This national series of events is centred around London. The week-long series of events showcases the UK as an epicentre of innovation. By taking a think-tank and collaborative approach, the event explores and debates fintech innovation, with topics varying every year. The event's partners include HM Treasury, Innovate Finance, the Department for International Trade, the Financial Conduct Authority, the London Stock Exchange, London & Partners and the City of London.

- **Innovate Finance Global Summit (IFGS)**
  This large event is traditionally based in London's historic Guildhall and brings the global fintech community to London. It showcases the industry and the global and cross-sector nature of financial innovation, and offers exhibition space and networking areas, enabling participants to network.

- **Money20/20 Europe**
  This global event (it is also held in the United States and Asia) is not usually held in London, but it is one of best-attended events by the capital's fintech players. It is a huge well-run showcase where startups, challengers, incumbents, tech firms, infrastructure providers, media and a wide range of other organizations engaged with fintech take part and mingle.

Key actors

The key players in the London fintech ecosystem include the large national banks, the smaller regional banks and building societies, the challenger banks and the specialist fintechs (see Figure 7.1). They are slowly morphing their propositions to address the new market realities (Megaw, 2019). The same applies to the smaller regional banks and building societies – even though these are less capable of investing in innovation at the scale of the large incumbent banks.

Other players are shaping the digital banking and financial services markets in the UK. The most interesting companies to keep an eye on fall into the following categories.

The incumbents

These are large universal banks serving all segments from retail to large corporates. They are still the dominant players in the UK market. Many are also active outside the UK. They include Lloyds Banking Group (LBG), Barclays, RBS/NatWest, HSBC and Santander.

The traditional challengers

These are smaller financial institutions that have much smaller market share than the incumbents. They have a smaller national footprint and a smaller range of products and services. These also include specialist banks. Some of the most recognized names in this group are Metro Bank, CYBG, Virgin Money (now owned by CYBG), Nationwide, The Co-op and all the building societies across the UK.

The digital challengers

These are businesses created to compete with the incumbent banks head to head. Their objective is to compete with the big banks by offering all or most of the services provided by the big banks, but with a better UX and a much lower cost base. They have a wide range of products – offered directly or through partners – and they eventually aim to serve all segments. Today, they are focused on retail and smaller business customers. They include the likes of Monzo and Starling Bank.

The specialist challengers

These provide a subset of the services offered by the universal banks. But they provide this subset of products much more competitively. For the time being they are content to be used side-by-side with the incumbent banks. They provide products such as money transfers, higher-interest savings, credit cards or mortgages. These include firms like TransferWise, Atom, Tandem, Curve and Monese. They also include challengers that target specific customer segments. Good examples of these are the fintechs and banks that target business banking customers. This grouping includes OakNorth, Tide and Cashplus.

The platforms

These are often built on top of infrastructure provided by the incumbent banks, using digital technology to change some of the fundamental banking services. These are crowdfunding platforms that enable bank customers to do things with their money that the incumbents would not normally allow them to do. These include providing or receiving direct loans to other customers or investing in startups. The leading challenger banks and fintechs in this space are Zopa, Funding Circle, Ratesetter, Crowdcube and Seedrs.

FIGURE 7.1 The London fintech ecosystem: Key actors

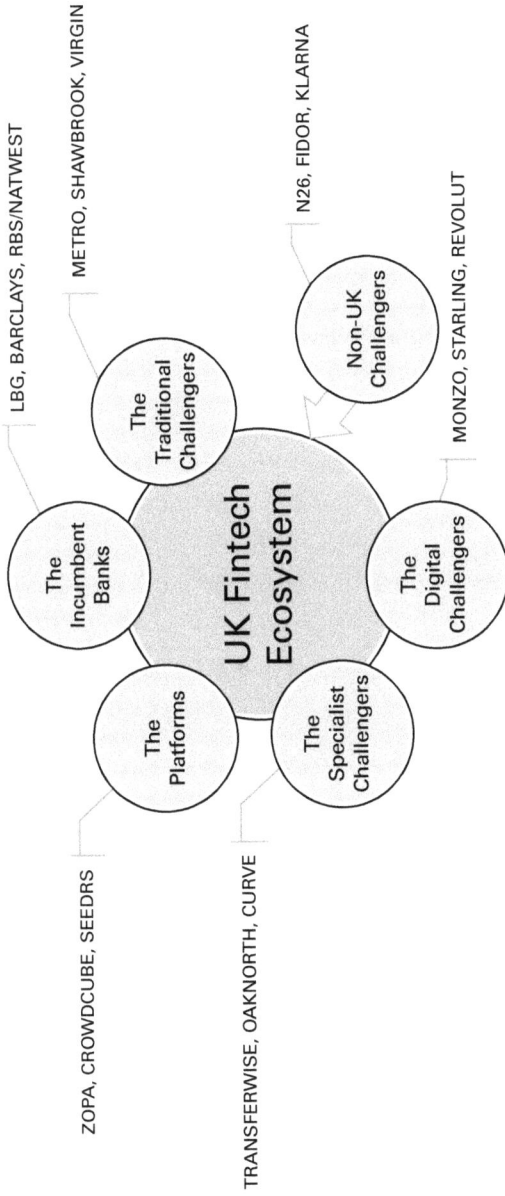

LBG, BARCLAYS, RBS/NATWEST

METRO, SHAWBROOK, VIRGIN

N26, FIDOR, KLARNA

MONZO, STARLING, REVOLUT

ZOPA, CROWDCUBE, SEEDRS

TRANSFERWISE, OAKNORTH, CURVE

The Incumbent Banks

The Traditional Challengers

Non-UK Challengers

The Digital Challengers

The Platforms

The Specialist Challengers

UK Fintech Ecosystem

The non-UK challengers

One of the outcomes of the UK leaving the EU has been that challengers based in Europe have delayed, slowed down or even reversed their UK market entry. The post-Brexit months and years will tell if the UK and London will continue to be seen as a desirable destination by challengers from outside the UK. Firms like N26 and Klarna are part of this cohort.

Key influencers

London fintech has developed through the years as a result of the vision, charisma, hard work and passion of thousands of individuals. It is hard – if not impossible – to pen a short list of influencers that is comprehensive and fair. We can talk about many influencers:

- corporate visionaries such as Zaka Mian, Ashley Machin and Ashok Vaswani who drove their banks to go digital;
- founders like Giles Andrews, Tom Blomfield and Anne Boden who created giants from an idea using their ingenuity and tenacity;
- believers in startups like Nektarios Lolios and Eric Van der Kleij;
- the voices of UK fintech including 11:FS, The Finanser and Duena Blomstrom;
- bet-takers who backed founders and sketchy business plans like Reshma Sohoni, Eileen Burbidge and Danny Rimer.

In all, the key influencers list for London is long and complex; far too long to attempt to provide a definitive list here.

Conclusion

London is fast becoming the leading global fintech centre. The convergence of people, regulation and capital has created an environment ideal for the creation of new businesses that will use digital innovation to challenge and transform the financial services industry. A few unique factors have made London's success possible:

- the geographic proximity of the financial institutions of the City and Canary Wharf to the creativity of the Silicon Roundabout;

- the presence of a large number of high-net-worth individuals who are not afraid of risk, and ready to take a bet on new ventures supported by an investor-friendly tax regime;
- the aggregation of high-quality educational institutions adjacent to a huge number of demanding employers willing to pay for the best talent across the globe;
- the presence of a prudent but innovation-friendly regulator.

These factors together have created a very supportive environment for fintech.

Today, London is second only to Silicon Valley (Walters, 2019) in size and diversity of its fintech innovation. The only possible spanner in the works is anything that could disrupt this situation. Technical, financial and political changes impacting the UK and the world in the coming years will determine whether London will continue in its upwards trajectory or otherwise.

References

Blackman, P (2019) Global Fintech Investment Hits Record $111.8B in 2018, KPMG, 13 February, home.kpmg/xx/en/home/media/press-releases/2019/02/global-fintech-investment-hits-record-in-2018.html (archived at https://perma.cc/8SMX-UFZT)

Capgemini (2019) World FinTech Report 2019, 7 June, www.capgemini.com/gb-en/news/world-fintech-report-2019/ (archived at https://perma.cc/QK4Z-2BP5)

City of London (2018) Record number of European workers in the City of London, 26 January, news.cityoflondon.gov.uk/record-number-of-european-workers-in-the-city-of-london (archived at https://perma.cc/49NE-3ZLY)

FCA (2017) Innovating for the Future: the next Phase of Project Innovate, 10 April, www.fca.org.uk/news/speeches/innovating-future-next-phase-project-innovate (archived at https://perma.cc/42XM-7VZ4)

FCA (2018) New bank start-up unit launched by the financial regulators, 31 December, www.fca.org.uk/news/press-releases/new-bank-start-unit-launched-financial-regulators (archived at https://perma.cc/62KZ-K4F8)

FCA (2019) Global Financial Innovation Network (GFIN) *FCA*, 24 October, www.fca.org.uk/firms/global-financial-innovation-network (archived at https://perma.cc/ST89-2ULC)

Gentleman, A, Busby, M and Syal, R (2019) 'Reckless' plan to cut off free movement alarms EU nationals, *The Guardian*, 19 August, www.theguardian.com/politics/2019/aug/19/reckless-plan-to-cut-off-free-movement-alarms-eu-nationals (archived at https://perma.cc/9ACH-CYF2)

Glencross, J (2019) The EIS has cost the government £3bn in tax relief, so why has it become more generous? *CityAM*, 3 June, www.cityam.com/eis-has-cost-government-3bn-tax-relief-so-why-has-become/ (archived at https://perma.cc/7NQP-Z9ZK)

HM Treasury (2019) UK FinTech: On the Cutting Edge, 24 February, www.gov.uk/government/publications/uk-fintech-on-the-cutting-edge (archived at https://perma.cc/6QXU-8JVT)

Howard, M (2016) The City of London was never the same after the 'Big Bang', *New Statesman,* 22 October, www.newstatesman.com/culture/books/2016/10/city-london-was-never-same-after-big-bang (archived at https://perma.cc/DA5Q-4EU3)

Imperial College Business School (2019) Fintech – Innovative Banking Course, www.imperial.ac.uk/business-school/executive-education/open-programmes/fintech-innovative-banking/?gclid=Cj0KCQiAl5zwBRCTARIsAIrukdNQGOHFnvZU-gOGrH4LdxuvoSZQ03MVJBJAx7DU-nA3d3aPhG5WNJcaApBCEALw_wcB&gclsrc=aw.ds (archived at https://perma.cc/5RCU-PKNN)

King's College London (2019) FinWork Futures Research Centre, www.kcl.ac.uk/business/research/centres/fintech-futures/finwork-futures-research-centre (archived at https://perma.cc/Z7TB-HCFY)

KPMG (2019) Venture Pulse: Q4 2018 Global Analysis of Venture Funding, *KPMG*, home.kpmg/xx/en/home/insights/2019/01/venture-pulse-q4-18-global-analysis-of-venture-funding.html (archived at https://perma.cc/4LSL-4UGK)

Lewis, R (2019) List of Small Business Grants in the UK, *Entrepreneur Handbook*, 19 September, entrepreneurhandbook.co.uk/grants-loans/ (archived at https://perma.cc/WF4Z-6DCK)

LIBF (2019) Programmes, Courses and Qualifications, www.libf.ac.uk/study/professional-qualifications/the-centre-for-digital-banking-and-finance/programmes-courses-and-qualifications (archived at https://perma.cc/2ZCV-2WKS)

London School of Economics (2019) Cryptocurrency and Disruption, www.lse.ac.uk/study-at-lse/Online-learning/Courses/Cryptocurrency-Investment-and-Disruption (archived at https://perma.cc/G78G-6335)

Megaw, N (2019) Race to Become UK Digital Banking Leader Hots Up, *Financial Times*, 5 October, www.ft.com/content/9e004184-e68d-11e9-b112-9624ec9edc59 (archived at https://perma.cc/L2DP-GDXF)

Rewal, J (2019) Innovation grants: the five biggest recipients in 2019, *Beauhurst*, 22 November, about.beauhurst.com/blog/5-biggest-innovation-grants-2019/ (archived at https://perma.cc/6U7S-TQKX)

Specialist Banking (2019) An Interview with Ricky Knox: 'It's about Time the Mortgage Sector Caught up with the Way People Live', specialistbanking.co.uk/article-desc- 7164_an-interview-with-ricky-knox-its-about-time-the-mortgage-sector-caught-up-with-the-way-people-live (archived at https://perma.cc/Q6E6-P6XY)

UKRI (2019) *How to Apply – UK Research and Innovation*, www.ukri.org/funding/how-to-apply/ (archived at https://perma.cc/B9F4-SQKW)

Wallop, H (2010) Metro Bank granted FSA licence, *The Telegraph*, 5 March, www.telegraph.co.uk/finance/personalfinance/7377565/Metro-bank-granted-FSA-licence.html (archived at https://perma.cc/23RG-BD2L)

Walters, R (2019) The UK fintech revolution, *Specialist Professional Recruitment*, www.robertwalters.co.uk/hiring/campaigns/the-uk-fintech-revolution.html (archived at https://perma.cc/4P44-LC2Z)

08

The Gulf

Background

Gulf Cooperation Council (GCC) landscape

The GCC is a regional inter-governmental political and economic union made up of the states of the Gulf: Saudi Arabia, the seven Emirates of the UAE (including Abu Dhabi and Dubai), Bahrain, Oman, Qatar and Kuwait.

Despite being a relatively new player in the global financial services industry, the Gulf region, particularly Dubai and Abu Dhabi, is now a significant component of the international fintech landscape (Fintechnews, 2019). The reasons for this are varied as we will see in this chapter; the stakeholders also vary from incumbents and regulators to governments and fintechs. However, what is overwhelmingly clear when working in the region is that there is a collective will to bring genuine collaboration innovation to the region, to nurture fintech growth within the region, to release a wave of capital to fund this growth, and above all to come up with solutions where fintech products and services meet the needs of the region's very diverse population. As with every region, there are some forward-thinking pioneers who see the opportunities and gain first-mover advantage, and GCC is no different.

Data is the new oil

As oil reserves decline, a regional awareness of the need to diversify various individual economies more deeply into areas such as tourism, real estate and financial services has emerged. All key participants in the region have realized that the data that comes from this diversification has value and could be the 'new oil'. The movement encompasses a diverse set of stakeholders ranging from ruling families, central banks, governments and regulators to financial services and telco incumbents, investors, and, of course, fintech has entrepreneurs from all corners of the Earth. All are taking positive steps to create a supportive and inclusive ecosystem that has gone a long way to providing solutions to meet the needs of all parties, including end-users, who in some countries in the region are largely made up of a migratory population, and whose lack of a financial footprint can make it notoriously difficult for incumbents to serve their financial needs. They are also moving with speed and, to the outside observer, with gusto and determination.

Accelerators, financial zones, innovation labs, new investors and proactive regulators have seemingly sprung up like oases in the desert, ready to source, support and succeed in the brave new fintech world. The promised prizes of inclusion and efficiency through technology have taken the region by storm and are now part of the everyday vernacular in financial services.

The fintech influence in the region

Established industry players such as incumbent banks, telcos and foreign exchange providers are only just waking up to the opportunities afforded by this relatively nascent area of fintech and want to exploit its potential. The 56 million people who make up the GCC (GCC-STAT, nd) are looking for customer-driven solutions to their financial needs. If that were not enough of a pool to fish in, Egypt and Jordan are also emerging as significant participants in the fintech landscape. This chapter will focus on the major centres for fintech: Dubai, Abu Dhabi, Saudi Arabia and Bahrain.

However, while the major cities in these countries are sometimes seen as pockets of extreme wealth, the wider population is largely underbanked and hosts a large number of migrant workers who struggle to access banks and payment services.

Key drivers

Change on this scale does not happen by accident or without an understanding of how to capitalize on some of the existing key drivers that combine to create the perfect 'fintech storm' in the region. There is a palpable collective will to succeed that is backed up by physical and financial resources to enable not just local success, but success that can be exported from and imported into the region.

Growth in fintech has happened very quickly over the past five years, overtaking growth in other industries in the region. Alongside this aggressive fintech growth, there are five areas that stand out as critical to this impressive transformation.

The perfect storm demographics

A lot of people! And a significant proportion of young people are tech-friendly, making them ideal for fintech adoption. Viewed as a whole, the MENA region (Middle East/North Africa) has approximately 300 million people in its realm. Of course, not all of them will be in the fintech target for early adopters or for that next critical tranche of customers who go beyond the believers and begin to contribute to a meaningful bottom line, but if the proposition is right for the region there is ample opportunity to test and prospect for buyers for solutions.

A population that embraces new technology

A recent report (MAGNiTT, 2019) in the region found that 83 per cent of UAE residents are receptive to adopting fintech solutions by non-financial institutions and 76 per cent trust at least one technology company more than their bank with their money. This is a much higher take-up rate than many other parts of the world and could be explained by the region's demographics and the fact that it does not have any long-standing heritage brands which normally have some loyalty with users. One of the positive by-products is that it makes the region a perfect testing bed for new fintech solutions.

The region is also home to a large migrant population from countries such as the Philippines, India and Pakistan, who are more likely to have access to the internet and smartphones than they are to a full-stack bank account with an incumbent. They come with a demand for expat capital transfer and repatriation.

Internet penetration and online payments

As we debate the rollout of 5G in certain parts of the world, and struggle to get a signal in some of the shires and villages outside global metropolitan regions in developed countries, the GCC countries boast one of the highest average levels of internet penetration, added to which over three-quarters of the population appear to be at ease with online payments.

Of the 3.9 billion internet users globally in 2018, 164 million of them were in MENA. The internet penetration rate in the GCC is the highest amongst all sub-regions of MENA. The penetration rate for the UAE was 91 per cent for 2018 and for Saudi Arabia 73 per cent in the same year. In comparison, the leading country in North Africa, Egypt, had a penetration rate of 43 per cent during the same time period (Puri-Mirza, 2019).

Access to capital: government and private funding

A forward-looking region, there are currently five government funds that support fintechs with over $1 billion of capital (MAGNiTT, 2019). Some of these government funds are distributed via fintech accelerators and incubators who also attract private capital from the region and abroad.

Investing alongside the government there is a healthy private capital scene emerging, albeit very regionally focused, with over 75 local investors, including family offices, having already taken the plunge and more joining their ranks every day. The region is very successful in attracting and retaining investment for fintech. Recent figures put the total inward investment into the MENA region at $237 million invested in 181 deals during the period 2015–19 (MAGNiTT, 2019).

Regulators back fintech with desert sandboxes and other initiatives

The complex landscape of regional regulations can be a challenge for entrepreneurs and startups to navigate; regulations are not consistent across borders in the GCC, and unlike trade zones such as the EU, being cleared to operate in one country, eg the UAE, does not allow a business to move easily into neighbouring nations. However, recognizing that this has in the past been a barrier for cross-border service providers, the Dubai Financial Services Authority (DFSA), Abu Dhabi Global Market Authority (ADGMA), Bahrain Central Bank (BCB) and others are working to improve this issue so that the region can develop and become a significant global player.

Abu Dhabi was particularly bullish on finding ways to engage the fintech community and the ADGMA made the region's first move into fintech with the launch of its Regulatory Laboratory, a fintech licensing regime to permit live testing in 2016 (Financemagnates, 2016).

Islamic fintech: additional driver and opportunity

There is another element that gives the region a clearly defined characteristic when it comes to financial services and fintech and that is the Islamic religion law, Shari'a, that governs the daily religious rituals of followers and encompasses financial matters as well. No longer confined to countries or regions where Islam is the predominant religion, the positive aspects of Islamic fintech solutions have struck a chord with financial institutions and end-users across the globe.

Regionally, digitally adept millennial Muslims, favourable regulatory regimes and government support have been partly responsible for the explosive growth in faith-based ethical finance in the form of Shari'a-compliant fintech solutions, which until recently had largely been overlooked by the mainstream financial services incumbents. Although Islamic fintech is a nascent industry, there is an opportunity to embrace the new transparency and choice that digital technology affords, and to do this at scale, going beyond applying a Shari'a-compliant lens to existing financial products and services.

One area where applying Shari'a principles would be very logical is in crowdfunding, where, according to expert and UK Islamic Finance Council (UKIFC) board member, Omar Shaikh, Islamic finance and fintech make a good match and opportunities emerge from this kinship:

> These [crowdfunding platforms] allow individuals to select where their money is deployed, but also how and indeed what level of return they chose to accept. By flexing the return dynamic it is possible to incorporate social returns alongside financial return. This approach to intermediation with enhanced transparency and choice is arguably better aligned with the *mudarabah* construct (owner of capital and the manager) compared to the existing structures used – restricted and unrestricted *mudarabah* Islamic banking deposit accounts.

The founders of Beehive, an SME P2P lending platform, and Yielders, an award-winning Islamic real estate investment platform, are leading examples of how to be successful and compliant. Mr Shaikh goes on to explain:

> Ultimately Islamic finance is the sale of a financial product that is deemed to be Shari'a-compliant by a board of Shari'a scholars. There is a high degree of transparency in products and services enabling financiers to see precise returns and remain compliant.

The sector can broadly be understood through three key lenses:

1 Negative screening: avoiding engagement with 'sin sectors' which are deemed to be harmful to society at large, such as alcohol or tobacco.

2 The ban on receiving or charging interest – returns can only be made through asset sale transactions (cost plus) or rent earned on underlying assets (operating/financing leasing).

3 Strong restrictions on excessive speculation and transactions with uncertainty, thereby heavily limiting the use of the derivatives market and only mutual insurance models being acceptable.

Another example of how Islamic fintech is becoming more integrated is the Dubai DIFC programme at the FinTech Hive, where the cohort is able to avail itself of the scholarly guidance and advice of the Dubai Islamic Economy Development Centre (DIEDC, 2019), established in December 2013 under the supervision of His Highness Sheikh Hamdan bin Mohammed bin Rashid Al Maktoum, Crown Prince of Dubai and Chairman of the Dubai Executive Council, to transform Dubai into the capital of Islamic economy.

Their current economic strategy (2017–21) focuses on identifying ways to measure and monitor the growth in Islamic finance, halal products and Islamic lifestyle encompassing culture, art, fashion and family tourism, as well as measuring their contribution to the UAE's national economy. Sharing knowledge, providing guidance and adding their voice to the ongoing development of regulatory frameworks, the DIEDC actively partners with key stakeholders in the region and also provides mentoring and support to Islamic fintechs and to those who are considering Islamic fintech or curious to learn more.

Key strengths

As with every region of the world, the characteristics that define the economic, demographic and regulatory environments shape a landscape where certain fintech verticals emerge as front-runners in the developing ecosystem. For the GCC, the main areas where fintech is making and can continue to make a significant impact are:

- P2P lending;
- crowdfunding;
- mobile payments and remittances;

- trading platforms;
- investment and robo-advisory services;
- insurtech;
- blockchain.

Emerging trends

Although not currently as predominant as those listed above, other fintech technologies are high on government agendas. We should also not forget that if we assume that 'data is the new oil' then impact will also be felt using AI and big data to improve banking and investment services, blockchain and distributed ledger solutions will also have a positive and much needed impact in the area of trade finance, particularly where SMEs struggle to gain full access, despite making up a significant proportion of input to GDP (as in other countries such as the UK, United States and parts of Europe) in a number of the region's countries (Global Property Guide, 2019).

We will explore these in greater detail further on in this chapter when we delve into accelerators, stand-out fintechs and key players in the region.

Talent

Every region where fintech is emerging feels the pressure of talent acquisition and retention. In smaller countries, as we will see in Chapter 11 on Tel Aviv, for example, there is an abundance of talent but also an exodus as the domestic market cannot support the scaling of fintechs. In London, talent has come from a wide spectrum of countries, with some of the UK's unicorn fintechs having been founded and developed by foreign entrepreneurs. What will be the impact on talent in a post-Brexit Britain still remains to be seen. What we have seen, for example in Paris, are government awareness and initiatives to upskill, attract and retain both domestic and foreign talent and to start sowing the seeds of tech skills much earlier in a child's education so as to develop a local talent pool. The GCC feels the same pain but is also making headway in this space.

Legislative changes

In the past, the region was fairly restrictive with regard to foreign workers. Visas were limited in number and came with red tape and restrictions which meant that recruiting skilled workers was expensive and time-consuming for companies. However, recent legislative changes in the UAE have provided a new opportunity for foreign investors and given a boost to fintech.

The changes to the employment laws in 2018 were lauded as one of the most significant changes to the UAE economy since the 2002 freehold law which enabled foreigners to buy property. The new laws allow foreign nationals to set up businesses outside of the countries' free zones and to own them 100 per cent. They also allow for 10-year residency visas to be made available for specialist workers in fields such as technology and academia, along with five-year visas for students in the country.

Commentators in the industry are of the opinion that the new rules will be a game-changer and boost the UAE economy, promising a new era of creativity and business continuity.

Educational initiatives

As with many other regional hubs, the GCC countries are aware of the need for a tech-educated local population, but also of the need to find solutions that enable qualified and exceptional fintech entrepreneurs and employees to enter, remain for an extended period of time, and make meaningful contribution to the region. To that end, there are a number of government and regulator-led initiatives in the area of both academic and professional education, filling a void left by some of the global universities who appear to have put their fintech programmes on hold in recent years. These schemes include the following:

- **Government support**

  The full fintech ecosystem is very keen to welcome the wider overseas fintech community to the region, and in addition to a new visa regime and extended student visas, the UAE has added government support talent development initiatives such as One Million Arab Coders, a programme launched in October 2017 in order to give young Arabs skills they will need for a future economy (The National, 2017).

- **Abu Dhabi Global Market (ADGM)**

  The Abu Dhabi Global Market contains an academy for financial education, which aspires to be one of the leading academies in the region, providing world-class financial research and training services, and helping to position Abu Dhabi as a leading global financial centre. Their offering of globally recognized educational and experiential programmes on a range of topics and qualifications in banking, finance, leadership, entrepreneurship, technical and soft skills is constantly evolving and improving, and taking full advantage of the appetite for digital learning as well as face-to-face interaction. Its partnership with the UK's leading banking and financial services education and qualifications institute, the venerable LIBF (in London and Abu Dhabi), is further evidence of how seriously the ADGM Academy takes its mandate.

Regulation

The regulation of financial services in GCC countries is not a one-size-fits-all scenario, and takes different forms in different countries, with a number of GCC countries taking a multi-agency approach.

As we have seen globally, regulation can be seen as a help or a hindrance to getting fintech to market, and there are some Gulf states that have nudged their regulators to fast-track new rules to not only shore up the legalities of the sector, but also in a bid for regional prominence in the field.

Regulatory sandboxes: not child's play

Taking a proactive approach, the region is home to nine sandboxes: closed, controlled environments set up to test frameworks established by a regulator to enable fintechs and incumbents to access potential innovations using live data, as well as enabling regulatory labs established by regional governments to support fintech innovation. Sandboxes can be found in Abu Dhabi, Qatar, Egypt, Jordan, Oman, Bahrain, Kuwait, Saudi Arabia and Dubai, and have taken their inspiration from the UK, where the Sandbox was launched by the FCA in the UK in 2015. It was the first of its kind, and it has had sceptics and supporters, but has since gone on to house a number of successful cohorts, proving the value in the concept and the results. It has also launched a new Global Financial Innovation Sandbox (GFIN), which is explored in Chapter 7 on London, and which counts ADGM and DFSA (Dubai) amongst its members.

Who regulates what in the region

UNITED ARAB EMIRATES

The regulatory landscape in the UAE consists of three principal bodies: the UAE Central Bank (Central Bank) and the Securities and Commodities Authority (SCA) as the 'onshore' regulators; and the Dubai International Financial Services Authority (DFSA) in respect of the Dubai International

Financial Centre (DIFC), a separate financial free zone located in Dubai with its own civil and commercial laws and court system:

- **Dubai Financial Services Authority (DFSA)**
  The Dubai Financial Services Authority is a body established under Dubai law as the independent regulator of financial services. It administers the Regulatory Law 2004, which is the cornerstone legislation of the regulatory regime. The Law establishes and enables the regulatory framework within which entities may be licensed, authorized, registered and supervised by the DFSA. Representatives from the DFSA actively engage with the fintech community via vehicles such as the FinTech Hive and are keen observers of nascent technologies which will need to interact with regulators in the validation and approval process of becoming regulated. The DFSA also administers the Markets Law which governs the activities and conduct of financial and market participants, the Law Regulating Islamic Financial Business 2004, the Collective Investment Law 2010 and the Investment Trust Law 2006.

- **Dubai International Financial Centre (DIFC)**
  The DIFC was established in 2004 and is a special economic zone in the financial district of Dubai. The 110-hectare district is a major global financial hub for the Middle East, Africa and South Asia markets and the DIFC has its own independent, internationally regulated regulator and judicial system, common law framework, global financial exchange, tax-friendly regime, and a large, cosmopolitan business community with more than 21,000 professionals working across 1,600 firms. The DIFC is responsible for the Dubai accelerator, FinTech Hive, which is housed on its premises.

- **Abu Dhabi Global Markets Authority (ADGM Authority)**
  ADGM Authority is the Financial Services Regulatory Authority in Abu Dhabi and oversees a sound regulatory framework of clear and transparent rules, benchmarked against international standards and global best practices. It is responsible for Federal Legislation, Abu Dhabi Legislation and Financial Services Regulations and Rules. ADGM initiated the region's first VC fund framework in 2017, a proportionate and risk-based approach to regulate fintech. In 2018, it introduced a comprehensive crypto-asset regime which puts a robust framework around crypto activity. In 2019, it launched regulatory frameworks for digital banking, digital securities, robo-advisory, and the use of APIs.

- **The Financial Services and Markets Regulations (FSMR)**
  The FSMR established the legislative and regulatory framework for financial services in ADGM and has been broadly modelled on the UK's Financial Services and Markets Act 2000 (FSMA) and other related legislation.

The list of regulators will soon be expanded to include the Financial Services Regulatory Authority as regulator for the Abu Dhabi Global Market, a recently-launched financial free zone located in Abu Dhabi similar to the DIFC.

KINGDOM OF SAUDI ARABIA

- **Saudi Arabian Monetary Authority (SAMA)**
  The SAMA has existed for over 60 years and is the central bank of the Kingdom of Saudi Arabia. Headquartered in Riyadh, it deals with monetary policy, promotes the growth of a sound financial system and supervises commercial banks, foreign exchange dealers, insurance, finance and credit companies.

- **SAMA FinTech Saudi Initiative**
  The SAMA FinTech Saudi Initiative and the recent decision to set up a regulatory Sandbox is already having a positive impact on FinTech investment in the country, and banks such as Riyadh Bank are looking to deploy their CVC fund alongside other investors, sending another positive signal to the entrepreneurial community.

- **Capital Market Authority (CMA)**
  In addition to the SAMA, Saudi Arabia also has the CMA, which is responsible for the financial, legal, and policing of the Tadawul, Saudi Arabia's stock exchange.

KINGDOM OF BAHRAIN

- **Central Bank of Bahrain (CBB)**
  Alone within the GCC, Bahrain has opted for a unitary approach. The financial regulatory system is governed by the Central Bank of Bahrain, and the same regulations apply across the country, with no regulatory free zones. The CBB regulates both the conduct of financial services business in Bahrain as well as the financial institutions that provide those services. The CBB argues that this approach creates a consistent and coherent regulatory model that can be applied across the board and it also provides a straightforward and efficient regulatory framework for financial services firms operating in the country.

Key institutions

Accelerators and incubators

Following the lead of the explosive growth and proliferation of accelerators globally, the region's governments offer their own versions of direct physical and financial support solutions in the form of fintech-specific accelerator programmes, which, on a local level, are very competitive amongst themselves and very enthusiastic when it comes to getting their message out to the global community. These programmes are going from strength to strength, not only showcasing the best that the regional fintechs have to offer but also acting as catalysts and havens for global fintechs to enter the region as part of their overall expansion plans. These successful accelerators bring together entrepreneurs, incumbent financial institutions, other large corporates, such as credit card companies and telcos, investors and the regulator in both a virtual and a physical space that encourages knowledge exchange, product and team development, investment and opportunities for commercial engagement with corporate partners.

Looking at each offering in more detail, there a number of homegrown and/or partner programmes running throughout the region:

- UAE
  - DIFC FinTech Hive;
  - Plug and Play (Abu Dhabi Global Market).
- Saudi Arabia
  - Monsha'at and NCB (National Commerce Bank) collaboration;
  - FinTech Hive.
- Bahrain
  - Bahrain FinTech Bay.
- Jordan
  - Finance Forward: MENA 2020.

UAE: Dubai

DIFC FINTECH HIVE

Established in January 2017 and located in Dubai's financial district, the DIFC is the home of the FinTech Hive, a fintech accelerator that strives for genuine commercial engagement, information exchange and establishing best practice standards that can be shared further in the region (eg the Jeddah programme launched in 2019). It not only offers an accelerator programme, but also co-working space, investor introductions, growth workshops from over 60 partner organizations and a good, active working relationship with the local regulators. Since they began, startups have gone from start to super-stars in a short space of time and provide genuine opportunities for growth and commercial engagement in the region. The Hive is a best-in-class example of how government, startups/scaleups and corporates can create a focused and thriving ecosystem from scratch (Marketwatch.com, 2019).

The Hive has just concluded its third cohort, and in 2019 launched a sister programme in the Kingdom of Saudi Arabia (KSA). The 2019 cohort features 31 companies, which is a 50 per cent increase in the number of participants on the previous year, and covers a broader scope of verticals including fintech, insurtech, regtech and notably Islamic fintech.

The programme consists of a three-month curriculum in which a group of selected finalists work closely with stakeholders, industry and growth experts, mentors and partners to create innovative and forward-looking solutions that aim to address the evolving needs of the region's financial services industry.

At the helm is Executive Vice President Raja Al Mazrouei who is on record as saying:

> FinTech Hive plays a crucial role in DIFCs efforts to shape the future of the regional financial landscape. It is part of an ecosystem that includes an enabling infrastructure, fit-for-purpose regulation, subsidized licensing and most importantly, access to some of the world's pioneering financial institutions (DIFC, 2019).

Amongst these pioneering financial institutions that DIFC partners with are:

- Emirates NBD (National Bank of Dubai);
- ADIB (Abu Dhabi Islamic Bank);
- Arab Bank (Associate Partner);
- FAB (First Abu Dhabi Bank, Associate Partner);
- National Bank of Fujairah;
- Standard Chartered;
- HSBC;
- Visa;

- Finablr;
- Riyadh Bank.

And from the insurance sector:

- Noor Takaful (Ethical Insurance);
- AIG;
- Axa Gulf;
- Zurich Insurance;
- Insurance House;
- CIGNA.

The DIFC programme also works closely with the state-owned telecom operator, Etisalat, which is important as many fintech solutions are mobile first and most of the population is mobile-enabled, and with Islamic Scholars form the DIEDC (Dubai Islamic Economy Development Centre) who provide guidance in the area of Shari'a compliance.

The finalists selected for the 2019 cycle of the FinTech Hive accelerator programme contained some best-in-class regional companies including:

- **DAPI (UAE)**
  Lays claim to being the first financial API (application programming interface) in MENA allowing fintech apps to leverage open banking regulations by initiating payments and accessing real-time banking data.

- **Eazy Financial Services (Bahrain)**
  Brings biometric technologies and innovative solutions to the banking and financial services industries.

- **FinFirst (Kuwait)**
  A digital lending aggregator that pairs SMEs with banks and NBFIs (non-bank financial institutions), fully automating KYC/AML (know your customer and anti-money laundering checks), loan fulfilment and credit scoring. Lowering the cost of applying for a loan and minimizing the hassle of application forms, it addresses a number of the key challenges identified in the region and opens up customer acquisition channels for lenders, a challenge which features highly on their list of challenges.

- **Hakbah (Saudi Arabia)**
  An Islamic fintech in the area of cooperative savings, and on a mission to revamp and digitize traditional financial practices.

SPOTLIGHT ON STAND-OUT PERFORMERS
Wealth and robo-advisory

- **Sarwa:** Founded in 2016 by Mark Chahwan, Sarwa was the first graduate of the DFSA's Regulatory Sandbox following nearly 12 months of testing and the first robo-advisory firm to get a full licence from the DFSA.

- **Beehive:** Founded in 2014 by Craig Moore and based in Dubai, the multi-award-winning Beehive is MENA's first regulated P2P lending platform, having obtained its licence from DFSA in 2017. Moore saw an opportunity to mirror the already successful P2P lending companies such as Funding Circle and Zopa in the UK, and to him the Middle East was an untapped market. Beehive is set to see cumulative loans made through its platform reaching the Dh500 million mark in November, the month in which it celebrates its fifth anniversary.

UAE: Abu Dhabi

PLUG AND PLAY ADGM

Part of the global Plug and Play Tech Center accelerator and investor platform, the programme in Abu Dhabi launched in 2015 and connects fintechs from around the world to corporates around the MENA region. Corporate partners include:

- BNP Paribas;
- Finablr;
- Riyadh Bank;
- FAB (First Abu Dhabi Bank);
- Boubyan Bank.

Fintech verticals covered include security, wealth and robo-advisory, payments, data analytics and customer engagement.

OTHER INSTITUTIONS

- **Hub 71**

  The Abu Dhabi government and major entities such as Mubadala, Softbank and Microsoft have partnered to set up Hub 71, a global technology ecosystem that brings together key enablers for startups to succeed.

- **Ghadan 21**

  As part of the Ghadan 21 initiative, the Abu Dhabi Investment Office has launched the AED 535 million Ghadan Ventures Fund to attract startups and VC funds to Abu Dhabi.

- **MENA**

  The MENA FinTech Association, a not-for-profit industry champion for the MENA fintech community, is also headquartered in ADGM. The big four accounting firm KPMG was one of its founding members.

SPOTLIGHT ON INSURTECH

Abu Dhabi-based Bayzat, the online platform that makes HR administration less painful, recently secured $16 million in a Series B funding round investment. Founded in 2013, Bayzat provides health insurance and small business HR software (Businesswire, 2019).

Kingdom of Saudi Arabia (KSA)

FINTECH SAUDI INITIATIVE

The FinTech Saudi Initiative launched in 2018 to support the fintech ecosystem, promote the Kingdom as a fintech hub, improve financial inclusion and encourage the rise of digital transactions. Part of Saudi Arabia's Vision 2030 strategy to support entrepreneurship and the enhancement of fintech services, the initiative addresses the challenges surrounding the previous, and to a large extent current, gaps in tech education, solutions for the SME community, which figure highly in trade finance, for example, and for the incumbent financial services.

With no previous blueprint for 'what good looks like' in fintech, either from a tech or a regulatory perspective, the Kingdom has been playing catch up in the region, but with Vision 2030 seems to have put down a proverbial stake in the fintech sand. Wisely, they chose to enlist the assistance of the global services of Deloitte, which also offered expert assistance in formulating the overall strategy for FinTech Saudi. They acted as evaluator and developer of a number of specific initiatives, including a fintech accelerator space, to add momentum to accelerating the growth of fintech in the region. The initiative also helps to attract international talent and investment.

According to Deloitte there were about 15 operational fintech startups in Saudi Arabia as of 2019 (Deloitte, 2019). While the industry is relatively small compared to other larger neighbouring markets such as the UAE, Saudi Arabian startups have experienced rapid growth which is partly due to the government efforts and initiatives to develop the ecosystem. The Saudi market size represents a significant opportunity for foreign fintech companies, given the country's massive purchasing power.

A physical space for fintech – The King Abdullah Financial District (KAFD) – is a new development under construction in Riyadh, Saudi Arabia. With 59 towers and over 3 million square metres, the $7.8 billion project is making the statement that Saudi Arabia has arrived in terms of financial services with the goal of becoming a major finance hub in the Middle East.

SPOTLIGHT ON REGTECH

Qoyod, an accounting cloud solution for small and medium-sized businesses in Saudi Arabia, has attracted attention from significant investors who believe the startup has the potential to scale quickly and exploit one of the largest MENA markets, Saudi Arabia. The startup allows local businesses to cover most of their accounting and bookkeeping needs, within the context of KSA statutory requirements, making it a valuable tool for SME owners (Farhat, 2018).

Kingdom of Bahrain

BAHRAIN FINTECH BAY

Smaller than the likes of Dubai but nonetheless packing a powerful punch, Bahrain FinTech Bay (www.bahrainfintechbay.com) is part of a global hub network that includes Silicon Valley and Singapore. Positioning itself as a fintech hub and the region's largest incubator, it offers co-working space for fintechs, access to over 30 corporates and partners who are looking to partner, engage with or incubate with fintechs, events, market and trend research, access to talent via the National Fintech Talent Programme, which is certified by the likes of Georgetown and Berkeley from the United States. It also offers access to investment via the Bahrain Development Bank's $100 million fund, and its dialogue with the regulator.

Since 2017, the Economic Development Board and the Central Bank have been working from a unified blueprint to lay the foundations for a successful fintech hub. Bahrain was the first country in the region to have a Sandbox, and it has gone on to lay out clear and transparent regulatory frameworks governing verticals such as crypto-assets, crowdfunding, robo-advisory and so on, while establishing a Fintech Innovation Unit to help guide fintechs through the regulatory process.

As part of the drive to become the number one digital destination in the region for fintechs, in May 2019 the National Bank of Bahrain (NBB) took the lead as the first bank in MENA to provide open banking infrastructure services for its customers. In order to accomplish this feat, they partnered with specialist fintech and open banking infrastructure provider, Tarabut Gateway. With Tarabut Gateway's technology, customers will be able to connect their NBB account to any bank in Bahrain, which is a powerful first, enabling a consolidated view of their finances via NBB's mobile banking apps and online portal.

SPOTLIGHT ON CRYPTO AND BLOCKCHAIN

Bahrain-based cryptocurrency exchange, Rain, became the first licensed cryptocurrency exchange in the Middle East when it acquired the Crypto-Asset Module (CRA) licence from the Central Bank of Bahrain. The company has since gone on to secure a seed round of $2.5 million (Bridge, 2019).

Kingdom of Jordan

FINANCE FORWARD: 2020

A multi-year, global accelerator partnership between Village Capital, a Washington DC-based, not-for-profit VC investor, trainer and support organization, PayPal and the MetLife Foundation, the inaugural Finance Forward: MENA 2019 accelerator programme took place in Amman and featured 11 early-stage ventures operating in the local environment (Boyd Digital, 2019). The participating companies cover fintech, but the programme is not exclusive to fintech as it also covers community resilience and economic mobility. Two finalists received grant capital from the MetLife Foundation totalling $50,000.

Cohorts from the 2019 programme include:

- **Fundbot (Beirut)**
  A digital factoring solution addressing working capital needs of SMEs by providing access to bank credit for invoices;

- **Finllect (Dubai)**
  A personal finance app that enables Gen Z to better understand and manage money;

- **Kaoun (Tunis)**
  Enables unbanked and underbanked individuals and businesses access to financial services through identification, payment and credit solutions;

- **Merakido (Cairo)**
  A gamified habit-building financial well-being app;

- **Rumman (Amman)**
  An automated micro-saving and investment application which allows people to invest for their future starting from as little as $1;

- **Solfeh (Amman)**
  A fintech micro-lending platform, providing same-day emergency cash advancements to salaried employees.

Access to capital

The MAGNiTT 2019 MENA FinTech Report has ranked fintech the Number 1 sector in MENA for the number of deals funded in 2018 and 2019. The sector even surpassed e-commerce and logistics in 2018 as the most invested industry by number of deals, which in a major international logistics hub is quite a feat.

Key players in private capital

Capital availability from the private sector has increased rapidly in the last four years with the number of global investors as a percentage of total investment remaining steady at between 28 and 36 per cent. Private funding is predominantly regional (MAGNiTT, 2019), with the number of private investors in MENA-based fintech startups reaching 37 in 2019, up from 16 in 2015. Of the 162 investors, 14 per cent were from outside the MENA region, which illustrates the way in which the ecosystem is beginning to mature.

KEY INVESTOR STATISTICS IN MENA-BASED STARTUPS
According to MAGNiTT 2019, the top investors have also been the most active investors, filling the coffers of multiple fintechs. Those who have completed more than five investments include:

- 500 Startups;
- Startupbootcamp;

- Pride Capital;
- Oman Technology Fund;
- Flat 6 Labs.

The majority of deals have been at early stage. However, notable later-stage transactions include:

- $30 million for Network International, $20 million for Paytabs and $10 million for Souqalmal;
- in the MENA region, 13 fintech startups have had an exit;
- the top five funded fintech startups include Network, Paytabs, Agreed, Yallacompare and Beehive and collectively have raised over $100 million in venture funding from various institutions including General Atlantic, Warburg Pincus, ICS, Saudi Aramco, Choueiri Group, Argo, Dtec, Wamda Capital, STC, Precinct Partners, Middle East Venture Partners and RTF;
- the region has seen two fintech IPOs from Fawry and Network International.

RIYAD BANK'S FUND

To add to the regional funding pot, in November 2019, Riyad Bank, one of the largest financial institutions in the Middle East, announced plans to invest $26.7 million into its newly launched fintech startup investment programme aiming to accelerate the launch of new financial products across the country.

Government funds

In addition to funnelling funds through the various accelerator programmes, the region's governments have initiated some fintech funds:

- The UAE is home to the Abu Dhabi Investment Office, Abu Dhabi Catalyst Partners and DIFC. Funding for fintech has been drawn down to the tune of $146 million, $1 billion and $100 million respectively.
- Bahrain is home to the Alwaha Fund of Funds and has distributed $100 million.
- Egypt has the Central Bank of Egypt which has funded fintechs to the value of $57 million.

SOFTBANK VISION FUND

One private–public funding partnership that has garnered significant attention in the press and the public eye is the 2016 Softbank – Saudi Arabia's

$100 billion technology investment fund, focused on emerging tech firms. Both Softbank and Saudi Arabia's Public Investment Fund (PIF) provided $25 billion and $45 billion respectively to the Softbank Vision Fund, while the remaining $30 billion was sourced from an undisclosed group of investors. New territory for Saudi Arabia at the time, the Softbank Group was already involved in a number of accelerators such as the Softbank Innovation Programme in which fintech startups are granted the opportunity to secure multi-million dollar funding rounds based on prototype development and test marketing results.

Key events

The region has a reputation for hosting world-class, world-leading conferences and exhibitions, being a central geographical transport hub, and both Dubai and Abu Dhabi have a number of dedicated conference and event facilities. Visitors, exhibitors and leading industry experts are drawn to the regional events and add to the continual credibility building of the young centre of excellence. By no means an exhaustive list, the following are some of the key conferences and summits in the region.

- **FinTech Abu Dhabi**
  One of the highlights of the autumn regional fintech calendar, FinTech Abu Dhabi attracts thousands of visitors, exhibitors and speakers with a global reach. The conference covers the key fintech themes of the day (up to 2019 there have been three events), an awards ceremony, a focus on female-led initiatives and a corporate innovation challenge.
- **FINTEX Middle East (Bahrain)**
  Held in the Gulf Convention Centre, Fintex ME attracts both fintech and incumbent organizations offering the latest in banking software as a service, cybersecurity, biometrics, cloud computing, data analytics, AI, blockchain and payments.
- **IFN World Leaders Summit (Dubai)**
  The World Leaders Summit has a focus on the latest finance and fintech developments in Islamic finance. The summit addresses a variety of topics including the role of technology in Islamic finance and investment, the asset finance management industry, regulatory frameworks and fintech ecosystems.
- **New Age Banking Confex (Dubai)**
  With a focus on the challenges presented by open banking and its impact on the traditional banking system, and the prevention and impact of

cybersecurity and cybercrime, two recurring challenges for regional incumbents, the New Age Banking Confex conference takes place in Dubai and attracts hundreds of banking and financial services leaders, security professionals and fintech solution providers.

- **Jordan Blockchain and FinTech Summit**
  Held at the King Hussein Convention Center, Dead Sea, Jordan, the Jordan Blockchain and FinTech Summit focuses on the development of the fintech, cryptocurrency and blockchain sectors, their current states and potentials, key challenges, problems and their solutions. The conference will allow the discussion of aspects of digital currency regulation in the country and main areas of decentralized technology integration including government, fintech, insurance, trading and more.

- **Finovate Middle East (Dubai)**
  The Dubai-based chapter of this global brand has a regional banking and fintech focus and attracts hundreds of visitors and dozens of international speakers. The event has a strategic partner in the UAE Ministry of Finance, and leading one of its fintech programmes is Raja Al Mazrouei, executive vice president of FinTech Hive at DIFC who comments: 'Finovate is a credible global event and Dubai is a crucial connection for global financial hubs. Finovate acknowledges the potential and opportunity for Dubai to lead the region in innovation and fintech.'

- **Future Blockchain Summit (Dubai)**
  Hosted by Smart Dubai at the Dubai World Trade Centre, and showcasing the latest innovations and applications in blockchain, Future Blockchain provides an inspirational meeting ground for upwards of 10,000 global visitors and participants, from industry leaders to startups within the blockchain ecosystem.

- **Annual Investment Meeting (Dubai)**
  The Annual Investment Meeting is a world-class event that has a reputation for meaningful knowledge exchange, networking, business match-making and cementing partnerships and commercial engagements. It attracts international investors, leading academics and industry experts with a focus on foreign direct investment opportunities.

- **Seamless Middle East (Dubai)**
  Seamless Middle East at the Dubai International Convention & Exhibition Center, is one of, if not *the,* largest event in the region, and attracts circa 10,000 visitors and hundreds of speakers, investors and incumbents in the

fintech and financial services ecosystem. The event showcases innovative solutions that aim to address the region's challenges and take advantage of the opportunities. Topics include financial inclusion, robo- and wealth advisory, insurtech, AI, regtech and so on.

- **FutureSec Summit (Saudi Arabia)**
New to the conference scene, and focused on security, the FutureSec Summit is keen to be seen as a beacon in sharing experience and learning. The inaugural summit took place in Saudi Arabia in 2019.

Conclusion

Where does this burgeoning fintech ecosytem go beyond 2020?

The pace of growth for the region's fintech ecosystem has been staggering and looks set to continue on its current trajectory for the foreseeable future. Ambitious government-sponsored plans that extend to 2030 should guarantee the continued existence of the accelerators, investor networks, legislative and regulatory frameworks required to continue the journey, moving on from what some might see as the low-hanging fruit of payments and remittances on to more sophisticated solutions involving blockchain. However, what seems clear is that all of the region is now maturing and embracing the collaboration and partnerships that arise once the disruptive child has matured into the reluctantly cooperating adolescent and on to embracing genuine collaboration opportunities as a young adult.

It also seems that the feeling is mutual in that it is not only fintechs getting on board with collaborating and partnering, but also the incumbents and the regulators. All signs bode well for providing genuine solutions and personal impact in a region that has a migratory and greatly unbanked population who embrace technology.

Continued growth of Islamic fintech

Islamic fintech is a young but growing sub-sector and ripe for the continued incumbent disruption in retail, commercial and investment banking services. Its values speak to a wide swathe of millennials and Gen Z and the region is providing support and opportunities for its particular type of innovation to be applied in real-world solutions and to flourish beyond the borders of Muslim-majority countries.

Positive signs

With fintech disrupting the global financial services market, the regional incumbents know they have to partner with the new players and onboard technology to stay relevant to their customer's needs. In Dubai, some of the partners in the FinTech Hive have been making great strides in partnering and also launching their own fintech initiatives, products and services.

Emirates NBD (Dubai) became the first app-based bank in the UAE, when it launched Liv (Liv.), their digital offering. Initially a UAE service, there are plans to launch beyond their borders. Having worked with some of the ENDB Innovation team, it is clear that the bank has embarked on an ambitious digital transformation and they see collaboration and partnership with fintechs as a key part of implementing their strategy. They work with over 20 fintechs on Liv and see solutions to their customer challenges emerge from these working relationships, be they foreign exchange, lending, payments or card services. They don't fear being disintermediated; they embrace the possibilities of working with a willing fintech ecosystem. They have an internal lab where fintech experiments can take place and are a very active partner on the DIFC FinTech Hive programme. HSBC is also a partner in the DIFC FinTech Hive Accelerator Programme, and after three years of taking part, HSBC sees the value in collaborating with fintechs who bring the innovation while the bank provides a regulated entity, a large customer base and the necessary capital to bring market-fit solutions that meet their customer needs to life. This blending of speed and agility alongside compliancy and a willing customer base could potentially give HSBC an edge in the region and beyond. Like other incumbents in the region, there is an awareness that internal builds from scratch can be costly and time-consuming, and time is one thing that GCC customers don't want to waste. Speed is key in getting solutions to market.

In Saudi Arabia, incumbent Islamic banks are now collaborating with fintechs to expand into new market segments and attract more customers. Riyad Bank, for instance has partnered with Gemalto to introduce a range of contactless payment wristbands.

Also in the UAE, and a little out of the ordinary, is the partnership between National Bank of Fujairah (NBF) and FinTech Galaxy. FinTech Galaxy takes a unique crowdsourced platform approach to connecting innovation challenges in the region to global and regional solution providers, via solutions such as a MENA fintech hackathon. Open to participants from all corners of the ecosystem from major local banks and the regulators to financial services professionals and leading tech firms, the fintechs taking part come up with innovative solutions for challenges in areas such as account aggregation, settlement, and digitization of the *murabaha* process (the purchase and sale of a commodity for profit vs a loan with interest) across financial services domains such as lending, trade finance, payments and ease of frictionless customer experience.

References

Boyd Digital: Global Financial News (2019) Village Capital and MetLife Foundation selects 11 startups for MENA accelerator programme [YouTube] www.youtube. com/watch?v=majgKSPUQcM (archived at https://perma.cc/UM8Q-RHJV)

Bridge, S (2019) Bahrain crypto exchange Rain secures MidEast's first licence, Bahrainedb.com, bahrainedb.com/latest-news/bahrain-crypto-exchange-rain-secures-mideasts-first-licence/ (archived at https://perma.cc/DWZ7-44NN)

Businesswire.com (2019) Bayzat, the Abu Dhabi-based tech startup, raises $16M in Series B funding, www.businesswire.com/news/home/20191021005534/en/Bayzat-Abu-Dhabi-Based-Tech-Startup-Raises-16M (archived at https://perma.cc/DE2A-WWBB)

Deloitte (2019) If you build it, will they come? Building a FinTech ecosystem from scratch in Saudi Arabia, www2.deloitte.com/uk/en/pages/financial-services/articles/fintech-ecosystem-in-saudi-arabia.html (archived at https://perma.cc/5BVR-8ZUJ)

DIEDC (2019) *Dubai's Capital of Islamic Strategy*, DIEDC, www.iedcdubai.ae/assets/uploads/files/DIEDC%20powerpoint_1464192004.pdf (archived at https://perma.cc/7DDK-3H6P)

DIFC (2019) Third cohort of DIFC FinTech Hive Accelerator Programme Applications Opened, DIFC, www.difc.ae/newsroom/news/third-cohort-difc-fintech-hive-accelerator-programme-applications-opened/ (archived at https://perma.cc/M25K-HY65)

Farhat, R (2018) Saudi accounting solution startup Qoyod closes a Seed round from Arzan VC, Wamda.com, www.wamda.com/2018/07/saudi-accounting-solution-startup-qoyod-closes-seed-round-arzan-vc (archived at https://perma.cc/7ZES-ZJHN)

Financemagnates (2016) Abu Dhabi launches first MENA Regulatory Sandbox for fintech, www.financemagnates.com/fintech/news/abu-dhabi-launches-first-mena-regulatory-sandbox-for-fintech/ (archived at https://perma.cc/JYV7-K7MX)

Fintechnews (2019) A Glimpse into Fintech in Saudi Arabia, fintechnews.ae/3734/saudiarabia/fintech-saudi-arabia-overview/ (archived at https://perma.cc/R2B3-BWNN)

GCC-STAT (nd) *GCC Population*, GCC Statistical Centre, dp.gccstat.org/en/Dash
Boards?2ncd0h4AYU12Vp2d9ze9w (archived at https://perma.cc/S83W-9RQL)

GlobalPropertyGuide.com (2019) GDP Per Capita in Middle-East (online),
www.globalpropertyguide.com/Middle-East/gdp-per-capita (archived at
https://perma.cc/6F6J-X4K2)

MAGNiTT (2019) 2019 MENA FinTech Venture Report (online), magnitt.com/
research/50675/2019-mena-fintech-venture-report (archived at
https://perma.cc/36MG-5EZU)

Marketwatch.com (2019) United Arab Emirates: DIFC FinTech Hive Accelerator
Programme, www.marketwatch.com/press-release/united-arab-emirates-difc-
fintech-hive-accelerator-programme-2019-04-03?mod=mw_quote_news
(archived at https://perma.cc/9U8J-HU9L)

Puri-Murza, A (2019) Internet usage in MENA: Statistics and Facts, Statista.com,
www.statista.com/topics/5550/internet-usage-in-mena/ (archived at
https://perma.cc/4GA4-BTB7)

The National (2017) UAE to train one million young Arab coders in the 'language
of the future', www.thenational.ae/uae/uae-to-train-one-million-young-arab-
coders-in-the-language-of-the-future-1.669868 (archived at https://perma.cc/
G565-J2HK)

09

Paris

Background

The City of Lights: a star in the European fintech firmament

Paris has historically taken the number one spot when it comes to elegance, engineering, amour and glamour, but it may surprise you to learn that in recent years it has also emerged as a beacon of disruption and change in the fintech arena, opening its arms and doors to all things fintech. Financial services have had a long-term home here, but now fintech is supercharging the scene on the Seine.

Be assured that this new starring role was no mean feat, as the traditional banking sector was less than willing to relax the membership rules of the universal banking club and allow new fintech players to take a seat at the table. In contrast, cities such as London and Berlin were much more responsive to fintechs and integrated them easily into their financial services sector earlier on.

A historical footnote with modern-day relevance

Although Paris is the topic of this chapter, it is important to add some historical context to its financial services and fintech positioning against the backdrop of its relationship with its nearest leading fintech centre, London, as well as to chart the historical ups and downs of the French banking industry as they are partially responsible for some of the modern-day innovation we cover in these pages.

History

It's not you, it's me

London and Paris have had a complicated relationship and a sort of histori-cal sibling rivalry for centuries. This played out into all sectors of business and commerce but particularly in financial services. Until the middle of the 19th century, Paris was the financial place to be, led by wealthy families and societies who financed wars and large industrial ventures, largely using deposits. The country saw its largest banks expand throughout the 1800s but then became imperilled by massive withdrawals at the time of the 1870 Franco-Prussian war.

The banking acts of 1894 started the regulation and control of the sector but also brought complaints from small businesses and entrepreneurs who began finding it difficult to access credit. The French finance minister decided to create a commission in 1911 which was responsible for filling this gap in the banking system by preparing a law that would favour the development of the *banques populaires*. This law was passed in 1917.

Although the population still held the banks in low esteem, they were nonetheless able to attract a relatively large clientele and began to develop and expand their operations and products considerably. In the early 1900s, Crédit Lyonnais grew enough to be comparable in size to some of the largest banks in the City in London. While the banking system developed through-out the 1920s, banking structures remained fragile, and it was only with the stabilization of the franc by Poincaré between 1926 and 1928 that the credit institutions were able to rebuild their resources.

As a result of the Great Depression in the 1930s, the major banks were exposed to massive demands for withdrawals, and large-scale bankruptcies occurred in 1930 and 1931, reducing the number of banks by a quarter. The banks who had managed to hold large liquid reserves succeeded in overcom-ing the banking crisis and this meant that France fared better than most of central Europe and indeed the United States of America.

Throughout the 1900s, the sector grew and in only a few decades the number of branch offices doubled. By the 1970s, almost all French families were using mainstream banking services. Banks also offered businesses and private clients a range of more and more diversified products such as long-term and medium-term credit, export credit, project financing, personal loans, housing assistance, mutual funds and so on. Deposits tripled between 1966 and 1976, and since that time bank money has represented four-fifths of the total amount of money in circulation.

Key strengths

A new banking revolution

As recently as 20 years ago, the French government was still largely in control of the banking industry, but the banking law of 1984 started a succession of moves that effectively abolished credit specialization and ultimately led to the deregulation of the banking system.

Until the creation of the European single currency and the European Commission regulations, the sector was mostly in the hands of national players, but the single currency opened the sector up and brought an influx of competition from foreign banks. Strong competition has resulted in substantial changes in the industry. Large-scale acquisitions and takeovers took place, concluding with a full-scale reorganization of the banking sector in France. In fact, France was an early adopter of digital banking when several banks started offering rudimentary banking services on France's PTT (Postes, Télégraphes et Téléphones) Minitel, an early precursor of the internet.

Now France is adjusting to the new conditions brought about by technology and changing customer demands. A new generation of innovative financial services companies has emerged, driven by new demands, enabled by mobility and data technology. Rapid changes have pushed the regulator to evolve its rules and be more supportive of innovation, and the country is emerging as a centre of excellence in fintech.

As a late bloomer, Paris has not wasted any time in positioning itself as a world leader in fintech, and this has been especially significant since the UK's decision to leave the EU was made. Acting in the spirit of the startups looking to seize the moment, the French government saw an opportunity to promote Paris as a fintech hub and set about preparing the sector with appealing funding schemes, super-cool co-working spaces and access to talent. As the country that spawned early fintech pioneers such as security firm Gemalto (www.gemalto.com) and payment processor Ingenico (www. ingenico.com) who tapped into the large French – and global – payments market, there is precedent for taking the digital initiative.

The attitude from the established incumbents has also gone a long way to help advance the fintech ecosystem. Laurent Herbillon, Open Innovation director at BNP Paribas explains why BNP Paribas, an incumbent, has got it so right:

Previously, banks concentrated more on 'make' vs 'buy' in what was a more concentrated landscape with fewer competitors. In the past four years, the emphasis at BNP Paribas has shifted more to the buy/cooperation side and leveraging the positive impact of bringing outside talent into the bank. This has been most clearly seen in areas such as AI/ML [machine learning], NLP, KYC, risk, distribution and the customer experience.

We embarked on a digital journey, and realized that we needed to start engaging more meaningfully with startups and scaleups.

Herbillon sums it up:

Importantly, this transformation was from the bottom up and the top down in the bank, avoiding the trap of setting up 'innovation labs off the ground' that were segregated from the mainstream. It was important to develop the spirit and mindset within the bank and that initiatives not be outside 'business as usual'. In fact, many of our employees showed great creativity, energy and imagination when interacting with startups in the proper conditions and environment. They started to value more and more cooperation with startups and to embrace the working relationship, reinventing and reinvigorating themselves.

This approach by the leading incumbent banks and the regulator has been the lynchpin to the success and speedy development of the fintech sector, helped by fantastic transport links via train, air and sea. France is now a centre of excellence for fintech, and some believe it is now a challenger to London for the crown of fintech capital of the world.

Alongside incumbents and regulators, the education system is also responding to the challenge to ensure that France stays ahead in the fintech industry by preparing and educating more secondary students in strategic industries such as AI and blockchain. With London on its doorstep as a major competitor, France will need to continue to offer incentives and innovation to keep the entrepreneurs coming to France.

Rapid growth has brought impressive impact, and the Paris region is leading the way as a European fintech hub. Key examples of this are:

- There are around 457 fintech, insurtech and regtech companies in France (Tracxn, 2019). Of these, over 250 are in activities regulated under different statutes by the French regulators ACPR and Banque de France.
- The fintech sector in France is responsible for creating over 800,000 jobs (89 per cent full-time roles).

- 2018 was a record year for French fintech with over €300 million in investments; this trend seems to be continuing, as 2019 is expected to reap over €600 million of investment.

- Paris hosts one of the largest fintech events in the world, The Paris FinTech Forum, which brings over 2,900 attendees from more than 160 countries.

Key verticals

The fintech sector encompasses a number of verticals and France is no different from any other city in that its constituent parts are represented across a variety of sub-sectors. Some are more established than others and the most significant growth areas are:

- Insurtech represents 17 per cent of the fintech startups in France and one-third have been created in the last two years. Alan, an insurtech startup which raised €80 million between 2018 and 2019, is a good illustration of the country's ability to lead the way in disruptive innovations and establish leading players not only locally but globally.

- Crypto, blockchain and initial coin offerings (ICOs) are booming, with regulators actively contributing to create the framework of a supportive regulatory environment. Ledger is a French success story. It developed security and infrastructure solutions for cryptocurrencies as well as blockchain applications for individuals and companies. In 2018, the French firm announced that it had secured $75 million in a Series B funding round, led by world-famous Draper Esprit.

- Lending, including P2P, direct lending and marketplace models, is also booming, with more platforms being created in niche markets such as green projects or real estate. Lumo is a renewable energy crowdfunding platform which started in 2012 and has been combining leading expertise in crowdfunding and renewable energies to accelerate green energy transition. It was acquired by Société Générale in 2018 (Société Générale, 2018).

- Investment and financing services remains the most crowded fintech category in France with 83 new startups emerging in the year to March 2019. One such example is Kesitys who is providing the next generation of trading software and who showcased its offering at the 2019 French FinTech Tour in London and Dublin. This sector hosts plenty of exciting businesses from consumer credit solutions, online brokers and crowdlending platforms. Players in this high-growth sector are worth watching; there may be some consolidation and acquisitions as those with the best technology start to become profitable.

- The banking/PFM segment is not growing as quickly, which is probably due to dominant players having a strong market share. Think of Qonto (B2B neobank recipient of $115 million investment from China's Tencent Group in early 2020), Lydia (B2C payment app turning into a kind of metabank), Bankin, Linxo and Budget Insight, for example. Also, European leaders keep eating market shares, such as N26 which in January 2019 overtook Revolut as Europe's most valuable mobile bank with a valuation of $2.7 billion (Smith, 2019). In a nutshell, these sub-segments are already quite mature and slowly becoming saturated in France, so that it appears complicated for new players to grow in 2019.

- Regtech is a key topic for the near future. The daunting increase in GDPR/AML/ MiFID2/PSD2/you-name-it compliance costs is pushing regulated institutions to implement and/or partner with tools to facilitate compliance checks and reporting. KYC and ID management remain hot topics. In this context, 2020 could be the year for these cutting-edge technologies to come of age.

Current challenges facing French fintechs

Unlike Tel Aviv, Silicon Valley or London where the population is tech friendly and at ease with being early adopters of new customer-centric solutions, the biggest challenge for French fintech is its low take-up by the public for services offered by these innovators. Early users tend to be the millennial generation and older generations tend to be more wary of security issues and the various harsh conditions (lack of harmonization, lack of regulation or legal answers, etc) in the regulatory framework. Perhaps the country's demographics are to some extent behind fintechs' slow adoption.

A Deloitte study (Deloitte, 2015) shows that, of the services offered by fintech companies, account aggregation is the most used by the French with 9 per cent of users. Services related to savings (crowdfunding, financial planning, automated advice) and connected objects are currently used by around 4 to 6 per cent. These low rates are due mostly to the low notoriety of fintech vis-à-vis the general public. Indeed, only about 1 in 4 people are familiar with these innovative financial services. This may also bode well for platforms and services in France. While the digital revolution is creating challenges it also represents incredible opportunities that are waiting to be seized.

Marketing and education campaigns for these services will lead to a greater uptake. Many have shown interest in fintech but are yet to make the foray into the sector. Of those questioned, 18 per cent declare themselves interested in the innovation that receives the least interest (P2P payments via social networks), whereas the most popular products – connected insurers and account aggregators – would attract up to 45 per cent of French people.

Station F: a billionaire's vision comes to life

Not the exclusive home of fintech, but right up there as a contender for housing the lion's share of the community is Paris's Station F, bursting onto the scene in 2017, and dubbed as the world's largest startup campus. Set across 366,000 square feet on the banks of the Seine, it is home to established tech players such as Amazon, Facebook and Microsoft as well as thousands of startups paying around €195 ($235) per desk per month, which is around half the price of other desks in Paris. These startups are the campus's main source of revenue, alongside rental fees from 32 VC firms.

Station F's mission is to connect corporates, organizations and universities to the pioneering entrepreneurs with startup enterprises. Fledgling companies are able to access a variety of accelerators and incubators, alongside co-working spaces and all the ancillary services required for business such as restaurants, cafés, bars and event spaces to help them move their ideas forward.

The enterprise was backed by Xavier Niel, a French telecom billionaire, who is a legend in his home country, having lavished millions on tech education and French startups, and who invested $285 million into the project, stating: 'The real force of Silicon Valley is the mentality, the spirit. There's no reason at all that can't be replicated in Paris.'

An important footnote to the infrastructure story is the government's $21 billion super-fast internet programme that launched in 2013. Equipping the whole of the country's cheaper-than-London real estate market with speedy internet connections could be very enticing to startups and incumbents alike.

The elusive unicorn

Despite the government's inducements and encouragement for fintech, inward investment still lags behind other European cities. KPMG's annual fintech survey estimated worldwide investment was nearly $112 billion in 2018 (BNP Paribas, 2018). By comparison, the $328 million invested in French fintech is a splash but not a wave of investment. London still tops the list for global fintech deals in 2019, surpassing Silicon Valley for the first time. With that level of competition on its doorstep, Paris will have to continue its Gallic charm offensive in order to attract the brightest and the boldest talent to its new-ish ecosystem.

Something that might help investors invest and entrepreneurs set up in Paris are the tax benefits announced in recent years: lowering corporation tax to 28 per cent and offering other tax incentives for having French-based employees, share distribution to employees and willing angels investing.

Although there is an uptick in investment, hugely inflated valuations and mega fundraises are rare for French fintechs, and the country struggles to see the emergence of fintech unicorns to compete with the likes of Stripe, TransferWise or Ripple. At the end of March 2019, however, the Franco-American unicorn Kyriba became the first with a valuation of $1.2 billion (Freeman, 2019). The other French contenders for the title are October, Lydia and Ledger. The third of these, specializing in hardware portfolios for cryptocurrencies, is also the big favourite and is aiming for a $10 billion valuation by 2024.

Talent landscape

Challenges and responses

No country or city escapes the challenges around identifying and attracting the required talent, as resources for world-class technology skills are stretched.

France is aware of the need to develop its workforce and does have top-class graduates in relevant subjects such as computer and data science. It has also recognized the need to develop its talent pool early on and has taken measures to prepare its workforce for the digital economy from school-age children.

The Paris region has announced its AI plan for 2021 with a focus on training and education, including the launch of a PhD-level scholarship with €4 million in funding. France is starting a programme of AI training courses specifically geared toward job seekers looking to develop their skills and is opening its first AI high school.

As well as poaching talent directly from the school and university system, France is also looking at schemes to reskill its existing workforce to ensure the country can keep ahead of the digital curve and stay attractive to the best worldwide talent.

The French government created the so-called 'French Tech Visa', a simplified, fast-track procedure for three types of international tech talent to obtain a residence permit known as the 'Passeport Talent'. The French Tech Visa is open to three categories of tech talent – startup founders, employees, and investors – and allows them to live and work in France. It is valid for four years, on a renewable basis. It is extended to immediate family members: spouses also receive residence permits authorizing them to live and work in France.

Another initiative launched in 2016, the 'Tech Ticket' package aimed at tech entrepreneurs includes a €45,000 ($47,000) grant, visa facilities and fast-track administrative procedures.

Prodigal sons and daughters

As France focuses its economy on fintech and digital innovations, it is seeing many of its citizens return from overseas locations as they see the opportunities in their home country. Successful entrepreneurs who went to the United States or the UK are now coming back to innovate in France. Success stories such as Ledger, a cryptocurrency wallet which raised €68 million, or Alan, an insurtech start-up which raised €80 million between 2018 and 2019, are good examples of France's ability to lead the way in disruptive innovations and become a leading player in the world.

The impact of the UK's decision to leave the EU has also led to a contingent of talented tech workers remaining in France when they may have otherwise been tempted to relocate to London (Jones, 2019).

Competition for top talent is fierce and it comes from incumbents as well as startups and all the service providers in between. If fintech firms are going to succeed in the battle for minds, they will need to attack the problem with creativity and pragmatism, along with a bit of Gallic panache.

Access to capital

So where is the money flowing?

On a European, and indeed on a global stage, London continues to blaze the capital trail with over 39 per cent of all European fintech investment landing in the capital (FinTech Global, 2019). According to Innovate Finance (the independent membership association that represents the UK's global fintech community), London overtook Silicon Valley in fintech funding for the first time in 2019 (Taylor, 2019). This is not to say that other key capital cities have been complacent, but, to date, London's nearest rivals are Berlin and

Paris who each gets just half that amount. In 2018, Berlin and Paris raised 21 per cent and 18 per cent of what London raised.

The funding of innovation through public–private partnerships is growing as governments all over the world start to understand the importance of this industry and seek ways to foster and encourage development in both fintech and the wider digital economy. The UK was one of the first countries to launch tax incentive schemes, with its investments in funds and platforms for post-seed investment and more recently with the Patient Capital Initiative from the British Business Bank. Other countries have begun to see the value in these schemes and launched similar initiatives. This includes France.

French government funding initiatives

In 2015, the French government concluded an extensive research exercise and announced a plan worth €10 billion, which includes €4 billion of its own capital contributions, aimed in particular at VC and innovative initiatives such as blockchain for 2017–20.

The fund was established to develop tech hubs throughout the country and provide financial support funnelled through various channels to help tech entrepreneurs. Several French fintechs have already benefited from this programme and have started to develop at an international level, including the consumer lending platform Younited Credit, payment app Lydia (French equivalent of PayPal's digital wallet Venmo) and Lendix, a pan-European SME lending platform (re-named October).

Venture capital and private capital

According to a study conducted by global professional services company Accenture, French fintechs raised $423 million in the first half of 2019, 48 per cent more than a year earlier (Machin, 2019).

The French state is also investing heavily alongside private capital through its VC arm BPI while other fintech-specific VC funds have emerged like NewAlpha Asset Management and Truffle Capital.

Other notable large private firms starting funds include BlackFin. This PE firm focuses exclusively on financial services operating in Paris, Brussels and Frankfurt and is addressing the needs of entrepreneurs at all stages of development across continental Europe through three funds: BlackFin I and BlackFin II for growth equity, and BlackFin Tech for venture capital (BlackFin

Tech, 2019). In 2018, BlackFin Capital Partners positioned itself as the largest independent Fintech fund in Europe after completing a €180 million final closing.

Their combined efforts appear to be paying off as French fintech firms have raised significant funding in recent years. SME loan crowdfunding platform Lendix raised €12 million (2016), KissKissBankBank €5.3 million (2016), Ulule €5 million in three rounds, Tiller €12 million (2018) and French startup Wynd raised another €72 million recently from Natixis, Sofina and BNF Capital (Dillet, 2019). The company has raised €112 million in total from investors including Sodexo, Orange and Alven.

Incumbent venture capital

Not to be outdone by the VC firms, the incumbents in financial services and insurance have established their own investment arms and funds and have made great inroads into investing and acquiring fintech propositions. Here is a sample of some of their successes.

BNP PARIBAS

BNP Paribas is a pivotal player in the fintech ecosystem and its willingness to work with and acquire fintech startups is a model that is the envy of many of its international peers. Being one of the largest banks in France means it looks to the global scene for inspiration and investment choices.

Through its investment fund, Opera Tech Ventures, it has cast a wide net and is keen to fund financial industry transformers with a global scope. Its focus is on disruptive and transformative innovations that shake the financial industry, and investments include:

- Chime Bank in the United States;
- Rewire, an Israeli company providing international workers with a digital banking platform to manage their lives;
- Token, an open banking platform that allows banks and third parties to interact on a digital global financial services ecosystem.

Laurent Herbillon, Director of Open Innovation for BNP Paribas, believes it is important to engage with accelerators, academics, startups and scaleups, making investments, creating partnerships and adding value to the global fintech and insurtech ecosystem. He says of the bank: 'We recognized that when we work with startups a one-size-fits-all approach is not the right approach. We adapted.'

SOCIÉTÉ GÉNÉRALE

Société Générale plans to 'transform to grow' as part of its new investment strategy and created their own €150 million fund, Société Générale Ventures, that is looking for disruptive and innovative propositions that cross a number of its business lines. The idea is to invest in companies that make Société Générale more attractive to its customers, but also to be able to offer their clients products and services that improve their business offerings. Investments are made into both external fintechs, such as Treezor, a core banking platform; Lumo, an online energy supplier (now acquisitions); Reezocar, a second-hand car financing solution; and also into propositions that are unearthed in its own moonshot programme, such as Moonshot-Internet.

CRÉDIT AGRICOLE CIB

Crédit Agricole CIB has already made an investment in SETL, specializing in multi-currency, multi-asset settlement on the blockchain, and the blockchain platform, Open CSD, for payments and settlements.

AXA VENTURE PARTNERS

Following on from the success of its first $110 million fund, AXA Venture Partners (AVP) has raised an additional $150 million for investment in companies in Europe, the United States and Israel. With a maximum investment of $6 million, the fund is on the look-out for enterprises such as software as a service (SaaS), SMEs and consumer solutions with a focus on fintech but also digital health. AVP has invested in over 40 firms at all stages of development since 2015 including fintech, insurtech, cybersecurity and AI.

Profile of the regulator

Such impressive growth in the French fintech ecosystem is due in part to having such a forward-looking government and regulator. The French regulatory authorities are well known for being meticulous, some might even go so far as to say, pernickety, which results in high-quality standards and regulations that are valued and respected throughout Europe.

In a very proactive move, the French stock market regulator Autorité des Marchés Financiers (AMF) took positive action three years ago when it established an internal department with the remit to lay the regulatory foundations to help establish the fintech sector. Not content to 'naval gaze', the

AMF also sought opportunities to learn and liaise from and with other regulators from around the world. It organizes events such as the Paris FinTech Forum and created the Banque de France integrated institution, ACPR (Autorité de Contrôle Prudential et de Résolution). The ACPR combines opinions on innovation from industry experts, academics and other experts in the fintech ecosystem.

France, as a member of the EU, is impacted by decisions, directives and rulings that emanate from Brussels.

The legal market in France and recent developments

France has an established and comprehensive set of regulations with respect to fintech, and there are a number of drivers behind this. Paris is home to a high concentration of financial institutions and asset managers. There is strong infrastructure established in payments, insurance and telecoms and the sector can rely on strong governmental and ministerial support.

French authorities and regulators have exhibited constant interest in fintechs, which are driving technological innovation and providing inward capital and job creation in the country.

Several initiatives have promoted the French fintech industry:

- In June 2016, the AMF set up its FinTech, Innovation and Competitiveness division to support the growth of the sector and encourage the adoption of new regulations.

- Fintech-friendly regulation that sets a threshold below which no authorization from regulators is needed to start a fintech business and the regulator has established a one-stop-shop to fast-track registration and authorization for foreign startups.

- At the end of 2017, the Swave initiative, incubator of fintech and assurtech startups, was launched with the support of the government.

- More recently in 2018, the politician Bruno Le Maire has, despite some setbacks, expressed his support to help define the framework for the initial coin offerings (ICO) and the cryptocurrency sector.

Regulations implemented in the last few years demonstrate the French government's commitment to quickly establish appropriate frameworks that foster the development of fintech companies while ensuring investors' protection.

The ecosystem

Key institutions

Launched in 2016, France Fintech is an association of more than 100 companies from the industry (France FinTech, 2019a). It is a non-profit organization whose mission is to promote community and best practice in the fintech sector in France and beyond. It acts as a representative body and a voice for French fintech companies, the public authorities and the regulator. It publishes industry news, runs events and selects relevant partner organizations and resources as part of its offering.

Its members make up a range of companies and institutions recognized as integral players of the ecosystem: tech leaders, investment funds, law firms, auditing and consulting, banks, insurance groups, industrial companies, public or associative entities, etc.

The objective of the organization is to develop the entire fintech ecosystem and create an environment conducive to the emergence of French fintech champions.

Incubators and accelerators

A large contingent of incubators and accelerators support the French fintech industry with more than 370 startup incubators scattered throughout the country, including 208 in Paris. Amongst the most active are:

- **Station F in Paris:** The world's biggest startup campus with thousands of startups in a 26,000 square metre space (Knowles, 2018).
- **Swave:** Paris&Co and its corporate partners Société Générale, NewAlpha Asset Management, Crédit Municipal de Paris, Exton Consulting, AG2R La Mondiale and Mastercard have set up a fintech incubator.
- **KAMET by AXA:** A healthtech and insurtech startup studio.
- **50 Partners:** A co-working space by le Loft dedicated to entrepreneurs with a flexible and affordable office offering for startups.
- **Truffle FinTech Incubator:** A large mutual fund by Truffle Capital.
- **L'Atelier:** By BNP Paribas, for fintechs and corporates.
- **Plug and Play Initiative:** BNP Paribas.

SPOTLIGHT ON BNP PARIBAS

Founded in 1978, L'Atelier became a 100-per-cent-owned subsidiary of the BNP Paribas Group in 2003. Today, L'Atelier's three main areas of expertise are prospective research, business transformation consulting services and business acceleration programmes.

Following the great success of Season 1 in 2015, L'Atelier BNP Paribas launched a second season of its fintech and corporate accelerator programme in 2016. It is a joint initiative with fintechs with a vision to provide optimal conditions for them to find the right 'market fit', including tailored business and technical support, introductions to BNP Paribas Group businesses and departments and free-of-charge hosting at its WAI (We Are Innovation) premises in Paris.

The Head of Accelerator Programmes at L'Atelier BNP Paribas, Emmanuel Touboul, explains:

> What we're offering startups is unique in the financial sector. The programme, which focuses directly on business development, has been designed with the sole aim of creating value both for the startups and BNP Paribas group businesses.

BNP Paribas has also started a Plug and Play Initiative which networks a powerful group of banking, insurance and fintech experts and invites fledgling firms to a network of mentors, executives and VCs to accelerate their time to market, fundraising, and revenue pipeline.

Key events

France hosts some notable events attracting delegates from the fintech industry from all over the world.

- **Paris FinTech Forum**
  The Paris FinTech Forum (PFF) is an annual event that is rapidly becoming one of the most exclusive digital finance and fintech events in Europe. PFF 2020 had over 2,900 attendees from over 75 countries and featured hundreds of panels and interviews with over 320 CEOs from banks, insurance companies, telecommunication companies, regulators and

fintechs from all across the world. The two-day event is organized by Altéir with the support of over 160 international partners and hosted in the former French stock market exchange in Paris.

- **Fintech R: Evolution**
  France FinTech organizes various other conferences, including FinTech R: Evolution @Station F as well as supporting the Paris FinTech Forum (France FinTech 2019b).

- **French FinTech Tour**
  Completing its third year in 2019, the FinTech Tour is a three-day event designed to increase French fintech adoption into other jurisdictions. The French FinTech Tour gathers senior and top executives from banks as well as insurance, investment and financial-related companies.

Key influencers

LAURENT HERBILLON

BNP Paribas has deliberately developed a strong relationship with startups, and specifically fintechs, based on four pillars: co-creating, accelerating, banking and investing. This cooperation is intended to support the bank's digital transformation while supporting the development of fintechs.

Herbillon, Open Innovation Director, says BNP Paribas has become a leading light in the fintech ecosystem due to its willingness to engage holistically with this emerging sector of the financial services industry.

The bank understood that to reap the benefits fintech and insurtech could bring, not only for them but the wider French economy, they would have to convince their employees, senior management and stakeholders that startups were not the enemy of the bank. The combined efforts of BNP Paribas employees and the startups would ultimately result in a positive impact.

Herbillon says:

> We quickly realized that we needed to start engaging more meaningfully with startups directly or via accelerators in order to start doing things like POCs [proof of concept] and MVPs [minimal viable product] vs experimenting with no clear aim. Our transformation was from the bottom up and the top down in the bank. We encouraged our teams to co-design with the startups and scaleups, and to feel empowered by the process. At the same time, senior management

actively encouraged employees to do things differently, to be okay with experiencing failure, and to learn from these setbacks. They supported internal innovation champions to engage with the people on the ground.

The impact of this new way of working took many forms, but BNP Paribas wanted to create a sense of community both within internal teams, who traditionally work in silos, and also with the external startup community, with whom they do not usually get involved. Among many initiatives, it engaged with the ecosystem directly or through partners such as Plug and Play with whom they launched a BNP Paribas Acceleration programme at Station F, one of the biggest incubation places in the world. Another result of this interaction was its Startup Engagement Kit (SEK) to enable a smoother process to MVPs and POCs in risk and compliance procedures, for example, making it easier to connect to the internal IT and legacy systems.

Herbillon says:

> All key players were involved in developing the Startup Engagement Kit and it also provided another way of educating our teams in this new method of working. We were in a good position. We had the place to work with the startups, the potential to use cases to apply the results to, and Plug and Play bringing the startup talent. We had well-defined challenges to work on together, with a business unit and budget holder involved, and rigorous vetting and engagement with the startups garnering mutual working respect.

The results for this dedicated programme are impressive: more than 45 POCs/MVPs over the past three years, a third of which have gone into production. This outcome sends a positive message to both the internal teams and the startup community, making it clear that BNP Paribas can work with and learn from agile startups.

LAURENT NIZRI

Nizri is founder of the strategy and innovation consultancy, Altéir Consulting, and founder of the high profile Paris FinTech Forum event. He is also Chair of ACSEL, a French association focusing on all aspects of the digital economy.

ROXANNE VARZA

The current Director of Station F, Varza has a CV rich in tech and startup heritage, as she was previously the head of Microsoft's startup activities in France, including Microsoft Ventures. She was also the editor of the respected publication

TechCrunch France, and played a leading role in a number of startups. An adviser to Silicon Valley companies looking to enter the French marketplace, she is also well known for 'paying forward' or 'giving back' to the wider community, and is the co-founder of Girls in Tech (Paris and London), an organization which educates and empowers women in technology, and provides coding courses, hackathons and start-up competitions for women.

LAURENT LEMOAL

LeMoal is CEO of PayU, providers of online payment services to merchants, and an executive team member at Naspers, the global internet business that covers a variety of sectors including entertainment, gaming and e-commerce. His role is to develop their global fintech proposition, with a particular lens on payments and credit, and to be part of the fintech investing team. LeMoal's educational journey took him to Italy and the UK, and his previous career saw him as a vice president at PayPal Europe and an analyst at the consulting firm McKinsey.

Other notable players

- **Younited Credit**
  Younited Credit, founded in 2009, has raised over $123 million; their offering of all manner of insurance products to consumers, businesses and institutions is broad and ambitious. The company benefited from a French government initiative, La French Tech (2019), setting up tech hubs aimed at delivering support on the ground and in funding to innovative companies that had potential to grow internationally.

- **Orange Bank**
  Launched in 2017, Orange Bank is a mobile bank offering from the telecoms giant and their first foray into digital banking. Aware of the need to diversify their offering and to maximize their position vis-à-vis mobile usage and deep customer data, Orange set out to offer a simple, easy-to-use banking solution to millions of customers.

- **Kard**
  A Paris-based electronic money offering for Gen Z aimed at the overlooked teen market. In the style of Revolut, it claims that opening an account is quick and easy and markets itself for community appeal. Its products include savings features and expense sharing. It raised $3.3 million in a pre-seed round in 2019.

- **Baobab**

  Provides digital and mobile solutions in the form of loans, savings and other products that have financial inclusion for small and micro-businesses and individuals in China and Africa. Founded by Arnaud Ventura in 2005, the company has nearly 4,000 employees and a very wide sweeping footprint across Africa.

- **SOeasi**

  A challenger bank launched by the home finance solutions provider, 570easi, that heralds the ethos of Islamic finance and is aimed at the underserved and underbanked population. It offers banking, savings, payments and wealth management solutions.

- **Ledger**

  Launched in 2014, and still leading the way, Ledger uses its proprietary technology to provide secure solutions for blockchain applications and security and infrastructure solutions for cryptocurrencies. Its operating system, BOLOS, integrates with a secure chip for the Ledger wallet line, or to a hardware security module for various enterprise solutions. The original team of eight members is now joined by more than 150 additional employees in Paris, Vierzon and San Francisco. It operates in over 170 countries with thousands of clients. In 2018, Ledger secured $75 million in a Series B funding round led by Draper Esprit with additional funding from Draper Venture Network funds, including Draper Associates, Draper Dragon and Boost VC, as well as FirstMark Capital, Cathay Innovation and Korelya Capital.

- **October**

  Formerly called Lendix, October was founded by Olivier Goy in 2014. It is a pan-European SME lending platform that facilitates lending to businesses from private and institutional lenders. Having raised in the region of $90 million and with operations also in Spain, they have set the ambitious goal of wanting to be the leading lending marketplace for continental Europe.

Where does the city on Seine go from here?

The signs for fintech and financial services are all very positive in Paris. There seems to be a concerted and joined-up plan between industry, academia and government to capitalize on the potential good fortune of Brexit, but also on waking up to the opportunities fintech presents that may have been accelerated by Brexit (Jones, 2019).

The country's new perspective on early tech education; incumbents such as Paribas and Société Générale who are leading the way in collaborating and investing in fintechs, helping to take them global; investment in infra-structure that enables collaboration and knowledge exchange; a responsive regulator; and an increasingly active investor community all bode well for the future of fintech and for financial services in Paris.

At times, history has been unkind to financial services, but the modern financial era presents an opportunity for those who survived and thrived in traditional corridors of commerce to evolve and remain relevant through a symbiotic relationship with the very disruptors who once threatened to make them obsolete. It remains to be seen if they heed the call.

References

BlackFin Tech (2019) The 2019 French Fintechs Panorama, medium.com/blackfintech/the-2019-french-fintechs-panorama-edf6c9452603 (archived at https://perma.cc/7EL2-LUAY)

BNP Paribas (2018) Startups which improve banking and finance, group.bnpparibas/en/hottopics/fintech/briefing (archived at https://perma.cc/7TQR-3BYH)

Deloitte (2015) Usages Mobile 2015: A game of phones, Deloitte, ww2.ac-poitiers.fr/ecogest/sites/ecogest/IMG/pdf/deloitte_etude_mobile-survey-2015.pdf (archived at https://perma.cc/AEF3-CZFL)

Dillet, R (2019) Wynd raises $82 million for its store management service, *TechCrunch,* techcrunch.com/2019/01/22/wynd-raises-82-million-for-its-store-management-service/ (archived at https://perma.cc/5GJB-89LL)

FinTech Global (2019) FinTech investment in France has grown almost ten-fold since 2014, FinTech Global, fintech.global/fintech-investment-in-france-has-grown-more-than-ten-fold-since-2014/ (archived at https://perma.cc/67N6-8F27)

France FinTech (2019a) Who are we? francefintech.org/qui-sommes-nous/#nosmembres (archived at https://perma.cc/J3GM-CB2Z)

France FinTech (2019b) Our Events, francefintech.org/en/nos-evenements/ (archived at https://perma.cc/Q6MK-9UW2)

Freeman, M (2019) Kyriba nets $160 million investment, pushing software firm's valuation above $1 billion, *San Diego Union Tribune,* www.sandiegouniontribune.com/business/technology/story/2019-03-27/kyriba-nets-160-million-investment-becomes-san-diegos-latest-unicorn (archived at https://perma.cc/7XX2-ZQY7)

Jones, H (2019) Brexit hits ability of UK fintech to lure top talent, *Reuters,* uk.reuters.com/article/us-britain-eu-fintech/brexit-hits-ability-of-uk-fintech-to-lure-top-talent-report-idUKKCN1R0005 (archived at https://perma.cc/CU7T-U2WS)

Knowles, K (2018) Station F is the world's biggest startup incubator: can it become the best? *Forbes,* www.forbes.com/sites/kittyknowles/2018/05/02/station-f-is-the-worlds-biggest-startup-incubator-could-it-also-become-the-best/ (archived at https://perma.cc/2V8D-VT2L)

La French Tech (2019) www.gouvernement.fr/en/la-french-tech (archived at https://perma.cc/29ZZ-ENHM)

Machin, L (2019) Accenture Global Analysis: UK fintech investment almost doubles, *Payment Expert,* paymentexpert.com/2019/08/16/accenture-global-analysis-uk-fintech-investment-almost-doubles/ (archived at https://perma.cc/5H8M-W648)

Smith, O (2019) With a $2.7 billion valuation, N26 overtakes Revolut as Europe's most valuable mobile bank, *Forbes*, www.forbes.com/sites/oliversmith/2019/01/10/with-a-27-billion-valuation-n26-overtakes-revolut-as-europes-most-valuable-mobile-bank (archived at https://perma.cc/ZVL9-RLK3)

Société Générale (2018) Société Générale is pleased to announce the acquisition of Lumo, the pioneering renewable energy crowdfunding platform, www.societegenerale.com/en/content/societe-generale-is-pleased-to-announce-the-acquisition-of-lumo-the-pioneering-renewable-energy-crowdfunding-platform (archived at https://perma.cc/H4FN-XSBA)

Taylor, C (2019) San Francisco has rising competition when it comes to big fintech startups, *CNBC*, www.cnbc.com/2019/04/09/london-threatening-san-franciscos-fintech-unicorn-lead-research-says.html (archived at https://perma.cc/EU6E-M2DT)

Tracxn (2019) FinTech startups in Parison, Tracxn, tracxn.com/explore/FinTech-Startups-in-Paris/ (archived at https://perma.cc/ZW8V-RDUS)

10

New York City

Background

Conjuring up images of skyscrapers, wide thoroughfares and shops crammed full of innovative and unique items luring you in off the crowded streets, New York City (NYC) brings its own particular new world style to the financial services and fintech industries.

Distinctive for its sheer size and importance to the world economy, NYC is ranked the top global financial centre in the Global Financial Centres Index (Long Finance, 2019). Attracting the army of workers needed to service such an accolade, the New York Metropolitan area is home to more members of the Fortune 500 than any other city, including household names in finance such as JPMorgan Chase, Goldman Sachs Group and Morgan Stanley (Fortune, 2019). The Big Apple also hosts major exchanges including the New York Stock Exchange and the Nasdaq – the world's two largest stock exchanges by market capitalization (Wikipedia, 2019).

New York's real gross city product (GCP) has grown every quarter since Q4 2011, often outpacing economic growth in the wider US economy (Stringer, 2019). There are over 4 million people employed in NYC (Volovelsky, 2019). Rates of employment are generally high across New York, although the financial services sector has seen some job losses recently (Stringer, 2019).

History

Deep in the tech archives

Although people tend to focus on the tech and firms that sprung up following the global financial crisis, there is a debt of gratitude to be paid to the programmers of the 1950s who gave the world the Fortran programming language (1957) working out of IBM's office on East 56th Street (*New York Times*, 2019). Not to be outdone, the bright folks at Bell Labs, in Manhattan before upping sticks to neighbouring New Jersey, invented C and C++ programming languages as well as the Unix operating system, familiar to every student of modern computing.

What followed was a string of success stories, and amongst them was Bloomberg LP, established by Michael Bloomberg and Thomas Secunda in 1981, providing reliable access to real-time market data and news, as well as a way for people to communicate with each other over Bloomberg chat, for which it has become the gold standard. xThe company expanded into television, investing and research, and although it still makes the lion's share of its revenue via the terminal, the new fintechs are coming up fast from behind and beginning to offer niche solutions to content vs the full stack. This is particularly evident in regtech and AI, and of course in 'chat', where the likes of Slack, Team and Symphony are now part of everyday working life. It's not all doom and gloom because there is no denying that Bloomberg has built up an incredible repository of data over the decades, which continues to stand it in good stead as it invests in data science companies such as Kaggle, which may be able to continue the leading edge if it is able to access and work with the data (CB Insights, 2018).

New York City has experienced great growth in its fintech scene over a number of years. Writing in 2014, Accenture and the Partnership Fund for NYC noted that:

> New York's fintech cluster has grown twice as fast as Silicon Valley's over the last five years – deal volume grew 31 per cent annually, compared to Silicon Valley's 13 per cent, and investment grew 45 per cent annually, compared to Silicon Valley's 23 per cent.
>
> SOURCE Accenture, 2014

Silicon Alley (Flatiron)

Banking and financial services dominate the NYC landscape, and as an industry, financial services has always had technology as one of its core ingredients. It was never a static industry when it came to tech. It may not have always been quantum computing, as AI has only been around for some 60 years, so some of the tech of 'fintech', although not new, is being used in innovative ways. In addition to having a concentration of financial institutions, NYC would also have had a concentration of technology along with the bright young (and not so young) things who were developing and driving new technologies to fuel their products and services.

Given this unique concentration, right in the centre of all the creative, design and branding people lining Madison Avenue, with talent from top-tier universities like Columbia and NYU Stern on site, it would have logically been assumed that NYC would have blazed the trail when it came to shaking up financial services and introducing fintech to the nation. When you add to this the fact that NYC was largely built by waves of immigrants who brought their grit and determination to create a brave new world and a new world economy, it is baffling as to how the crown of fintech and financial services innovation, and initially the cream of the upstart crop, was not found along the avenues and alleys of NYC, but rather on the byways and beaches of the West Coast, and more specifically in Silicon Valley. Traditionally the home of the upstart tech startup, Silicon Valley is also a source of investors with deep pockets and of talent with the likes of Stanford, Berkeley and UCLA, for example, on its patch. However, apart from its expertise in payments technology, Silicon Valley is not a financial hub, so New York needed to play catch up.

In fact, it is said anecdotally that when Maria Gotsch, the co-founder of the trail-blazing FinTech Innovation Lab and CEO of the New York Partnership Fund, got the mandate from her then employer, Accenture, to discover where the financial centre sought out innovation, the unanimous answer from all CIOs and CTOs assembled was California, Boston and London (Gelfand, 2018). No one, it seemed, was taking a bite out of the well-equipped Big Apple when it came to innovation. So, it is even more notable that the impressive and very successful turnaround with regard to the fintech ecosystem in New York owes a great deal to the drive, determination and vision of Maria Gotsch who was unflappable in the face of doubt and disbelief.

Gotsch's project started in 2010. She soldiered on, and by 2017 VC-backed fintechs in Silicon Alley were raising 15 per cent more equity funding annually than their counterparts in Silicon Valley (Gelfand, 2018). Notable exits from FinTech Innovation Lab alumni include software storage system innovators Inktank (class of 2013), acquired in May 2014 for $175 million by Red Hat; online bill monitoring innovators BillGuard (class of 2012), acquired in 2015 by Prosper Marketplace for an estimated $30 million; and big data and visualization innovators Centrifuge Systems (class of 2012), acquired by Culmen International in 2019.

Recent alumni fundraising successes have included YayPay, a NYC-based startup focused on optimizing accounts receivables operations using machine-learning, which at the end of 2018 had raised $14 million in funding (Finsmes, 2018).

New York City's fintech ecosystem

One of the distinctive characteristics of the NYC fintech sphere is that the pool of tech businesses is a lot smaller than that in Silicon Valley, making it a more compact and communicative ecosystem, benefiting incumbents, disruptors and investors. However, somewhat surprisingly, according to Crunchbase (the respected source for funding information and insights on businesses), there are 660 fintech companies in NYC (Crunchbase, 2019). This is more than Silicon Valley (253) and San Francisco (442), so the fintechs in NYC still have to be stand-out propositions in order to attract investors.

Building on the concentration of financial institutions and their willingness to engage and collaborate with the fintech community, a recent report by the University of Cambridge's Judge Business School ranked NYC highly in the world as a fintech hub, citing the strength of its traditional financial institutions and Wall Street as the driving force behind the city's success (GFHI, 2018). The report focused in particular on the strength of NYC as an innovation ecosystem, ranking the city as the best global urban fintech ecosystem in the world as measured by macro-economic factors, the strength of its universities and the regulatory environment (GFHI, 2018).

Beyond finance, New York has strengths in disciplines closely related to fintech. New York boasts the highest percentage of AI and machine-learning job positions in a single US metro area (Startup Genome, 2019). Big data, and cybersecurity technologies also feature highly on the scene (Startup Genome, 2019).

In a recent special report, TechCrunch also identified that NYC is building a start-up culture grounded in companies which are 'deeply technical and deeply committed to building the future of enterprise infrastructure and applications' (Crichton, 2018). The report argued that, in contrast to the Bay Area, which is known for SaaS applications, NYC has a strong presence in companies working on underpinning infrastructure applications.

Brooklyn: bridging the gap

It is easy to forget that NYC is more than the island of Manhattan: it is comprised of five boroughs and its neighbour Brooklyn also has a vibrant tech ecosystem that stretches beyond the borders of the main island.

Established in the 1600s by the Dutch, and not physically connected to NYC until the 1880s, Brooklyn owes its name to the Dutch town of Breukelen but owes its current hipster reputation to technology. However, all that has changed as space became a sought-after commodity and there was more of it in Brooklyn than Manhattan, which attracted the likes of the marketplace Etsy to begin with, and then others followed (Tanzi, 2019).

SPOTLIGHT ON BROOKLYN

Some of the fastest-growing industries in Brooklyn since 2013 include:

- blockchain: 1,300 per cent growth, from one start-up in 2013 to 14 in 2018;
- cryptocurrency: 333 per cent growth, from three startups in 2013 to 13 in 2018;
- fintech: 229 per cent growth, from seven startups in 2013 to 23 in 2018;
- payments: 200 per cent growth, from 10 startups in 2013 to 30 in 2018.

A hive of activity

A city of over 8 million inhabitants on a piece of land that measures 302 square miles is by definition going to be a hive of activity and very, very, very crowded (Bowles *et al*, 2019). This same personality of the city that never sleeps found its way into the tech ecosystem, and NY boasts over 9,000 startups, numerous unicorns, over 100 accelerators, incubators, and co-working spaces (Startup Genome, 2019). Fintech found its place within the landscape, both literally and figuratively.

The Flatiron Building is located on 5th Avenue and 23rd Street. Completed in 1902, it was originally meant to be the Fuller Building, named for the construction company for which it would be the headquarters. However, the triangular shape of the building gave it the popular name 'Flatiron'. As a home for this initially unwieldy and rapidly expanding ecosystem, the iconic building and its environs, or 'Silicon Alley' (a name harking back to the days of the dotcom boom when the area housed and hot-housed the mainly media tech startups of the day), have become the focal point for fintech in Manhattan.

With Barclays Rise a stone's throw away and the Flatiron School for tech skills now global, this is one area where fintech is taking a bite out of the Big Apple – Big Apple real estate.

Strength in collaboration

An interesting characteristic of the NYC fintech ecosystem is the open desire for collaboration between fintechs and incumbents. With hundreds of thousands of fintechs, there is a real opportunity for regular and meaningful interaction between incumbents, be they investors, accelerators or procurers, and fintechs.

A B-Hive report on the New York fintech ecosystem published in 2018 noted that in 2010 only 37 per cent of investment in New York went to 'collaborative' fintechs (B-Hive, 2018a). Collaborative fintechs are companies who partner with larger incumbent firms. By 2015, that number had climbed to 83 per cent (B-Hive, 2018b). Globally, this trend for CVC is on the rise, but in New York, Citibank, via their Innovation Lab (or The Farm, as it's known in fintech circles), has been investing in collaborations with fintechs for the benefit of their own teams as well as their client teams for a number of years and ahead of other incumbents.

As the fintech industry moves increasingly towards incumbents of all sizes working more collaboratively with fintechs at scale (as opposed to startup) stage, either on a challenge–solution basis, or a use case basis, parties from both sides of the working relationship will no doubt benefit from the unique situation New York enjoys with close physical proximity to and good working relationships with incumbents and fintechs.

Access to capital

Alongside London and San Francisco, NYC is one of the fintech deal capitals of the world. As at August 2019, New York fintech companies attracted $1.93 billion of investment, just behind London ($2.11 billion) and San Francisco ($3.02 billion) (London & Partners, 2019). Considering it was a relative late-comer to the fintech scene, this is an impressive performance.

In other areas of tech in NYC there has really been no real shortage of readily available funding for the past decade, so when fintech was ready to receive, they were ready to give. What has been a new and welcomed addition to the investor landscape are the CVC funds investing alongside traditional VCs, and this is a trend that continues to rise.

There are many investors in the landscape and a number which focus solely or significantly on fintech, so take a look at some of the most active investors.

- **1/0 Capital**
  Invests in consumer credit-focused businesses that cover areas such as education, mortgages and asset-backed securities with an emphasis on technology. Its one exit is Paribus, which helps consumers benefit directly from fluctuating price reductions.

- **Anthemis Group**
  Co-founders Amy Nauiokis, Yann Ranchere and Sean Park established the New York office in 2015 (after they set up shop in London), and continue to partner with innovative incumbent financial institutions, such as the Spanish giant BBVA and Barclays Bank. Active investors, some of their successes include the sale of portfolio company Fidor Bank to the French BCPE (who have since parted).

- **Aquiline Capital Partners**
  Founded in NYC in 2005, Aquiline not only invests in NYC but also globally in service-driven and risk-heavy businesses in the financial services industry. Sectors include fintech, property, insurance and securities. Their six investments so far cover membership software with ClearCourse Partnership in the UK, Bitcoin payment solutions for enterprise with BitPay, reinsurance in the form of Trebuchet Holdings, and client onboarding and life cycle management with Fernergo.

- **Digital Currency Group**
  With a base in NYC, this specialist growth adviser and investor in Bitcoin and blockchain companies also owns and operates CoinDesk, the media and events platform for the blockchain community, a Bitcoin brokerage firm (Genesis Trading) and a digital currency asset management firm (Greyscale Investments).

- **ValueStream Ventures**
  This early growth stage fund based in NYC has a team that have been investing together since 2013. They invest in fintech, data analytics and B2B software but at the stage where, although there is revenue, the VSV team can still add value and help to fuel growth. They have had a number of exits, including include Loan Hero (POS financing) and Trigger Finance (DIY investing with rules).

- **Core Innovation Capital**
  Based in New York and LA, the firm adopts a values-based approach to VC investment in financial services and technology and focuses on investments that promote social mobility and economic stability. The firm's relationships span banks, credit bureaux, card networks, processors, money transmitters, regulators, advocates and investors. Entrepreneurs benefit from the firm's partnership with consumer finance think tank, the Financial Health Network (formerly CFSI).

- **FinTech Collective**
  A team that includes two entrepreneurial and exited co-founders with global tech experience and a seemingly more hands-on approach to working with their portfolio founders, FTC has invested in areas that include digital banking, lending, capital markets, payments and insurtech.

- **Fintech Ventures Fund**
  Invests in 'technology-enabled financial services companies', including non-bank lending, payments and insurtech. Portfolio companies include FundThatFlip, LQD Business Finance and IOU Financial business lending. Veteran financial services guru Serguei Kouzmine leads this forward-thinking team of investors.

- **IA Capital Group**
  A private investor group managing the Inter-Atlantic funds, and investing in growth insurtech and fintechs, including payments, asset management, retirement products and insurance services. The group has been on the scene for nearly 20 years.

- **NYCA Partners**
  One of the world's leading VC firms focused on fintech and innovation as it relates and connects to financial services in general. Their third fund of $210 million closed in 2019. One of their highest-profile partners is Hans Morris, who took Citigroup's institutional business to another level, and was president of Visa. Their portfolio, which covers areas such as payments, credit models, financial infrastructure and digital advice, is impressive and includes Affirm, Axoni, Acorns, Payoneer, Common Bond and Fluidly.

- **Ribbit Capital**
  Ribbit has invested in over 250 fintech companies, including unicorns Robinhood, CoinDesk, Wealthfront and Cross River Bank.

- **QED Investors**
An impressive portfolio which includes Remitly, ClearScore, NuBank and SoFi, QED is an early-stage investor in companies disrupting financial services in the United States, UK, and Latin America.

- **Amex Ventures**
An experienced corporate venture investor, Amex is looking for innovation that can be deployed for both its consumer and business customers, as well as its own internal business units. It has more than 60 financial services-related portfolio companies ranging from payments, commerce and security to fraud prevention and data analytics.

- **Citi Ventures**
Designed to explore new technologies and providers with a view to how they could be mutually beneficial to Citi, its clients and the fintech, Citi Ventures accelerates the engagement, growth and development of the solution provider via incubation and/or investment. Their portfolio includes Plaid, BlueVine, Betterment, Pindrop and Trulioo. The team is led by Vanessa Colella, Citi's CIO and Head of Ventures.

- **Capital One Growth Ventures (COGV)**
The venture arm of Capital One credit card and services, COGV invests through the strategic lens of Capital One and its customers. With offices in Virginia, San Francisco and New York, some of their portfolio companies include Dave, Feedzai, Paydiant (acquired by PayPal), MoneyLion and Credit Sesame.

- **Goldman Sachs Principal Strategic Investments**
Looking to invest in innovative technology businesses that can co-create and add value to Goldman Sachs offerings and clients, the investment fund invests $2–50 million in a variety of fintech areas that include payments, big data, security, and social finance.

Profile of the regulator

If the UK is known for being a principle-based regulatory system, the United States is very well known for being rule-based. It is also very well known for having circa 30 regulators that have something to do with financial services and therefore some will cover fintech.

Coming under the watchful eye of the regulators, there are a number of institution types that make up regulated financial services, some consumer facing and others more B2B. They include:

- those that take deposits – large and small;
- investment banks;
- non-bank entities;
- private equity;
- brokers and brokerage houses;
- mortgage originators;
- card payment originators;
- credit unions;
- payday lenders;
- automobile and vehicle lenders;
- unsecured lenders;
- student specific lenders.

This is quite broad coverage, and it would include some of the fintech community. The current situation regarding regulators and New York fintech is something of a mixed bag. On the one hand, the Consumer Financial Protection Bureau (CFPB) is looking to engage with the fintech community both domestically and globally, and on the other hand, the NY Department of Financial Services (DFS) is actively attempting to block the Office of the Controller of the Currency (OCC) from creating a new fintech charter, which has the incumbent banking community up in arms as they are concerned that fintechs are getting special treatment and being offered more relaxed regulatory frameworks (Monaka *et al*, 2019).

Consumer Financial Protection Bureau (CFPB)

The CFPB is a federal agency that protects, educates and empowers consumers as they navigate the complex, abundant and sometimes potentially treacherous consumer financial landscape in the United States, covering everything from student loans to payday loans, credit cards and everything in between. It was born out of the Dodd–Frank Wall Street Reform and Consumer Protection Act which regulates financial services, protects the consumer and is designed to prevent another financial crisis (Amadeo, 2019). It was signed into law in 2010 under President Obama, and the current US President, Donald Trump, has been very vocal about wanting to see it repealed, easing the constraints on traditional financial institutions.

The CFPB keeps an eye on incumbents but also debt collectors, vehicle lenders, and payday lenders, and other alternative finance providers, which could be part of the fintech community. New Yorkers seem to be very active complainants about everything from mortgages to consumer debt to credit cards, and the agency seems to hear their pleas for assistance (Stringer, 2017).

Dipping its toe in the fintech water with Project Catalyst, the CFBP actively engaged with the fintech community via various means, such as informal office hours, in order to better understand emerging innovation, the potential pitfalls and benefits for consumers, and where they would need to intervene and fulfil their obligations under the Dodd–Frank Wall Street Reform and the Consumer Protection Act.

As a follow on, the CFPB launched a Regulatory Sandbox in 2018, known as the Office of Innovation, to help fintechs and other financial services organizations advance their innovative ideas without being bound and gagged with red tape. The initial focus was on consumer products, keeping with the spirit of ensuring that consumers are offered inclusive, competitive products and services.

At the helm of the CFPB was Paul Watkins who came from the Arizona Attorney General's Office, Arizona having created the first US Sandbox in March 2018 (Kelly, 2018). This Arizona Sandbox has attracted a number of European fintechs looking to use the opportunity as an entry point into the USA – a fact which is not lost on the Department of Commerce in Washington DC, who are very aware of the arrival of UK and German fintechs on their shores.

Further adding to its international credentials and understanding, the CFPB was also an early participant in the FCA's GFIN initiative, serving on the Coordination Group, and is now joined by other members such as New York State Department of Financial Services, Office of the Attorney General of Arizona, OCC, the Federal Deposit Insurance Corporation (FDIC), and the Securities and Exchange Commission (SEC) amongst others.

The case of New York State v the OCC

Of course, it was never going to be all smooth sailing when it came to the regulators and fintech. The current banking regulations are not fit for fintech purpose and navigating the regulatory maze is challenging for fintechs. Some say this is the reason that change and progress has been slow to come in the United States, where cheques, for example, are still being used (albeit less often) and contactless payments are relatively new.

As if it were not complex enough already, there is an additional layer in the separation of the state and federal regulators. This sometimes makes for an uneasy relationship, which is clearly evident in the recent confrontation between the OCC which is mandated by the National Banking Agency to issue bank licences, and the NY State DFS which is leading the charge against fintechs being granted special national banking charters and taking this crusade to the courts. The nation – and the world – are watching this tech tango very closely as the implications go far beyond the borders of NYC.

The OCC was one of the early thought leaders when it came to assessing the frameworks and regulatory structures of fintechs, having begun to examine the regulatory implications that fintech innovation might create and where the potential obstacles and roadblocks to progress might lurk. One of the results of this introspection was the establishment of the Office of Innovation, and more controversially, the proposal to create an organizational and regulatory framework for fintechs to operate nationally under one regulator with one set of rules. It took some time, but the US government response came through in the summer of 2018 in the form of a Treasury Department report that was the culmination of a study and recommendations on fintech.

The Treasury recommended regulatory reform in four categories:

1 adapting regulatory approaches to changes in the aggregation, sharing, and use of consumer financial data, and to support the development of key competitive technologies;

2 aligning the regulatory framework to combat unnecessary regulatory fragmentation, and account for new business models enabled by financial technologies;

3 updating activity-specific regulations across a range of products and services offered by non-bank financial institutions, many of which have become outdated in light of technological advances; and

4 advocating an approach to regulation that enables responsible experimentation in the financial sector, improves regulatory agility and advances US interests abroad.

SOURCE *A Financial System That Creates Economic Opportunities: Nonbank Financials, Fintech, and Innovation*, US Department of the Treasury, July 2018, p 9

Criticism was levied from some corners, but given the regulatory complexity and general conservative nature of the country when it comes to financial innovation, the report represented quite a big step forward.

Perhaps surprisingly, at the same time, the OCC announced that it would start accepting applications for its special-purpose fintech national bank charter. Again, quite a major step forward, and one that did not go unnoticed by the New York State DFS and the Conference of State Bank Supervisors who are challenging the proposal. In *Lacewell* v. *OCC*, the state and federal regulators came to metaphorical blows with the final outcome not expected until an interpretation is reached in 2020. The state in the form of DFS has challenged the OCC on the point of a national charter for fintechs. This case has significant potential impact not only for fintechs but also for federal banking laws which are not designed to accommodate a type of dual banking system.

Challenged in its attempts to offer special national bank charters to fintechs by the New York DFS, the OCC must re-group. There was a ruling handed down by a federal court in Manhattan that asserted that allowing such a national charter would then leave the door open to other providers such as online lenders, alternative payment solutions and crypto-asset exchanges to operate without a banking partner in tow (Clark, 2019).

Although there is acrimony in the air at the moment, this is not to say that there hasn't been a sea-change in the relationship between the fintech community and the regulators – because there has. In fact, in the summer of 2019, the NY DFS made public a new Research and Innovation Division responsible for licensing and supervising virtual currencies and assessing efforts to use technology to address financial exclusion, identify and protect consumer data rights, and encourage innovations in the financial services marketplace (Adriance, 2019).

In addition to this, Maria T Vullo, former superintendent of the New York State DFS, joined the FinTech Innovation Lab New York as a regulator-in-residence for 12 weeks in April 2019 (Accenture, 2019) and the Federal Reserve Bank of New York held its first-ever research conference on fintech in March 2019 (Federal Reserve Bank, 2019).

Collaborating with other hubs

There are also signs that the New York regulators are embracing international fintech collaboration. For example, in July 2019, the NY DFS and Israel's financial regulators signed a memorandum of understanding to encourage and enable cross-border innovation and competition in fintech between the two hubs, which already share a close relationship (Israel MFA, 2019). Specifically, it covers:

- referrals with the aim of improving fintech speed to market;
- best practice and information sharing on trends, expertise, regulatory change and innovation;
- being a friendly source of local information and support with regard to regulations and authorizations.

The ecosystem

The popular saying that no man is an island is particularly apt to the fintech scene on the island that is NYC. Having established a vibrant and growing ecosystem in the City, NY simultaneously and perhaps unwittingly also estab-lished its top-tier positioning in the fintech world and has created a magnet for the talented, the ambitious and the curious in the global fintech community.

Accelerators, co-working spaces, conferences, meetups, hackathons… it's all going on. And although a good deal of the activity is centred around Silicon Alley, the community members are making good use of the whole of NYC.

Amongst the key stand-out participants are the following.

THE PARTNERSHIP FOR NYC AND ACCENTURE FINTECH INNOVATION LAB

This 12-week programme helps early-stage enterprise tech companies refine and test their value proposition with leading financial firms. Since its incep-tion, the programme has worked with nearly 70 companies, helped them raise $1 billion and seen seven acquisitions. Largely the brainchild of its CEO, Maria Gotsch, during her time at Accenture, their model, triumphs and tribulations are a beacon and inspiration to other cities.

MARIA GOTSCH

President and CEO of the Partnership Fund for NYC (the investment arm of the Partnership for New York City), co-founder of the FinTech Innovation Lab, and previously at a Deutsche Bank company, Gotsch has been spear-heading fintech innovation in NYC for a number of years. On the FinTech Innovation Lab, she said:

> When we established the FinTech Innovation Lab 10 years ago, few financial institutions were sourcing technology in New York. Now there is a rich ecosystem of fintech entrepreneurs, venture dollars and corporate engagement

here that has enabled fintechs to scale and create jobs locally. New York is now a leading centre of fintech - particularly for enterprise solution. (FinTech Innovation Lab, 2019).

TECHSTARS

Born out of an original association with Barclays Bank, the Techstars programme is now global. Their New York programme is a 13-week accelerator that quickens the pace of, and provides the circumstances required for the growth of 10 companies each year, including fintech. Mentors, industry experts, investors and guides to storytelling all help early-stage founders and teams to grow. Since its inception, the programme has had over 160 cohort members with a collective value of over $1 billion. As accelerator programmes go, Techstars sets the gold standard for those with a global reach (www.techstars.com/content/tag/barclays-nyc/).

JENNY FIELDING

The MD of Techstars NY, Fielding is also the founder and general partner at The Fund, an early-stage investor in only NYC-based companies.

EMPIRE STARTUPS

Founded in 2011, this fintech community builder was born out of a NY fintech meetup group, and has grown from strength to strength, offering conferences and world-famous week-long events (also in San Francisco). The community of just under 20,000 strong is global and includes founders, investors and financial services professionals.

JON ZANOFF

Managing director of Barclays Techstars New York and co-founder of Empire Startups, Zanoff earned his stripes in investment banking before embarking on a leading role in the NY fintech ecosystem.

OTHER NOTABLE MENTIONS

- **Michael Schlein**
  President and CEO, Accion (Investing), and chairman of the NYC Economic Development Corporation. A former investment banker, Schlein is passionate about making financial inclusion a reality in his work with micro-finance and impact investing. In 2014, Bill de Blasio, the Mayor of NYC, appointed Schlein chairman of the NYC Economic Development Corporation tasking him with re-igniting the vibrancy of the NYC economy.

- **Susan Oh**

  Founder, Muckr.AI and Blockchain for Impact (BFI). A civic technologist, multi-award-winning Oh is seeking ways in which AI and blockchain can be used for social good at large. Her co-founded venture, Muckr.AI, uses machine-learning to measure the trustworthiness of content based on source behaviour. Not content with purely commercial endeavours, she is also a governing member of Blockchain for Impact, a non-profit in partnership with the UN General Assembly.

- **Jeremy Balkin**

  Head of Innovation, HSBC Retail and Wealth Management (including Global Private Banking), USA. Based in NYC, Balkin is an award-winning author of *Investing with Impact* and *The Millennial Book*. He is a fitness lover, a graduate of the Harvard Kennedy School, a mentor to a number of fintech startups and a believer in corporate–scaleup collaboration in financial services.

Talent landscape

New York City has been a magnet for talent from around the country and around the world for quite a long time. Immigrants flocked to the City to make a better life for themselves and their families. Young graduates and professionals seeking adventure alighted from other US states to study, make their mark or make it big. Politicians, educators and business leaders all know the economic value of a first-class academic environment, and thanks to investors such as Sallie Krawchek, CEO and co-founder of Ellevest, a digital financial adviser for women, everyone is waking up to the bottom- and top-line benefits of having more women as owners: NYC has more than 410,000 women-owned businesses, more than double any other US city. Approximately 47 per cent of NYC's technology workers are foreign born (Tech:nyc, 2019). Talent, as it is in other fintech hubs, is a critical resource and a constant struggle to retain and attract. Thankfully there are a number of institutions leading the way when it comes to relevant education, and here are a number of examples.

Key institutions

Academic

Fintech courses have only been in existence for five years or so, and university courses generally take two years to get from inception to the lecture theatre or classroom, but there have been a number of leaders in the academic space who make good use of the vibrant fintech and deep financial services ecosystem in NYC. They include the following.

- **Fordham**
  The Gabelli School of Business offers an undergraduate fintech course aimed at Finance majors.

- **NYU Stern Executive Education**
  The course covers six areas that include innovation, technology, startups vs incumbents, valuations, risk and societal and policy implications of technology. Industry professionals teach alongside academics and case studies shed light on fintech disruptors.

- **Cornell Johnson**
  Part of a three-year MBA, the fintech courses are taught in NYC, and cover all aspects of fintech but also the entrepreneurial side of the subject, including business models, in order to work in teams to create and present their original solutions. Until these courses were launched, NY really had no leading entrepreneurial engineering offering. In close proximity, New Jersey had Stevens Tech, for example, but when Maria Gotsch won the support of Michael Bloomberg, the academic wheels began to turn, and things started to fall into place.

- **The New York Institute of Finance**
  The Institute offers the financial services professional everything from an introduction to fintech to advanced data science in course lengths from 14 hours to five days, in both on- and offline formats.

Key events

There is always something going on in NYC, be it a meetup, a global conference, a pitch event or just a general meeting of the minds. However, a number of events and specialist information sources stand out from the crowd:

- **New York FinTech Week**
  The brainchild of the 15,000 strong and constantly growing community organization that networks, links, connects, profiles and promotes fintech, innovative incumbents, investors and mentors, Empire Startups' flagship fintech event in NYC (and San Francisco) usually takes place in the spring, attracting thousands looking to debate, discuss, learn, showcase

and envelop themselves in all things fintech. Not content with one week of activity, throughout the year they offer meetups, pitch events, job boards, podcasts and newsletters.

- **CB Insights Fintech**
  The highly respected research firm CB Insights hosts their flagship fintech event, bringing thousands of fintech and financial services professionals together under one roof. Investors, incumbents, fintech unicorns and those aspiring to be mythical creatures all converge on NYC to talk business, network and add to the research.

- **Finovate**
  Short-form demos and expert insights offer a unique format that most of the industry enjoys. Hotly anticipated fintech demos (Revolut was once a pitching fintech here) and financial services professionals come together to debate and discuss key topics of the day and of the future, to unveil new products, services, partnerships and team members, and to applaud upcoming starts and be inspired to continue to innovate.

- **New York City FinTech Women**
  With over 2,000 members, this community is all about educating and empowering women in fintech. They run a series of events, including fintech Female Fridays, dedicated to educating, supporting and providing opportunities.

Stand-out fintechs

There are dozens of incredible fintechs and forward-thinking incumbents that help to weave the rich tapestry that is the New York fintech scene, but some of the stand-out companies that merit a mention are:

- **Etal** (founded 2016)
  A credit card business that wants to help people strengthen their credit rating while giving them cash back and a no-fee service. The founders came from financial services and partner with some of the leading credit rating agencies and credit card providers in their quest to open up credit to previously excluded and marginalized groups.

- **MoneyLion** (founded 2013)
  A consumer platform using AI and ML for borrowing, investing and saving.

- **Axoni** (founded 2013)
  A blockchain solution for capital markets being deployed in some of the world's largest financial institutions. Parties in a trade receive continuously updated transaction records with full transparency and synchronized payments (Majewski, 2019).

- **Common Bond** (founded 2011)
  Founded by David Klein, Michael Taormina and Jessup Shean, who ironically met at graduate school, and who empathized with and understood the collective pain of student borrowers, Common Bond saw and responded to the opportunity to help bring down the cost of student loans by refinancing borrowings, while helping investors get a better return on their funds. To date they claim to have funded over $2.5 billion in student loans. That is an awful lot of valuable learning.

- **Fundera** (founded 2013)
  A curated vendor marketplace for small business loan providers.

- **SeedInvest** (founded 2011)
  Founded by Ryan Feit and James Han in NYC, SeedInvest was one of the early entrants into equity crowdfunding in the US, helping to get the JOBS (Jumpstart Our Business Startups) Act, laying out the regulations for both accredited and non-accredited equity investors and platforms, over the line. With a $25,000 minimum investment threshold, it offers a 'broad church' approach from very early- to late-stage investments, hardware to software, fintech, health tech, AI and robotics, to name a few areas.

- **OnDeck** (founded 2009)
  Mitch Jacobs founded OnDeck in 2007, but really entered the public psyche in 2014 when its IPO raised $230 million. OnDeck is a B2B lending platform helping to get funds to SMEs more quickly and easily than it would be using an incumbent. It had a partnership with an incumbent in JPMorgan Chase from April 2016 to 2019 that focused on small business loans.

- **Venmo** (founded 2009)
  Venmo was originally a music startup designed to be able to communicate with bands in order to obtain mp3s, then became a simple way to pay someone in a social network, before being sold to Braintree in 2012 for $26.2 million. The brainchild of two Penn grads, the mobile app makes it easier and safe to send and receive funds from any other Venmo user.

The future is bright

New York has managed an amazing tech comeback, and there is no turning back now. Like the phoenix from the ashes of the dotcom era, the City has risen once again to take on a new tech mantle – the fintech mantle – for the United States. With its perfect storm of a density of financial services, depth of tech and design talent and deep funding pockets, the city that never sleeps has created a thriving ecosystem. There are hiccups along the way with regulatory tussles and Euro-invaders entering the challenger bank and alternative finance arenas, but there is a palpable momentum and shared will to succeed, expand and retain the fintech crown and all the spoils that accompany such an accolade.

References

Accenture (2014) *The Rise of Fintech: New York's opportunity for tech leadership*, Accenture, pfnyc.org/wp-content/uploads/2017/04/The-Rise-of-Fintech_2014. pdf (archived at https://perma.cc/5Q4M-HCQV)

Accenture (2019) Maria Vullo joins FinTech Innovation Lab New York as Regulator-in-Residence, Accenture, newsroom.accenture.com/news/maria-vullo-joins-fintech-innovation-lab-new-york-as-regulator-in-residence.htm (archived at https://perma.cc/P46G-DMLR)

Adriance, S (2019) New York DFS announces new division overseeing fintech [blog] Covington & Burling LLP, www.lexology.com/library/detail.aspx?g= 11b68a17-24ab-45b6-830c-afdd7f2ea317 (archived at https://perma.cc/ Z7VP-CF8X)

Amadeo, K (2019) Dodd–Frank Wall Street Reform Act, *The Balance*, www.thebalance.com/dodd-frank-wall-street-reform-act-3305688 (archived at https://perma.cc/8MU7-6QXH)

B-Hive (2018a) *The NYC Fintech Map*, B-Hive, b-hive.eu/news-full/2018/5/26/ the-nyc-fintech-map (archived at https://perma.cc/6VB4-3A3L)

B-Hive (2018b) *New York, USA: General & Fintech Landscape*, B-Hive, static1. squarespace.com/static/578f3f1d15d5db7814d05191/t/5b3372f7f950b7 fadb937cda/1530098446516/New+York%2C+USA+Report+2018.pdf (archived at https://perma.cc/2A5W-NQZ9)

Bowles, J, Dvorkin, E and Sharp, N (2019) *Brooklyn's Growing Innovation Economy*, Center for an Urban Future, nycfuture.org/research/brooklyns-growing-innovation-economy (archived at https://perma.cc/TW8A-MUKH)

CB Insights (2018) *The Disruption of Bloomberg LP*, CB Insights, www.cbinsights. com/research/report/bloomberg-terminal-disruption/ (archived at https://perma. cc/FAX8-MZWH)

Clark, D (2019) NY regulator's lawsuit derails federal push to charter fintech companies, *New York Law Journal*, www.law.com/newyorklawjournal/2019/10/22/ny-regulators-lawsuit-derails-federal-push-to-charter-fintech-companies/?slret urn=20191103170922 (archived at https://perma.cc/65CM-VSBW)

Crichton, D (2018) *Special Report: New York's Enterprise Infrastructure ecosystem*, Techcrunch, techcrunch.com/2018/04/21/new-yorks-enterprise-infrastructure-ecosystem/ (archived at https://perma.cc/ET8S-55LQ)

Crunchbase (2019) *City of New York FinTech Companies 2019*, Crunchbase, www.crunchbase.com/hub/city-of-new-york-fintech-companies#section-overview (archived at https://perma.cc/U45F-4UW3)

Federal Reserve Bank (2019) The First New York Fed research conference on fintech (2019), Federal Reserve Bank of New York, www.newyorkfed.org/research/conference/2019/fintech (archived at https://perma.cc/GZY6-GK7S)

Finsmes (2018) YayPay raises $8.4m in funding, Finsmes, www.finsmes.com/2018/12/yaypay-raises-8-4m-in-funding.html (archived at https://perma.cc/E5SU-TY3T)

FinTech Innovation Lab (2019) FinTech Innovation Lab New York now accepting applicants for 2020 class, www.fintechinnovationlab.com/fintech-innovation-lab-new-york-now-accepting-applicants-2020-class/(archived at https://perma.cc/E5SU-TY3T)

Fortune (2019) Fortune 500 and 1000 by MSA, City, and State (2019), *Fortune*, fortune.com/fortune500/2019/search/?hqcity=New%20York&hqstate=NY (archived at https://perma.cc/8UVG-3M34)

Gelfand, A (2018) Up by the roots: Inside New York City's push to become a global fintech capital – and what its ascent can teach other cities, *Harvard Business School*, www.alumni.hbs.edu/stories/Pages/story-bulletin.aspx?num=6641 (archived at https://perma.cc/9VE6-DGE5)

GFHI (2018) *The future of finance is emerging: New hubs, new landscapes global fintech hub report*, GFHI, www.jbs.cam.ac.uk/fileadmin/user_upload/research/centres/alternative-finance/downloads/2018-ccaf-global-fintech-hub-report-eng.pdf (archived at https://perma.cc/L7BT-NPTQ)

Israel MFA (2019) Financial regulators of New York and Israel announce agreement on FinTech cooperation, Israel Ministry of Foreign Affairs, mfa.gov.il/MFA/InnovativeIsrael/DoingBusiness/Pages/Financial-regulators-sign-Israel-NY-FinTech-cooperation-MOU-9-July-2019.aspx (archived at https://perma.cc/VD8R-SG9N)

Kelly, J (2018) Arizona Sandbox gives fintech start-ups a regulatory path to US, *Financial Times*, www.ft.com/content/aac62a22-c196-11e8-84cd-9e601db069b8 (archived at https://perma.cc/C5NH-7PDB)

London & Partners (2019) *A fine year for fintech: Global trends from a UK perspective*, London & Partners, www.innovatefinance.com/wp-content/uploads/2019/09/sibos_fintech_report_v8.pdf (archived at https://perma.cc/7LSE-EPYA)

Long Finance (2019) *The Global Financial Centres Index (2019),* Long Finance, www.longfinance.net/programmes/financial-centre-futures/global-financial-centres-index/ (archived at https://perma.cc/NY7X-P8WA)

Majewski, M (2019) Top 10 fintech companies in New York to watch in 2019, www.netguru.com/blog/top-10-fintech-companies-in-new-york-to-watch-in-2019 (archived at https://perma.cc/6AA2-PY9X)

Monaka, N, DeCresce, C and Hooper, R (2019) FinTech in the United States: overview, Thomson Reuters, uk.practicallaw.thomsonreuters.com/w-017-4511?transitionType=Default&contextData=(sc.Default)&firstPage=true&bhcp=1 (archived at https://perma.cc/H66Y-Q7BU)

New York Times (2019) It started with a jolt: how New York became a tech town, 21 November, *New York Times*

Startup Genome (2019) *Global Startup ecosystem report (2019),* Startup Genome, startupgenome.com/reports (archived at https://perma.cc/PT96-5CHH)

Stringer, SM (2017) CFPB and NYC: How the Consumer Financial Protection Bureau Empowers and Protects New Yorkers, New York City Comptroller Scott M Stringer, comptroller.nyc.gov/wp-content/uploads/documents/CFPB_and_NYC_How_the_CFPB_-Empowers_and_Protects_New_Yorkers.pdf (archived at https://perma.cc/G3VM-W2DZ)

Stringer, SM (2019) NYC Quarterly Economic Update (2019), New York City Comptroller Scott M. Stringer, comptroller.nyc.gov/reports/new-york-city-quarterly-economic-update/ (archived at https://perma.cc/HQ3A-89NZ)

Tanzi, A (2019) New York City's population is shrinking: Demographic trends, Bloomberg, www.bloomberg.com/news/articles/2019-04-18/new-york-city-s-population-is-shrinking-demographic-trends (archived at https://perma.cc/UYY9-UUV2)

Tech:nyc (2019) NYC Tech Ecosystem Overview (2019), Tech:nyc, www.technyc.org/our-ecosystem (archived at https://perma.cc/S4C7-Z85D)

Volovelsky, E (2019) *Labor Statistics for the New York City Region,* Department of Labor, www.labor.ny.gov/stats/nyc/ (archived at https://perma.cc/2YUJ-769P)

Wikipedia (2019) List of Stock Exchanges, Wikipedia, en.wikipedia.org/wiki/List_of_stock_exchanges (archived at https://perma.cc/RD7W-JKSP)

11

Tel Aviv

History

A nation that has its foundations in tolerance, tenacity and taking risks for the benefit of the greater good, Israel's fintech landscape mirrors some of its nation state building blocks, and nowhere in this relatively young country and nascent industry is this more apparent than in Tel Aviv.

As so aptly pointed out by the Startup Ecosystem ranking of 2017, 'The capital of Israel is Jerusalem, but the capital of the Startup Nation is undoubtedly Tel Aviv' (B-Hive, 2018). Named The Mediterranean Capital of Cool, Tel Aviv is well known for its vibrant nightlife, funky Bauhaus architecture and rich cultural offerings, but in recent years the 'hill of spring' has also become a hive of startup activity, attracting innovators of all sizes to its tightly knit and supportive ecosystem (Alford, 2008). Perhaps somewhat astonishingly, it has one of the highest startup densities in the world, and between 1999 and 2015, the country saw the creation of more than 11,585 startups inside its borders, with a population of only 9 million (Worldometers, 2019). Within this burgeoning group of innovative and disruptive startups and scaleups are 570+ fintechs, and there are no signs of this growth slowing down (Nechushtan, 2018). An example of the success and the international respect and regard given to the ecosystem of Israel was the record-breaking purchase of the vision-based self-driving vehicle startup Mobileye by Intel for an eye-watering $15.3 billion in 2018 (Lunden, 2017).

Silicon Wadi

In the early days of fintech in Israel, there were fewer than 100 startups and less than $15 million to go around. Now five times the number and many multiples of available investment funds, Israeli fintech has grown to include approximately 570 startups, collectively raising billions of dollars to date (Nechushtan, 2018).

Some of the key verticals or sub-industry categories they address include:

- cybersecurity;
- digital payments;
- personal finance;
- gaining ground: insurtech.

For the size of the country, and the concentration of financial services and insurance companies that sees five banks owning 90 per cent of the market share, domestic competition is not really a driver in this phenomenal fintech story. So just how did this tiny, but in no way insignificant, country perched on the eastern edge of the Mediterranean become such a force in the fintech world?

Key strengths

An independent non-profit organization that links governments, NGOs and business with Israeli innovation, Start-up Nation Central (SNC) plays a key role in connecting fintech innovators with financial services and multinationals looking to genuinely engage with the disruptors, creators and talent. They, very aptly, summarize the key ingredients in what has become a self-sustaining ecosystem in Tel Aviv which are: leveraging the strengths of a tightly knit startup community; an actively engaged investor community; and a forward-thinking regulator and multinationals who see the benefits of research, testing with, partnering with and sometimes acquiring startups. The Tel Aviv fintech ecosystem has used these key drivers to create one of the most unique and successful self-sustaining virtuous circles in the world.

From humble beginnings: an immigrant nation finds its natural resources

As citizens of a country that is not rich in natural resources and impacted by ongoing regional trading restrictions, Israeli entrepreneurs have focused on their other 'natural resources', such as tech skills, and industries which are not bound by borders or the natural elements and that can be incubated, developed and scaled for both domestic, but more importantly, international consumption.

A nation born of immigrants with grit and determination, or *chutzpah* as the locals call it, seemingly unflappable in the face of adversity, Israelis' have an entrepreneurial flair with higher than average higher education levels (OECD, 2016). At 46 per cent, and just second only to Canada, the percentage of Israel's population who have gone through tertiary education is very high compared to other countries. This push helps this small country punch well above its weight when it comes to fintech.

A perfect testing ground for tech

With a domestic population that is not large enough to scale to a significant level, Israel is seen by some as the perfect 'wood burner' environment for new fintech ideas, providing a fertile testing ground for the innovative solutions created in places like Tel Aviv that need to be exported in order to realize their full potential. This testing ground is not limited to startups and can sometimes see multinationals partnering with larger Israeli organizations, such as Microsoft and Bank Hapoalim, Israel's largest bank, to build a blockchain solution for digital bank guarantees.

The heritage of the defence industry

Of course, it's not all about formal education; there are a number of other significant influences on the success story that is Tel Aviv and elsewhere in Israel. The positive impact of the Israeli Defense Forces (IDF) on the fintech industry in Israel cannot and should not be underestimated, particularly in relation to cybersecurity where it has taken a dominant position in the global fintech landscape.

As conscription is mandatory in Israel, every Israeli will experience 24/7 living and working with their divisions, overcoming challenges and adversity using their grit, wit and intelligence, creating strategies that divisions can deploy and learning to manage teams. In other words, skills that are necessary in the startup environment (including 'bootcamps' or accelerators). This makes them attractive candidates for multinationals looking for more than competent talent. If you add the professional and technical skills gained during military service in areas such as biometrics, big data and real-time analytics, all of which are now integral parts of fintech and financial services, it is not hard to see why this small country produces serial entrepreneurs and globally experienced professionals that gives it an edge.

Government support

In addition to the entrepreneurial training ground provided by the military, the State of Israel is a key supporter of all tech industries in the country, and fintech is right up there with the rest. The Israel Government has taken a proactive role in the growth of fintech for a number of years, for example, encouraging entrepreneurs and leveraging the country's academic, scientific and tech workforce while often providing funding options. In addition to acting as a neutral interface in order to facilitate knowledge exchange between complementary parties, what follows are some key examples of how this willingness and proactiveness has been translated into practical steps. It is by no means an exhaustive list.

THE INNOVATION AUTHORITY

One of the ways in which government supports fintech is through the Innovation Authority (formerly the Office of the Chief Scientist of Israel's Ministry of Economy) with practical tools and funding initiatives including incubator programmes and grant funding.

There have also been a variety of government-backed financial support initiatives and incentive programmes, reaching as far back as 2011, to encourage large financial institutions to open permanent R&D centres and hubs in Israel to tap into the tech and entice the talent to their teams, but also to give back by having a local presence. This is borne out by the fact that more than 40 multinationals and financial services giants now have a presence in Israel. The talent identified on some of these schemes often went abroad to gain experience and knowledge, which was sometimes used to start their own ventures back on home soil. One could say that it's a sort of virtuous circle.

YOZMA GROUP

Another government initiative centred on funding and took the form of a VC fund leveraging public funds to boost private investment in order to ramp up R&D investment. From 1993 to 1998, the government matched 40 per cent of the money put into 40 companies by private investors, increasing the value of the fund from $100 million in 1993 to $250 million in 1996. The initiative also spurred over 30 foreign investment funds to set up in Israel. Israel spends more than any other country on R&D – 4.25 per cent as a proportion of GDP – and values this natural resource. The legacy of this scheme continues as private investors continue to play an active role in funding Israeli fintechs (Apolitical, 2017).

International financial institutions and large multinational corporations

A number of large financial institutions and multinational corporations (MNCs) have been so taken with the fintech possibilities and welcoming commercial environment on offer in Israel that they have launched permanent innovation centres. Citibank, Barclays and AXA are those with the highest profiles.

- **Citibank Innovation Lab**
  Seeing the need for a fertile testing and innovation lab, and taking advantage of the government support package, Citi established their first Innovation Lab in Tel Aviv in 2011. Buoyed by their success, they opened their Big Data Lab in 2013 in order to make strategic vs purely financially driven investments. With over 200 applicants to date, there have been some successes such as PayKey in mobile payments, and Ladingo with their e-commerce shipping solution. And also success in getting the Citi teams excited about the possibilities of working with startups.

- **Barclays Techstars**
  The teams at Barclays Techstars are global accelerator aficionados, combining the might of the UK bank with the US Techstars programme to select the entrepreneurs and propositions they feel have the best chance of success with their help. Ten fintechs are chosen to take part in an intensive 13-week programme that helps to accelerate their solutions and to help take them to market. Supported by the wider Barclays and Techstar networks, industry experts, mentors and other service providers, the cohort members are put through their paces as they prepare for the next stage of growth and are showcased to interested investors (including the Rise Growth Investment fund which is targeted at companies entering the accelerator). Key to the selection process is that at least one team member is a 'techie' and in Tel Aviv this is one criterion that is easy to meet! The fourth batch of hopefuls entered the programme in 2019, and the focus areas for this cohort include data protection, blockchain, mobile payments and tax reporting. Wave, which is trade finance on the blockchain, was one of the better-known 2015 graduates of the accelerator programme whose solution has been deployed with Barclays.

- **Deloitte's Innovation Tech Terminal (ITT)**
  This is a collaboration between Deloitte US and Israel for the benefit of Deloitte's clients, and startups. Services on offer include scouting tours to

identify and meet with the innovators and immersion tours for those who want to delve deeper.

- **AXA Kamet Ventures**
Established in 2016, Kamet Ventures is the incubator arm of AXA Insurance. Tel Aviv's Setoo, which offers a variety of insurance-as-a-service products, is one of their investees and is also licensed by the FCA in the UK.

Active and solid investor landscape

Tel Aviv has a good mix of both local and foreign investors and covers the full spectrum from startup to scaleup and beyond. We've already mentioned some of the ways in which the government funding initiatives around R&D have had significant impact, and encourage public–private funding efforts, but there is also a very healthy VC industry in town alongside business angels who have a global presence but are in search of Israeli businesses. Amongst the funders are also large tech firms, such as Google, Facebook, Intel, IBM, Microsoft and others, looking for corporate investment, acquisition and merger opportunities. For example, Waze satellite navigation systems was acquired by Google and also set up significantly sized R&D facilities to be ahead of the curve.

Access to capital

No fintech business, be it a startup or a later-stage scaleup, is immune from having to raisee capital. The quest for the elusive but essential traction (sales, intention to buy, etc) depends on many factors: the length of the sales cycle, the intensity of the tech development and the challenge to find willing partners and collaborators in order to secure proof of concepts and pilot programmes. But capital, as well as cashflow, is the lifeblood of a fintech business, and Israel has a very vibrant investor community.

Included in the ranks of funding providers are:

- **Viola Group**
An Israeli-based VC firm that invests in Israeli-affiliated companies, including fintechs, that are affiliated with Israel, but may not necessarily be based there, eg eToro, the online social trading platform.

- **iAngels**
  Accredited investors from around the world are able to invest alongside iAngels via their crowd-investing network in companies with an Israeli presence. They provide deal flow and work very closely with Start-up Nation in order to be right on the pulse of the ecosystem.

- **Sequoia Capital**
  Established in 1972 and headquartered in Israel, Sequoia, which is perhaps better known in Silicon Valley, invests in fintech as well as a variety of other tech sectors. With funds totalling just under $15 billion and exits including the likes of Instagram, this is a fund to be reckoned with.

- **83 North** (formerly Greylock IL)
  A global firm with over $800 million under management, 83 North invests in European and Israeli firms and entrepreneurs at all stages in both B2B and B2C propositions.

- **Moneta**
  A VC fund that invests in early stage data technology firms that are fintech (and insurtech) focused. One of Israel's most active investors, they have a seed fund established in 2015, and a later-stage fund for revenue generating companies set up in 2018.

RECORD-BREAKING INVESTMENTS FOR GROWTH

According to an interview in December 2019 with Yair Fonarov of Start-Up Nation Central, 2018 broke all half-year records for Israeli fintech, totalling $830 million in equity deals (Nechushtan, 2018). Of this amount, $100 million was raised by eToro, the social trading and investing platform. Even without the eToro deal, H1 2018 remains the highest-funded half-year ever at over $400 million. In figures yet to be published at the time of writing, three quarters of the way through 2019 saw $1.5 billion in equity investment, so once again, breaking records and signalling continued growth.

According to Business Insider Intelligence (Nonninger, 2019), in 2018, funding was secured across 58 deals, only four more deals than the year before. With significantly more money flowing in, this would indicate larger-sized investments, signalling a higher level of maturity and confidence in the market, a more bullish attitude from investors and funding for significant growth vs early-stage infusions.

As these companies have grown, they have also explored a wider variety of funding options, and very sensibly some have looked at the later-stage bridging and venture debt instruments from the likes of Silicon Valley Bank.

This is particularly evident with online lenders looking to expand loan books. Debt funding of this type is an indication of an increasing maturity level within the fintech ecosystem and bodes well for the future growth. Figures compiled by SNC 2018 highlight the fact that:

> $441 million in debt (more than twice the entire 2017 amount) was raised by four companies across six deals in H1 2018. Three of these companies are online lending startups that are entering a new phase in their effort to grow: BlueVine (an online invoicing company for small businesses), Behalf (working capital for small businesses) and BLender (a peer to peer lending platform).

Figures are updated annually by SNC, so do visit their website regularly.

HIGHLY EXPERIENCED ENTREPRENEURS WHO GIVE BACK

Success breeds success. As far back as 2007, Israeli tech entrepreneurs have had significant success, eg Fraud Services acquired by PayPal for $169 million in 2008. There is a culture of 'giving back' or 'paying it forward', depending on your lens, that is pervasive amongst the fintech scene in Tel Aviv. Even casual conversations with entrepreneurs from Tel Aviv inspire the listener to want to be part of adding value to the ecosystem. Their enthusiasm is truly infectious. It happens not only at pitch events, accelerators and research facilities, but also in the cafés and bars which typify the relaxed, sociable city. A city of serial entrepreneurs who share their journeys so that others may learn, enveloped in a culture that embraces the positive aspects of overcoming failure, is a powerful combination for success (Nechushtan, 2018).

Academic institutions

There are a number of academic institutions that are leading the way when it comes to fintech, which is hardly surprising given the higher than average percentage of the population that obtains graduate and postgraduate degrees. There is a general thirst for knowledge in Israel in general and, more specifically in Tel Aviv, for fintech knowledge.

There are also a number of leading academics who have taken the bull by the horns and created and delivered courses across the fintech spectrum. What follows is a sample of the vast academic landscape.

HEBREW UNIVERSITY

Professor David Gershon leads the MBA at the Hebrew University Fintech Center, where he and his colleagues have constructed long and short, in-person and online courses that cover topics such as:

- introduction to fintech;
- regulation and regtech;
- entrepreneurship in fintech;
- blockchain and cryptocurrencies;
- innovation in insurtech;
- fintech analytics.

Course content delves deeper into fintech verticals such as:

- peer to peer lending;
- crowdfunding;
- consumer and business credit;
- payments;
- wealth and investments;
- IoT/telemetrics;
- blockchain;
- cryptocurrencies, mining, exchanges;
- regulatory compliance;
- data analytics.

BEN GURION AND BE'ER SHEVA UNIVERSITIES

Leading the way in cybersecurity are Ben Gurion and Be'er Sheva universities. With the additional financial and promotional support of government, Be'er Sheva houses the Fintech Cyber (FinSec) Innovation Lab, a broad church ecosystem, to help turbo-charge the growth of cyber startups and attract investment to these companies.

Talent landscape

With such a prolific higher education system churning out highly qualified students in relevant subject matter, and with a solid foundation in startup skills gained in the military, one would think that there would be a glut on the supply side of the talent equation. However, one would be wrong. Despite understanding, anticipating and addressing the educational and ongoing experiential needs of the talent pool (eg stints working in large financial services organizations and other multinationals both in Israel and abroad), Israel, and Tel Aviv more acutely, suffers from the same lack of good and reasonably priced talent as does the rest of the world. Increasing numbers of multinationals entering the market and the very active VC scene means an abundance of talent hunters vs talent gatherers on the ground.

Unsurprisingly, the result is that it is a buyers' or an employees' market:

> Wages in the tech sector continue to rise faster than in the rest of the economy – Israel is the world leader in terms of the ratio of the tech sector earnings to earnings in the rest of the economy: 2.5.
>
> SOURCE Innovation Israel, 2018

The ecosystem

If variety is the spice of life, then Israel, and therefore Tel Aviv, are experiencing an explosion of taste and flavour when it comes to the makeup of the ecosystem. Accelerators, hubs, incubators, events, conferences, funders and incumbents all lay out the welcome mat to the fintech startups and scaleups.

By no means exhaustive, here is a sampling of some of the leading lights.

START-UP NATION CENTRAL (SNC)

Founded in 2013, with Eugene Kandel currently at the helm, and taking inspiration from Dan Senor's book, *Startup Nation: The Story of Israel's Economic Miracle,* SNC is a non-profit that provides a curated gateway to fintech and other innovative technologies in Israel. Proponents of meaningful, mutually beneficial and genuine startup – corporate commercial engagement, SNC takes a leading role connecting global corporates to Israeli-based startups, while making sure the local innovators gain something in the exchange. Helping corporates to identify their challenges, SNC can facilitate an introduction to possible local solution providers. Having hosted literally hundreds of multinationals, investors, government officials and NGOs, SNC has made introductions to more than 100 startups resulting in POCs, collaborations and investments.

- **Start-up Nation finder**
  An online platform that maps the ecosystem and contains information on all fintechs and investors in Israel with a mechanism to connect with them directly.

- **The Floor**
  Located at the Tel Aviv Stock Exchange, The Floor seems to be challenging the traditional accelerator, incubator and venture builder

models with their 'business challenge first – solution second' approach. Working with some heavy hitting incumbent banks, such as Santander and RBS, The Floor, established in 2016, seems to have made a name for itself with the international financial services community. Its perspective is now similar to models and programmes in other parts of the world but would have been quite revolutionary when it set out. In 2018, it secured a $5 million investment from the Chinese fund, Fosun, and it also has a branch in Hong Kong. Unsurprisingly, there is a heavy cyber element to the core team.

- **Israeli Bitcoin EmBassy**
  Based in Tel Aviv, this grassroots organization is a physical location for global Bitcoin enthusiasts to promote, discuss, debate and deliberate on the development of and regulation impacting all things Bitcoin.

Stand-out performers

Tel Aviv lays claim to circa 200 of the 570 Israeli fintech startups, some very new and others that have stood the test of time. Although many of them excel and all deserve our collective praise, here are a few of the brightest stars in the fintech firmament.

- **eToro** (founded 2007, Tel Aviv/London)
  Co-founded by Yoni Assia during the financial crisis, eToro was a pioneer in the online trading space, creating a model that revolves around a social trading platform with live streamed data, and community building, and offers users the opportunity to access trades and invest in currencies (including cryptocurrencies), commodities and indices. An interesting option is that users are able to 'follow' any investor on the network, allowing the eToro system to duplicate each trade made by the followed investor in the follower's account.

- **Fundbox** (founded 2012, Tel Aviv)
  Fundbox provides a draw-down facility to small businesses once they have 'had a look inside your business' and are satisfied the business is able to make the repayments. By providing short-term funds to businesses waiting to be paid, they effectively provide liquidity or working capital that is repaid with a clearing fee over 12 weekly instalments. No invoices are bought, sold, auctioned or traded so it is not an invoice financing solution. To help them get a more accurate picture of a customer's finance and risk profile, Fundbox plugs into the businesses' accounting software to locate and analyse relevant data points.

- **Forter** (founded 2013, Tel Aviv)

  Forter is a SaaS business that provides real-time fraud prevention solutions for online merchants. Its software verifies a combination of publicly available information and social networks, and deeper data using aggregation technologies. Its solution brings to bear big data analytics, machine learning, identity analysis and real-time behavioural sensors to track a user's interaction on the site including click analysis, heat maps and flow analysis.

- **Sirin Labs** (founded 2013, Tel Aviv)

  Having raised just under $158 million by crowdfunding in 2017, cybersecurity firm Sirin Labs created the first 'ultra-secure blockchain smartphone', Finney, that provides features such as P2P resource sharing, built-in cold wallet and a behavioural and machine-learning-based intrusion prevention system based on blockchain technology.

- **Hello Pepper** (Leumi group, founded 2017)

  Unlike pure fintech startups in that it was launched in 2017 by its parent company, Pepper is 117-year-old Bank Leumi's digital-from-the-ground-up mobile bank offering that was the result of disrupting from within and is the first of its kind in Israel. Said to be opening more accounts on a daily basis than the older, main, bricks-and-mortar bank, offering an investment app as well, Pepper, which has been seen as ripping up the traditional banking rulebook, has been praised for its use of tech, and in particular AI, and has global ambitions that start initially in the United States.

Key influencers

- **Eugene Kandel**

  The CEO of Start-Up Nation Central, Kandel is an Israeli economist and an Emil Spyer Professor of Economics and Finance at the Hebrew University of Jerusalem. He was the former head of the National Economic Council, and economic adviser to prime minister Netanyahu.

- **Yuval Tal**

  Founder and president at Payoneer – a fintech unicorn – an early e-commerce payment pioneer, Tal is a serial entrepreneur and investor who has helped shape the payments space. Originally from Jerusalem, he moved to Tel Aviv, where he studied mechanical and biomedical engineering. He has gone on record as saying that the IDF is good breeding ground for entrepreneurs as it makes you do things that are very hard, take your punishment when necessary and get the credentials to prove to others that you are a highly capable individual.

A local success generating hundreds of millions of dollars in revenue, Payoneer was founded in 2005, and is one of the largest online money transfer platforms in the world with a focus on B2B payments across borders. Its client list reads like a who's who of global success stories, and includes Airbnb, Amazon, Fiverr, Google and Upwork. Prior to founding Payoneer, Tal founded Borderfree, also cross-border payments, which he went on to sell to Pitney Bowes.

- Benjamin Nachman

  Founder and chief executive officer at Credorax, Nachman's background is a powerful combination of law and technology. He founded Credorax, a global e-commerce payments acquirer and processor, in order to connect families to their finances within the family unit, enabling parents and grandparents to allocate funds to retailers, charities and so on, for their children via a marketplace controlled by Jassby.

- Eyal Hertzog

  Hertzog is a co-founder and the product architect of Bancor, whose protocol enables the creation of smart tokens on the Ethereum blockchain. The Bancor Foundation raised $153 million worth of Ether cryptocurrency by selling its digital tokens, making it one of the largest token sales in the world. An early adopter and creator of end-user online ecosystems, he lit the way in user-generated currencies and blockchain solutions.

- Rakefet Russak-Aminoach

  This former CEO of Bank Leumi was once named in *Fortune* magazine's '100 Most Powerful Women' list, and is credited with understanding, and bringing to bear, the power of digital technology as part of the transformation of the country's biggest bank. One of her greatest achievements while in role is arguably the launch of Pepper, the digital bank platform for Leumi, which is now looking to enter the United States.

Profile of the regulator

Anyone considering embarking on a fintech journey in Tel Aviv, or elsewhere in Israel for that matter, should definitely consider taking legal advice and speaking with other founders who have previous experience working in Tel Aviv because technically there are no fintech-specific laws or regulations in Israel. That said, the Ministry of Finance and the regulators who touch fintech products are very positive about supporting fintech innovation so there is a positive approach and goodwill.

However,

> [e]ach fintech product may be regulated in accordance with the general laws in Israel on a case-by-case basis. For example, cryptocurrencies are soon to be regulated under the new Supervision of Financial Services (Regulated Financial Services) Law 2016 and may be regulated in accordance with the Israeli Securities Laws. Robo-advice services that provide investment advice will be regulated under the Investment Advice Law.
>
> SOURCE Sacks *et al*, 2019

Seemingly a blend of both principle- and rules-based regulation, Israel has a generally supportive regulatory environment in terms of flexibility and awareness of innovation. The Bank of Israel, which supervises regulatory revision for a number of fintech verticals such as P2P lending, has established an assistance centre aimed at helping fintech companies navigate the working journey with incumbent commercial banks, which is one of the ways it encourages open-mindedness and a receptive attitude to change when it comes to fintech regulations.

One of a number of key organizations involved in regulating fintech products, the Bank Supervision Department at the Bank of Israel is joined by:

- The Commissioner of the Capital Markets, Insurance and Savings (CMIS);
- The Israeli Money Laundering and Terror Financing Prohibition Authority (IMPA);
- The Israeli Security Authority (ISA) – established in 1968, ISA is the national securities regulator for Israel, and, in 2018, it established a fintech Innovation Hub to encourage discourse and learning.

Israeli Capital Market Authority: new developments afoot

In response to changing market demands, particularly around the need to engender and encourage more competition, Israel's regulator has started examining the distribution system for its licensing regime for fintech and has established a dedicated team for the purpose. In a similar set of circumstances to the UK regulator, the FCA, back in 2014/15, the Israeli Capital

Market Authority is experiencing more demand for licensing than anticipated so they have taken offensive action and established a fast-track route.
According to Israeli daily newspaper *Calcalist*, there are circa 2,000 applications currently in with them across all financial services, but including
blockchain and more general fintechs as well (Orbach, 2019).

Global Financial Innovation Network (GFIN)

Not wanting to be on the periphery of the international scene, the ICMA
has joined the FCA-orchestrated GFIN along with 30 or so other international regulators as the group looks to debate and define frameworks for
global collaboration. There is currently no active domestic Sandbox offering, having made an attempt in the past, but there are moves afoot to revisit
the concept.

Alongside the regulators is the Israeli Export and International Cooperation
Institute. Based in Tel Aviv, and operating within the Ministry of Trade and
Labour, this is a public–private partnership that helps startups advance and
develop their propositions and partnerships abroad, and also introduces
overseas companies to the Israeli fintech landscape, while also ensuring that
the domestic consumer benefits from this learning and receives a more
competitive offering as well.

Key events

There is always something going on in Tel Aviv, be it formal or informal, but
here is a taster of what might be found in this very fintech friendly city.

- **FinTech Junction**
  Having run for a number of years, FinTech Junction is one of Israel's largest
  and best-known conferences focusing specifically on technology and
  innovation in the financial services industry. Topics include cybersecurity,
  blockchain, AI, open banking, payments, ID, and P2P lending, for example.
  Each year it attracts thousands of professionals both near and far. The
  attendee list has breadth and depth, counting C-level corporate executives,
  entrepreneurs, investors, fintech startups, incumbent banks and other
  financial institutions, accelerators and government bodies among its ranks.

- **FinTech Aviv Meetup**
  Based at Rise TLV, FinTech Aviv is a meetup with a relaxed vibe that aims to be a meeting of the minds for all participants in the fintech industry. It welcomes entrepreneurs, investors, disruptors, innovators and would-be innovators.

- **DLD Tel Aviv**
  Not fintech-specific, but encompassing fintechs and related technologies such as AI and machine learning, DLD is one of the biggest and most high-profile tech events in Israel. It generally takes place in September, and sees startups and large corporates hoping to unearth a startup gem, celebrate and exchange ideas on all things innovation in the startup space. Comprised of a number of events, but anchored in the Digital Conference, DLD takes place in a variety of venues during the Innovation Festival.

- **Token fest: The Business of Blockchain**
  Thousands of international developers and enterprise professionals converge on Tel Aviv for this blockchain summit which has topics that cover ICOs to crypto-economics and digital commerce.

Moving forward

With such a vibrant and supportive fintech ecosystem, globally focused, highly motivated and proactive entrepreneurs, and a talent pool that is the envy of fintech hubs around the world, Tel Aviv is well positioned to continue its current fintech success story. It is true that the domestic market and surrounding region is not large enough to satisfy the business model needs of businesses established in this hot-bed environment, but there seem to be no shortage of large corporations prepared to set up innovation shops in-situ in order to tap into the emerging tech, government support and active funding scene. A unique combination of grit and determination and cutting-edge technology foundations, be they military or academic at their source, have given this small but mighty nation a respected position in the global fintech scene. With no signs of the key drivers abating and continued outreach via conferences, trade missions, research bodies and entrepreneurs themselves, this bodes well for all parties in the Tel Aviv fintech ecosystem.

References

Alford, H (2008) Seizing the day in Tel Aviv, *New York Times*, www.nytimes. com/2008/07/20/travel/20telaviv.html (archived at https://perma.cc/Z783-XCQM)

Apolitical (2017) *The government venture capital fund that boosted Israel's start-up economy* (online), Apolitical.co, apolitical.co/solution_article/ government-venture-capital-fund-boosted-israels-start-economy/ (archived at https://perma.cc/68W6-VLP7)

B-Hive (2018) Tel Aviv's business and fintech landscape, B-Hive.eu, b-hive.eu/ news-full/2018/3/28/report-tel-avivs-business-and-fintech-landscape (archived at https://perma.cc/K9YH-JPDD)

Innovation Israel (2018) *Human Capital Report 2018*, innovationisrael.org.il/en/ news/human-capital-report-2018 (archived at https://perma.cc/XP9Y-HMU4)

Lunden, I (2017) Intel buys Mobileye in $15.3B deal, moves its automotive unit to Israel, *Techcrunch*, techcrunch.com/2017/03/13/reports-intel-buying-mobileye-for-up-to-16b-to-expand-in-self-driving-tech/ (archived at https://perma.cc/ S36D-WJA9)

Nechushtan, M (2018) *Start-Up Nation Central Fintech Industry Report 2018*, Start-Up Nation Central, www.dropbox.com/s/cp9n2avk4fblpcd/Start-Up%20 Nation%20Central%20Fintech%20Industry%20Report%202018.pdf?dl=0 (archived at https://perma.cc/SXR5-6TZA)

Nonninger, L (2019) Israeli fintechs had a record breaking 2018, *Business Insider,* www.businessinsider.com/israeli-fintechs-record-funding-in-2018-2019-1?r=US&IR=T (archived at https://perma.cc/B7KX-QW8Y)

OECD (2016) *Education Policy Outlook, Israel (2016)*, OECD, www.oecd.org/ israel/Education-Policy-Outlook-Country-Profile-Israel.pdf (archived at https://perma.cc/8EPY-VCBS)

Orbach, M (2019) The Capital Market Authority is working to quickly arrange licenses for fintech companies, *Calcalist*, www.calcalist.co.il/internet/ articles/0,7340,L-3768555,00.html (archived at https://perma.cc/TR4G-MBJQ)

Sacks, A, Yosefi, A and Bur, I (2019) *Fintech Regulation in Israel,* Herzog Fox & Neeman, www.lexology.com/library/detail.aspx?g=966fb9d6-0282-4dc5-893c-81b5d87fd07f (archived at https://perma.cc/97NM-NDH4)

Senor, D and Singer, S (2011) *Start-up Nation: The story of Israel's economic miracle,* Twelve, Boston, MA

Worldometers (2019) *Israel Population,*Worldometers.info, www.worldometers. info/world-population/israel-population/ (archived at https://perma.cc/G6K4-U5BG)

12

Shenzhen

Background

Perhaps better known globally for manufacturing, and for doing it better and more quickly than any other country, China has embarked on a journey of reinvention when it comes to financial services and more specifically when it comes to combining its love of technology with finance delivered on a grand scale, resulting in some pretty astonishing fintech success.

In recent years, China has accelerated the pace of innovation in financial services and taken its place on a global stage as an important centre for fintech innovation and adoption. Its legacy in financial services being not as well-developed as in Western countries was a blessing in disguise for China. It found itself without the need to unshackle itself from the chains of outdated programming languages, hindering C-suite mindsets and a population weaned on cumbersome, complicated, margin-driven products and services. This lack of legacy, combined with the advantage of access to high-quality universities and a highly skilled workforce, has seen Beijing, Shanghai and Shenzhen emerge from this enormous landscape as key hubs for financial innovation. This chapter focuses on Shenzhen, the city across the Bay from Hong Kong.

With a population of just under 13 million on a landmass of just over 2,000 square km, for a long time Shenzhen lived in the shadow of its more famous and Western-facing rival city, Hong Kong. In an effort to turn this rivalry into an ascendency, a number of steps have been taken by both industry and government, and it would appear, at least for fintech in the region, their efforts are beginning to bear fruit.

Since 2016, the Shenzhen province alone has spent more than $600 million on programming and initiatives in order to attract global professionals and academics to its shores, and currently it has the largest economy in southern

China's province Guangdong. As part of the 1978 Chinese Economic Reform, Shenzhen became China's first Special Economic Zone (ECZ) and, as a result, was granted more free-market-styled policies, complete with business incentives to help attract more foreign investment and technology development. The strategy seems to be working. The city and the region have seen an influx of global accelerators, investors, academic partnerships and talent, including some returning national wanderers, and global gatherings of industry experts from across the fintech landscape, with particular emphasis on blockchain.

As an indication of its success in achieving its initial goal, in 2018, the government announced that Shenzhen's GDP (CNY 2.422 trillion) surpassed Hong Kong's (CNY 2.4 trillion) for the first time (Hua, 2019). However, such impressive growth has not come without risk and some pretty spectacular fallout as evidenced by the 2018 collapse of a number of P2P lenders who were able to function largely unfettered, bringing the industry to its knees. Seen by some industry experts as a natural cull, perhaps it is an early lesson that will serve as a reminder for future growth.

As is often the case in the face of extreme financial irregularity and the danger of systemic risk to a nation's financial system, the Chinese government's response to the fintech industry was swift and sharp. Regulations remained flexible and focused on scale, but were tightened in certain areas such as online payments, which is a huge industry for China, with the People's Bank of China (PBOC) requiring all companies engaged in online payments businesses to 'cut off' direct settlement with commercial banks at the end of 2017 in an attempt to stem the flow of and prevent further money laundering.

History

In the way that Birmingham, the UK's second city, might have been seen as a lesser-known relation to London but now has its own fintech hub complete with a fintech accelerator programme, or the way Dubai has skyrocketed to transform itself from an oil-based economy to a fintech hub, Shenzhen has been cast somewhat in the shadow of its better-known sister city, Hong Kong. However, like other erstwhile seemingly sleepy backwaters it has seen the opportunity in fintech and grabbed it with both hands, resulting in extraordinary success stories and a thriving ecosystem that seems determined to put out the welcome mat to global industry and academic visitors.

For much of its history, Shenzhen was a fishing village nestled in the Pearl River delta. Deltas in nature create a rich, fertile soil that is a welcoming and nourishing home for vegetation, and, in a way, Shenzhen has created a similar environment for the fintech industry, building out from its leading role in hardware, its special status as an economic zone and its proximity to the glittering lights and financial dynamos of Hong Kong. The city's fortunes embarked on a journey of transformation in 1980 under Deng Xiaoping's 'open door' mandate when Chinese officials took advantage of Shenzhen's unique proximity to Hong Kong and chose the city to become one of the county's first ECZ, providing economic incentives to attract foreign and domestic investors. It quickly became a hardware hub, known globally as the 'world's factory floor', pumping out masses of industrial and consumer products, including Apple's iPhone.

Shenzen is now one of China's most innovative cities, with a population that exploded to 12.5 million from approximately 100,000 in 1980. Making good use of its abundant supply of engineers and ameliorating local government policies, it has overtaken Hong Kong in attracting new-economy companies, earning it the title of the Silicon Valley of China. Having shaped itself as an advanced technology sector facilitating and supporting the rapid growth in the fintech sector, alongside Beijing and Shanghai, Shenzhen has experienced a rapid rise to become one of the top three fintech centres in China.

Key strengths

Catapulting Shenzhen into the stratosphere of the fintech universe did not happen by accident, and as with other global fintech hubs there are a number of key political, demographic, technological and economic drivers that helped to enable this regional success story. For some time, the Shenzhen authorities have had an ambition to duplicate or surpass Hong Kong's success as a leading global financial centre and have taken steps to promote and push the region into becoming a financial hub to rival its neighbouring city.

The two cities have long been competitors and collaborators, and the recent political tensions in Hong Kong have led to questions as to whether or not it is possible for Hong Kong to maintain its leading status as the region's global financial centre, prompting Shenzhen officials to leverage this uncertainty and position the city as the new financial heart of the Greater Bay Area.

The government has instituted a plan to elevate Shenzhen into a global model socialist city and continues to push financial reform. The head of the Finance Bureau for the Futian district, Zhu Jiang, recently disclosed a new plan for the district with a Financial Work Bureau which would research global trends in finance and technology and play a key role in Shenzhen's mission to become a new kind of international finance centre, which would be named the International Financial Technology Gathering Demonstration Area.

These initiatives bode well, but there is still much to be done if the Hong Kong model is to be approached, and the other two largest international financial centres, New York and London, are to be challenged. An important key to its success is capital flow. Hong Kong has thrived on free flow of trade, information and, more importantly, capital, which is essential to build a global financial hub.

Hong Kong also operates on an internationally aligned legal system, Common Law, which is globally accepted for conducting business, while Shenzhen's legal system operates on Chinese law which is not yet internationally accepted. A further hindrance to the region's development is the 'Great Firewall' that regulates the internet and censors news, reducing the opportunity for the free flow of information which is vital for making timely, well-informed business decisions.

Despite the obstacles, the government is determined to accelerate the region's development and Shenzhen has several key strengths:

- It is forecast to be one of the 10 largest city economies in the world by 2035, with a gross domestic product reaching $800 billion based on 2015 prices, according to Oxford Economics (Chan, 2019).

- It has been designated home to more than 3 million businesses, many of whom are at the forefront of innovation in their sectors, including local tech giants such as Huawei, Tencent, BYD and ZTE, and foreign companies such as IKEA and LinkedIn.

- In 2016, it witnessed the birth of the Financial Blockchain Shenzhen Consortium (FISCO), signalling to the world that it had the intention to become the leader in blockchain technology, and in particular how it can be applied to security and compliance in financial services.

- Light-touch regulatory environment: love it or loathe it, the light-touch regulatory environment in place between 2013 and 2015 aided the tremendous growth of fintech. An unfortunate consequence of this unfettered growth was the resulting wide-scale fraud (particularly in marketplace lending) and systemic financial risks prompting the Chinese government to implement a regulatory framework. At the same time, the PBoC established a fintech committee in an effort to coordinate policies for lending, insurance and payments and to improve the quality of fintech offerings.

- Demand from a tech-enabled demographic – with a population of 1.43 billion citizens in 2019, there is no shortage of potential demand from domestic consumers for fintech products and services. Living standards in many areas of China are higher and improving, smartphones are more and more prevalent nationwide and online payment already dominates the payment channels. With a growing middle-class population, there should also be an uptake in insurance products and services where Shenzhen is strong, as it is the home of the very successful Ping An Group.

- Customer behaviour – a nation of shoppers and sharers, online. The country spawned the tech giants Tencent and Alibaba and the resulting widespread adoption and use of e-commerce, the internet and social media, as well as social commerce, is prevalent throughout China. Crucially, the online payments that power these domestic mega-sites are not sitting on the side-lines of consumer financial tools but are seamlessly embedded in the lives of their users; something that the Chinese unicorns have done incredibly well as opposed to their counterparts in the West, who are playing catch up. The population that is at ease with being online, QR codes, facial recognition, finance and paying online could also be the population that takes the lead and becomes comfortable with electronic cash in China. Alipay and WeChat Pay have created digital currencies and in many urban centres credit cards and fiat currency is no longer accepted.

- Funding – according to Accenture, the 2018 value of fintech deals in China overall was $22.5 billion, representing 46 per cent of fintech investment globally (Accenture, 2018). Shenzhen features highly in this list of companies receiving funds with Ant Financial raising $14 billion of that total.

Talent landscape

Despite having an exceptionally large financial services professional population to draw upon (7.6 million), as China took its place as a leader in the fintech industry it encountered the same sharp rise in demand for talent and skills that the rest of the world experienced. They have, however, addressed this issue in their own way and initiatives and programmes in place seem to be yielding results.

According to EY in their 2017 research into China and the UK's relationship, China has over 500,000 financial expertise elites, ie individuals with higher education, an overseas working background and more than 10,000 fintech specific elites (EY, 2017). The preponderance of such talent as well as STEM talent (science, technology, engineering and mathematics) is due partly to the universities excelling in these subjects and partly due to having to meet the demand created by the international tech giants in the region.

In addition to academic and industry initiatives, the government is also doing its part in winning the talent war in the Greater Bay Area by the many economic and knowledge creation reforms in place in Shenzhen and in particular in Futian, where Ping An, currently the world's seventh most profitable company, is based. These 'regional perks', in addition to the abundant and affordable physical space in Shenzhen, highly prized in a land so densely populated, make it easier to attract and retain talent in the financial services and technology sectors, as evidenced by its efforts yielding a 20 per cent rate in experienced overseas 'returnees' (EY, 2017).

As if these conditions were not enough to tempt talent to the region, the fintech community is offering higher salaries, fewer working hours, stock options in some very high-performing firms and faster promotion opportunities than their traditional financial services competitors.

Access to capital

Capital in Shenzhen, and indeed in all the key fintech hubs in China, is in ample supply and actively flowing into welcoming fintechs. China also has a very active IPO market, from a history of difficulty in securing later-stage funding, and completing more IPOs in the past 10 years than the leading US and UK exchanges. To add to this favourable environment, the Chinese government operates more than 750 government-guided funds, which often come with physical space attached, in order to help and support startups and early-stage companies.

The lure of tax and data incentives

There are also initiatives afoot to help entice fintechs to the region, including tax policies and startup incentives where 'new high-tech enterprises' are taxed at 15 per cent compared to regular 25 per cent rates, access to data services such as the Social Credit System (a system to assign a credit score to every citizen and business), and the Emerging Industry Innovation Fund (£3.9 billion) established in order to promote digitization.

Shenzhen fintech startups have access to various VC funding and fund-raising activities and the Shenzhen Capital Group (SCGC), a government-backed group, is one of China's most prominent VC firms. According to Crunchbase data, SCGC, founded in 1999, has invested in a known total of 171 companies, including 14 lead investments in the last four years (Dowling, 2017).

Putting some specifics on the size of the space:

- As of June 2019, 378 investments were made in the technology sector with an amount of CNY 37.270 billion.
- 91 transactions exceeded $100 million, reaching a total value of CNY 204.163 billion and accounting for 69.19 per cent of total startup investments.
- Tencent, the tech firm known for WeChat, has invested in over 46 global unicorns over the past few years.

The most active fintech investors in China

According to KPMG, fintech investment in Asia Pacific got off to a modest start in 2019 after experiencing a record-shattering level of investment in 2018, due in part to a number of very large investments in China (KPMG, 2019). Not surprisingly, the market levelled off a bit in the first half of 2019, adjusting downwards due to the lack of mega-deals in China and in reaction to the geo-political tensions between the United States and China impacting trade and investment. To add to these circumstances, Beijing regulators have been focusing their attention on the fintech industry, and as with any sector in the spotlight, fintech is feeling the impact of scrutiny and circumspection.

TABLE 12.1 Active investors

Most Active Investors	Top FinTech Deals
Source Code Capital	Qudian, Smart Finance Group, INK, feidee.com, Nongfenqi, Huifenqi, zichan360, licai.com, Lantouzi, Xiao Hu Group, juaicai.com, BMQB.com, ABC Fintech, Lean Work
IDG	China UMS, Qingsongchou, Shuidihuzhu, EasyTransfer, Tongdun, Qiandai, Tongbanjie, wacai.com, Wecash, 100credit.com, Yixin, Formax, TransferEasy
Sequoia	ddjf.com, Shoujidai, Xiaoyusan Insurance, Zhongan, Pai Pai Dai, Jinfuzi, feidee.com, 19pay, rong360.com
BANYAN Capital	Zhongrongjin, Qiandai, Shuidihuzhu, Yuanbaopu, Qinbao, QuantGroup, Jcaimao
BAI	Yixin Group, Fenqile, Nongfenqi, Meixin Global, Bigo Live, Baca, Linklogis
Marathon Venture Partners	Baozhunniu, Knowlegene, ejsino.com, Cihon, gevent.com, au23.cn, Totodi
Bluerun Ventures	Qudian, Shuidihuzhu, au23.cn, Totodi
Qiming Ventures	ABC Fintech, wacai.com, SequoiaDB
China Creation Ventures	Id5.cn, Yixin, Sinowel, rong360.com
Vertex Ventures	InstaReM, Turnkey Lender, Maxent

SOURCE China Internet Report, 2018

Accelerators and incubators

Shenzhen has all the ingredients that make it a perfect landing pad for global accelerators looking to take advantage of a highly developed tech environment, generous government support packages, abundant land space, a talented workforce, academic prowess and an active and well-stocked investment community. Although it is a comparatively nascent industry in Shenzhen, it is attracting a lot of interest from some heavy-hitting global players who are putting down local roots, including the following.

- **Hande Finmaker**
  An SME finance organization for its core business, this Shenzhen-based finance firm has also launched a fintech accelerator with an emphasis on blockchain, but also other tech, and an education programme as well as an innovation fund.

- **Ping An–SparkLabs Fintech Accelerator**
  This is a collaboration between Ping An Technology and SparkLabs. SparkLabs, co-founded by William Chu, Jay McCarthy and Frank Meehan, has been operating since 2013 as a global network of accelerators and VC firms. It fosters innovation in modern finance by nurturing global technologies and has also launched its own seed and Series A funds to invest in early-stage technology businesses.

- **Plug and Play Tech Centre**
  The Silicon Valley-based global accelerator programme that featured in Chapter 8 on the Gulf, also makes its presence known in Shenzhen. With other Plug and Play offices in Beijing, Shanghai and Chongqing, the team believe that Shenzhen has the right mix of both hardware and software industries, investors and entrepreneurs in order to be a successful member of the global Plug and Play platform, connecting Shenzhen to the original Silicon Valley at the same time. The 12-week early-stage startup accelerator programme runs twice a year, and fintech is one strand of the programme alongside ecology, real estate, internet of things, and so on.

Most important players

The list of the some of the best-known companies in Shenzhen reads like a who's who of global fintech and financial services. Companies that cross product and service lines, starting with an initial proposition such as retail payments, and then expanding their offering to other verticals such as lending, are not uncommon in China. What starts as a market leader in one sector becomes a market leader in a conglomerate. What is also not uncommon is the enormous size of a funding round in comparison to other parts of the world. Hundreds of millions of dollars are abundant, while billions are still rare but do exist.

Stand-out performers

According to the research partner to the VC and corporate intelligence community, Tracxn (Tracxn, 2019), among the 153 fintech startups based in Shenzhen, only a handful hold the majority market share (Table 12.2).

TABLE 12.2 Stand-out performers

Name	Business Description	Funding ($ million)	Year
OneConnect	Provider of software solutions based on technologies such as blockchain, AI, etc	650	2015
WeBank	Launched by Tencent, and licensed in 2014, WeBank is China's first digital bank that offers personal micro-loan products and financial management tools	450	2014
Linklogis	Linklogis is a provider of supply-chain finance, risk models, and micro- or small-sized loans	265	2016
Ping An	Shenzhen is home to Ping An, which runs the QEX, whose forex quotas could easily be widened to take more HKD-RMB business. Ping An is the world's seventh most-profitable company and one of the clear leaders in the global fintech industry	4.800	1988
Dashu Finance	Provider of unsecured loans	211	2014
Jubaohui	Provider of online products such as loans, crowdfunding	200	2014
Touna	A P2P lending platform that provides individuals and SMEs with financing services	102	2012
Jinfuzi	An online wealth management platform for products such as mutual funds and trusts	102	2012
Juzilicai	An online platform that pools money from investors for consumer lending, offering a fixed interest return rate	100	2014

In addition to this impressive list, the following companies are being touted as the top Shenzhen startups for 2019 and poised for spectacular growth in the coming year (HexGn, 2019):

- **Qulian Technology**
  Launched in 2016, Qulian is a Shenzhen blockchain and distributed ledger technology solutions platform with a Series B round of $1.5 billion with lead investors Xinhu Zhonbao Co Ltd and China Gaoxin Investment Group Corp.

- **Shenzhen JFZ Capital Management Co**
  Tapping into the growing wealth within the domestic population, JFZ is an online wealth management service targeting high-net-worth individuals. It offers a variety of different products and covers asset classes that include PE, M&A and private placements, as well as funds.

- **Shenzhen Suishou Technology**
  Shenzhen Suishou Technology is a mobile finance software subsidiary of Chinese enterprise management software developer Kingdee International Software Group (established 1993). An example of how a core product can spin out into a full product offering, the company offers a complete suite of finance and insurance products and services via five main platforms covering areas such as wealth management, consumer loans, credit card applications, securities trading and insurance, including a personal finance mobile app and a mobile credit card management app.

- **Wei Zhong Shui Yin**
  Founded in Shenzhen in 2014, and counting Ant Financial as one of its shareholders, Wei Zhong Shui Yin processes and analyses enterprise data to provide financial services and other clients with credit investigation and risk mitigation services. Their cloud-computing database covers most of China's provinces as well as most major sectors.

Profile of the regulator

Unlike the UK or the US where there is well-developed but evolving principle- and rules-based regulatory framework that applies to fintech and financial services, making it simpler for both disruptors and end-users to navigate and apply regulation and guidance to products and services, currently there is no single law or body which regulates fintech products, services and businesses in China. One consequence of this fluidity is that a number of fintechs are giving the four to five largest state-owned banks a run for their money by offering what feels like banking services. Wise to this, and showing great foresight and pragmatism, these leading banks are also exploring fintech partnerships much earlier than their foreign counterparts. For all concerned, depending on the product or service, different regulatory bodies, administrative measures and guidelines apply. As is often the case with grey areas, the ambiguity or lack of clarity in regulation can result in unsavoury practice (as China saw with the P2P lending scheme scandals of 2018) but can also help spark the imagination, resulting in positive disruption and innovation.

In general, there now seems to be an acceptance that stricter, clearer regulation and regulatory reforms, particularly in Shenzhen, where there is a foreign as well as domestic fintech presence, is a good thing for confidence, investment and further adoption. In Shenzhen, they are working hard on legal reforms, setting up special courts and arbitration centres as part of a plan to provide clarity and certainty in order to continue to attract global business. However, in order for regulation to be a force for good in certain parts of the country, there will need to be a coordinated effort and buy-in from all, or at least more, of China's regulators to ensure a smooth implementation of any policy decisions.

Key regulator and regulations

One of the key bodies when it comes to regulation in financial services in Shenzhen is the Local Financial Regulatory Bureau of Shenzhen Municipality.

TABLE 12.3 Regulator and regulations

	Regulator	Specific Legislation
Online payment	People's Bank of China (PBoC)	Administrative Measures for Payment Services Provided by Non-financial Institutions
P2P lending	China Banking and Insurance Regulatory Commission (CBIRC)	Provisional Rules for the Management of Services Activities of Internet Lending Information Intermediaries
Equity crowdfunding	China Securities Regulatory Commission (CSRC)	Implementing Scheme of Dedicated Regulation on Risk of Equity Crowdfunding
Funding sales online	China Securities Regulatory Commission	Administrative Measures for Sales of Securities Investment Fund and Administrative Measures for Supervision of Money Market Funds
Insurance sales online	China Banking and Insurance Regulatory Commission	Provisional Measures for Supervision of Internet Insurance Services
Online trust business and consumer financing	China Banking and Insurance Regulatory Commission	N/A
Blockchain information service	Cybersecurity Administration of China	Administrative Rule on Blockchain Information Services

SOURCE Shenzhen Government Online, 2019

It has several main duties, including:

- implementing laws, regulations, and policies;
- monitoring, observing and feeding back in order to improve the financial environment;
- promoting physical and technological development and innovation in Shenzhen;
- supervising small loan firms and finance houses such as leasing and commercial guarantee firms.

The Bureau is not alone in regulating or guiding fintech and financial services firms and is joined by a number of bodies and corresponding legislation (see Table 12.3).

The ecosystem

As with all developing ecosystems, there are a number of key protagonists who take a more active role and they include incumbents, associations, institutions and world-leading fintechs. Shenzhen has its representatives and they include the following.

Banks

Perhaps not what you would expect from such a large country, but China's financial services industry is dominated by five large banks:

- Industrial and Commercial Bank of China (ICBC) is China's largest bank with corporate and personal banking products, financial asset services and e-finance.
- Agricultural Bank of China (ABC) operates corporate banking, personal banking, treasury operations, and others.
- Bank of China (BOC) is the central bank of China.
- China Construction Bank (CCB) provides deposits, loans, fund management, foreign exchange and other services to individuals and corporate clients.
- Bank of Communications (BoCOM) provides general banking and mainstream financial services.

CCB–Tencent fintech partnership

Although these five banks have a significant foothold in financial services, they are not unaware of or unwilling to benefit from the opportunity to partner with some of their competitors or tech providers. One example of this is the joint innovation lab of CCB (China Construction Bank) and Tencent. In what is perhaps seen as a surprising partnership by people outside of China, plans have been announced for a joint fintech innovation lab between the state-owned CCB and the tech giant Tencent (WeChat, 2020). The lab, which will create a knowledge-sharing and communication platform, will be named 'Construction Bank–Tencent Financial Technology Joint Innovation Lab' and will be led by Tencent's cloud business unit. It will involve collaboration in technologies that include AI and big data, as well as blockchain and cloud-computing. It will also draw on the knowledge resources of the Entrepreneurs Harbour of South China College of CBB University and Tencent's technology.

Other institutions

- **Shenzhen Fintech Research Institution**
  Together with PBoC, the Local Financial Regulatory Bureau of Shenzhen Municipality established the Shenzhen Fintech Research Institution with a primary purpose of carrying out fintech and digital-currency-orientated projects initiated by the Shenzhen municipal government and the central bank.

- **Shenzhen Internet Finance Association (SZIFA)**
  SZIFA, established in July 2015, with Ping An in the presidential role currently, is the self-regulating organization that was set up with the support and guidance of the Shenzhen Municipal Government and the Shenzhen Municipal Government Financial Services Office. The association calls out and disciplines members who bend or break the laws and guidance for their industry, contributes to government policy and acts as an external voice for the member community. There are more than 200 members and SFIZA counts amongst its ranks a number of well-known internet financial companies, representing the top echelons of the internet financial industry in Shenzhen.

- **Financial Blockchain Shenzhen Consortium (FISCO)**
  Established in 2016, the FISCO is a not-for-profit organization with more than 100 members including financial institutions and financial information

service companies, all dedicated to the development and application of blockchain technology in financial services. They operate an open-source platform involving working group members in the continual development of the blockchain solutions.

Key events

As with other global fintech centres, Shenzhen is awash with fintech events, be they smaller meetups or global conferences, both in the city and across the Bay with its neighbour Hong Kong.

Leading the way in technology such as blockchain means that some of these events are no longer provincial in scope, but have taken on global proportions, attracting visitors, speakers and exhibitors from around the world. The following is a taste of what happens in the region.

- **The Global FinTech Investment Summit Shenzhen**
  Building on the theme of science meets capital, and with the aim of fostering global collaboration and partnerships with industry and leading universities such as MIT and Peking University, the summit attracts global financial institutions, universities, Nobel Prize winners, investors and startups. Continuing to develop startup fintech solutions in areas such as lending and investment, the District of Nanshan, known by some as 'Nanshan FinTech City', is the home of this global summit. Showcasing the fintech potential of Shenzhen, feeding into policy developments and housing demonstration and innovation sites, Nanshan is looking to be a driving force in the continued upwards trajectory of fintech growth in Shenzhen.

- **Blockchain World Forum Shenzhen**
  This is a global event that attracts all stakeholders in the fintech and blockchain ecosystem. Regulators, academics, industry experts and incumbent financial institutions sit side by side with tech developers, investors and startups, discussing and debating the challenges to be overcome and the opportunities on offer in the blockchain industry. Following a traditional format, there are keynotes from experts, panel discussion and use case studies which help to highlight and share learning and best practice. The event also provides opportunities for partnerships to develop with a view to identifying solutions for some of the industries likely to be significantly impacted by blockchain solutions,

such as financial services, law, insurance, government and public services, energy, the arts and real estate.

- **Hong Kong Fintech Week**
Touted as the world's first cross-border fintech event, the Hong Kong Fintech Week was held in both Hong Kong and Shenzhen in 2019, highlighting the increasing importance of Shenzhen in fintech. Regulators, investors, founders and incumbents are joined by financial services professionals from all four corners of the world to explore topics such as blockchain, payments, messaging, cybersecurity and banking. Organized and hosted by InvestHK, Finnovasia and Finovate, partners include the Hong Kong Monetary Authority (HKMA), the Securities and Futures Commission (SFC), the Hong Kong Insurance Authority and Hong Kong Exchanges and Clearing Limited.

Key influencers

Shenzhen is home to a number of global powerhouses of the fintech industry, and befitting such an environment are the pioneering entrepreneurs and business leaders who have helped to transform the landscape, the industry and the lives of those working in the industry, while simultaneously accumulating vast amounts of wealth, and some would say, power. Taking the opportunities that technology and timing have afforded them, using their global educational and commercial experience, where applicable, and executing on their bold visions has propelled a number of entrepreneurs into the fintech stratosphere. By no means an exhaustive list, the following are some stand-out performers.

The 'Ma' triumvirate or the 'three horses'

The Ma trio (the Chinese character for the surname 'Ma' means 'horse' or 'pony') is undeniably one of, if not *the,* most powerful triumvirate of financial services, fintech and insurtech entrepreneurs in the world. Amassing billions of dollars in net worth between them and trillions in revenue, these three men have altered the fintech landscape on a grand scale:

- **Jack Ma**
A co-founder and former executive chairman of the e-commerce and financial services Alibaba Group (1999), including its affiliate company,

Ant Financial (formerly known as Alipay). The powerhouse that is Ant Financial is leading the way in using AI for risk assessment, marketing, transaction risk and customer service. Over 120 companies in e-commerce, insurance, government and finance make use of Ant's superior technology. According to *Forbes*, Ma achieved $40.78 billion of real-time net worth. From humble beginnings, the self-made billionaire is ranked Number 1 on China's Rich List for 2019. The initial IPO of Alibaba in 2014 set a world record in terms of shares sold, and Ma led the successful business as chairman until he stepped down in 2019 to pursue other works.

- **Pony (Huateng) Ma**
  The co-founder and CEO of Tencent (1998), one of the world's largest internet and technology companies, and one of the world's largest social media firms with QQ instant messaging, the predecessor to WeChat, and WeChat itself (2011) – between them these two apps dominate China's biggest mobile instant messaging service – and one of the world's largest investment corporations, Ma graduated from Shenzhen University and is a first-generation Shenzhen migrant.

- **Minghzhe Ma**
  Chairman, executive director and founder of Ping An (which means 'peace and safety') Insurance Group (1988), a Chinese conglomerate and China's largest life insurance company that saw the market opportunity in the growing middle class and expanded beyond insurance into the edges of fintech, diversifying into banking and financial services, attracting hundreds of millions of internet or online finance customers along the way.

Other influencers

- **Ericson Chan**
  The CEO of Ping An Technology, the Chinese insurer's tech affiliate, and a board alternate director of the Hong Kong Interbank Clearing Limited. Chan, a former banker at Standard Chartered, is a mentor for the SuperCharger Fintech Accelerator programme and a fintech member of ASIFMA. He has been a member of the Disruptive Innovation in Financial Services Committee of the World Economic Forum since 2014.

- **Anthony Sar**
  The CEO and co-founder of Finnovasia, one of Asia's largest fintech community organizations, and the force behind Hong Kong FinTech

Week, Sar is a leading fintech event organizer in Asia, striving to promote cross-border collaboration, knowledge exchange and commercial engagement. His previous roles include co-founder and managing director of Innovative Trips, a Hong Kong-based company specializing in creative, educational innovative trips for individuals and corporations to visit locations such as Russia, China, Hong Kong, India, Japan, Singapore, South Korea and Taiwan to explore new ideas, learn from experts and meet with the local community.

Where does Shenzhen go from here?

The signs are there that China's regional cities are now finding their voice in fintech and this looks set to continue. There seems to be a softening of the hard edges that previously existed in Shenzhen's relationship with Hong Kong, with more collaboration in place, benefiting both cities and the region as a whole. Whether or not Shenzhen can – or needs to – overtake Hong Kong as the key financial hub in the region remains to be seen, but as far as fintech, and more specifically blockchain and insurtech are concerned, Shenzhen is more than holding its own.

International cooperation

The international community engagement also shows no signs of slowing down when it comes to accelerators, investors and cross-germination of promising startups from Silicon Valley in the United States and Silicon Roundabout in the UK. Global incumbents see the opportunities in partnering with tech and the potential commercial advantages afforded them by the Chinese government laying out the welcome mat, so this should also continue, particularly in the blockchain space.

Regulation

Given the recent issuance of virtual banking licences across the Bay in Hong Kong, and the lessons learnt from having a more laissez-faire attitude towards regulation, particularly in the P2P arena, it would be logical to assume that the trend towards tighter and increasing regulation will continue. This will be particularly relevant if Shenzhen continues to extend welcoming arms to overseas fintechs and financial services who will possibly be reassured by additional guidance and structure.

Talent

Globally, the skills required for successful fintech ventures are in short supply, so continuing to create an environment that woos diaspora professionals back to their home country or those who wish to migrate from other regions of China to Shenzhen will be a vital part of winning the talent war.

The partnerships and collaborations with the likes of MIT in the United States and Peking University closer to home will be instrumental in winning the talent war as well as producing some cutting-edge research.

Funding

To all intents and purposes, it looks like the freight train of fintech funding is set to continue hurtling along the track. It is a likely assumption that new mega-deals will appear at some point, but what is more important is a constant and consistent flow of capital and guidance where it is needed and can have the most impact.

References

Accenture (2018) *The Win-Win Proposition*, Accenture, www.accenture.com/_acnmedia/pdf-98/accenture-the-win-win-proposition-apac-fintech-momentum.pdf (archived at https://perma.cc/G3LC-5REL)

Chan, E (2019) Can Hong Kong maintain its status amid protests despite Beijing's push to turn Shenzhen into a financial hub? *South China Morning Post*, www.scmp.com/economy/china-economy/article/3025600/can-hong-kong-maintain-its-status-amid-protests-despite (archived at https://perma.cc/9P3N-X37J)

China Internet Report (2018) *South China Morning Post*, Yeung, E, www.scmp.com/china-internet-report (archived at https://perma.cc/K554-DSCU)

Dowling, S (2017) How one China-based VC, backed by the government, invests at home and abroad, *Crunchbase News,* news.crunchbase.com/news/one-china-based-vc-backed-government-invests-home-abroad/ (archived at https://perma.cc/H26G-8NQS)

EY (2017) *China and UK FinTech: Unlocking opportunity*, www.ey.com/Publication/vwLUAssets/ey-china-and-uk-fintech/$File/ey-china-and-uk-fintech.pdf (archived at https://perma.cc/WT95-TF64)

HexGn (2019) *Top Shenzhen startups to watch out for in 2019*, HexGn, hexgn.com/top-shenzhen-startups-to-watch-out-for-in-2019/ (archived at https://perma.cc/G7KC-A7MB)

Hua, C (2019) Shenzhen surpasses HK in GDP, *Chinadaily.com.cn,*

www.chinadaily.com.cn/a/201902/28/WS5c7720fda3106c65c34ebd70.html
(archived at https://perma.cc/9VTB-A34L)

KPMG (2019) *The Pulse of Fintech 2019*, assets.kpmg/content/dam/kpmg/xx/
pdf/2019/07/pulse-of-fintech-h1-2019.pdf (archived at https://perma.cc/3WHL-
WY4Z)

Shenzhen Government Online (2019) Local Financial Regulatory Bureau of
Shenzhen Municipality, http://english.sz.gov.cn/govt/agencies/l/201811/
t20181122_14606271.htm (archived at https://perma.cc/5MTR-BMNQ)

Tracxn (2019) *FinTech start-ups in Shenzhen*, tracxn.com/explore/FinTech-
Startups-in-Shenzhen/ (archived at https://perma.cc/B448-ZHH8)

WeChat (2020) CCB and Tencent reach strategic cooperation to build fintech lab,
mp.weixin.qq.com/s/kxL6wnWdYYLHGkJ39jd51A (archived at
https://perma.cc/5MTR-BMNQ)

13

Final Thoughts

What is fintech and why does it matter?

Origins

Many of you reading this book will either be studying fintech, banking or associated subjects, working in financial services or fintech, or researching the subject and looking to gain knowledge and insights. You've probably heard the term 'fintech' many times, and, like many others, have asked yourself 'what is this fintech thing and where did it come from?' This is a much more common question than you might think.

In answering this question, we went back to the industry's roots and began by exploring why banking exists and how it has evolved over the centuries. Our starting point was in the medieval relationship bank where every product was a bespoke proposition exactly matching the customer's needs and capabilities. Fast forward a few hundred years, and we reviewed the industrial bank of the 18th century, focused on selling financial products rather than providing financial solutions. The customer no longer got the right product for his/her needs but had to accept that a 'good-enough' proposition was the best they would get.

Continuing our evolutionary expedition, we went on to understand the automated version of the industrial bank – the IT bank, which took root in the 1950s and saw customers' needs reduced to simplistic data points processed by a remote mainframe computer. The empathy or understanding of real customer needs of centuries gone by was no more. Our journey then uncovered the arrival of digital banking and how it differs from its non-digital, or analogue, predecessor, where – if done well – it could revive the importance of the UX and of the relationship bank, coming full circle to the customer once again being offered a financial product designed for them specifically. Importantly, we explained how digital technology could do the seemingly impossible and allow for extreme customization to be offered to millions of customers.

Visions and goals

Having charted the evolution of these significant and sometimes cataclysmic changes, we took a closer look at what is triggering this change – what are the visions and goals of change. We delved deeper into how evolving technology is impacting the banking proposition and how data processing capability is enabling customers to bank without having to go to the bank. The modern bank is always in a customer's pocket inside their mobile phone. We posited that all this change would not be possible without customer adoption and the slow but unstoppable acceptance of digital and mobile technology in sectors such as retail, information, travel and media which led to consumers not only accepting digital banking but demanding it.

We examined how, more than any other industry, the role of the regulator is driving innovation in banking and is fundamental to change. It became clear that certain regulators (especially the UK ones) are a genuine force behind the pace and rise of digital change and the growth of fintechs in their market.

Last but not least, we considered the phenomenon of the large amounts of capital flooding into the fintech market, be it angel, venture or corporate venture funding. We explained why in the last five years the amount of financing offered to financial services startups has exploded and why savvy investors see fintech as a smart move.

In taking a close look at disruption, we introduced the concept of the neobank, and attempted to describe what the bank of the future could look like. This new entity would be extremely flexible and adapted to its customers' needs and capabilities. It would offer three products: payments, credit and a capital protection capability all integrated in smart, automated, data-rich intelligent guidance and advice.

Implementation

Visions and goals are laudable but are nothing if they are not transformed from an idea or ideal into tangible results. In an effort to understand and explain how different financial organizations are implementing digital change, we discussed the three phases of change from adapting the current business, to evolving it, to then creating the premises for a real transformation. Transformation can come from inside an organization, from external sources or from a combination of both, and we reviewed the delivery option from build in-house, partner with specialists, or acquire businesses that would lead the change.

Once a course of action is decided, a delivery plan must be agreed and implemented. Investigating how this change might be delivered led us to explore the emergence of global fintech hubs where people, innovation, capital and regulation interact to create unique ecosystems that enable the development of future business models in banking and financial services.

Genuine innovation in financial services is rarely a solitary exercise; rather it is driven by shared outcomes. By studying what we called the fintech tribes, we looked at how businesses across the globe have used the conditions specific to their local hub to create solutions and businesses that address problems shared globally. In this context, we discussed five tribes, from the bank challengers to the infrastructure builders, touching payments, the unbanked and social banking in our trajectory.

The hubs

This new world is not confined to one country, region or continent. Across the globe from London to Shenzhen, nimble, customer-driven fintechs are capturing market shares, diminishing returns for the giants of financial services and creating access to a better type of banking and finance in their markets. They are being helped and supported by local ecosystems encompassing investors, academics, governments, regulators, accelerators, networking groups and so on.

The second half of the book presented a series of profiles of the different geographical hubs where change is afoot in both financial services and fintech. We got under the skin of what makes them distinctive, what challenges they face and how they are resolving these potential roadblocks to progress. For each market profile, we charted its history, the structure of the existing banking infrastructure, the access to talent, capital and technology and the impact of regulation.

A global perspective

For the first leg of our journey, we visited six major hubs: London, Paris, the Gulf, New York City, Tel Aviv and Shenzhen. Some of these hubs are at the forefront of the evolution in financial services and are leading the fintech charge from the front; others are newer entrants to the ecosystem, propelling themselves into leading roles in their regions. Either way their impact is being felt far beyond their borders.

These profiles are very much the results of the authors' perspectives and experiences. They are meant as an introduction to enable the reader to understand the nature of each hub and to be used as the first step in engaging with the changing face of banking.

Outlook

One of the things that emerged when researching for this book was that there is genuine expectation from the market that the banking sector is going to go through some very troubling times in the near future. In fact, it is not uncommon to hear opinions that the collapse of the global financial system is inevitable. Whether you share this extreme view or not, what is clear is that the banking sector is in for a bumpy ride.

The global reset which may be months or still years away will cause wide-scale disruption and will impact all players in the financial ecosystem, and therefore is not a subject that should be ignored when discussing the fintech evolution/ecosystem.

In its *2019 Global Banking Annual Review*, consulting firm McKinsey (McKinsey, 2019) closes with these words:

> The call to action is urgent: whether a bank is a leader and seeks to 'protect' returns or is one of the underperformers looking to turn the business around and push returns above the cost of equity, the time for bold and critical moves is now.

Later in the year, the former governor of the Bank of England, Mervyn King, said that we are: 'Pretending that we have made the banking system safe… we are sleepwalking towards [a new financial] crisis' (Bambrough, 2019). Rating agency Moody's is no less gloomy, believing that the outlook for global banks is negative: '… reflecting slowing long-term economic growth trends and growing political risks' (Moody's, 2019).

The gloomy theme that is underlying predictions for the future is very much underscoring the need for change, to adapt to new realities and to embrace the notion that in banking and finance, business as usual is no longer an option.

What next?

One of the biggest drivers of this uncertainty is the advent of digital disruption in the sector. There is a need to better understand how digital innovation is changing the fundamentals of the industry, the implications of these changes, and how to harness this disruption for the good of all participants and most importantly customers.

1. Staying still is not an option

As the fintech revolution continues its march on financial services, slowly bringing big tech giants into the industry, the need for change becomes truly urgent. The torrent of investment raining down on the fintech community has been record-breaking and is showing little sign of slowing down. The banks are faced with increasingly demanding regulatory environments, collapsing returns on equity across the globe and relentless competition from new entrants. These are meeting the needs of frustrated retail, commercial and corporate customers with cost bases and capabilities that the banks cannot match without huge capital outlays and most recently the forays into the industry by the big tech giants. The banks' only option is to change.

2. Possible scenarios

This is not a simple task. The future of banking is certainly digital, but it is unclear what it will ultimately look like. There is a myriad of scenarios proposed by academics, consultants, the media, banks, the regulators and fintechs, to name just a few. The actual make-up of the financial services of the future will most likely be an amalgamation of three scenarios:

- **FinTechs win**: Challenger banks and fintechs win. Incumbent banks will be replaced by new providers with different business models that customers embrace. The banks will close or be taken over by the fintechs.
- **Banks win**: The banks leverage their reserves and large customer bases and become digital. The incumbents either learn to be innovative and transform on their own, or they buy the fintechs that challenge them or – both. Fintechs will not be able to compete.
- **Big tech wins**: The banks and fintechs are disintermediated by the big tech and social platforms. The banks and fintech can only reach their clients through channels provided by the tech firms. They are placed into

competition with each other, ending in a race to the bottom in terms of price. Many cease operating – most become captives of their tech channel.

3. What really matters

While we don't have a crystal ball and cannot see into the future, what we can see is that the most likely outcome will be a hybrid of the above scenarios, with two certain outcomes: eventually all banks will be digital and in the end customers will be better off.

That's all that really matters!

References

Bambrough, W (2019) A former Bank of England governor warned the 2008 crash that inspired Bitcoin could happen again, *Forbes*, 28 October, www.forbes.com/sites/billybambrough/2019/10/27/a-former-bank-of-england-governor-warned-the-2008-crash-that-inspired-bitcoin-could-happen-again/#4c4f6c7c4214 (archived at https://perma.cc/92YK-S5M9)

McKinsey (2019) *Global Banking Annual Review 2019: The last pit stop? Time for bold late-cycle move,* McKinsey and Company, www.mckinsey.com/industries/financial-services/our-insights/global-banking-annual-review-2019-the-last-pit-stop-time-for-bold-late-cycle-moves (archived at https://perma.cc/EXB8-FEE9)

Moody's (2019) *Banking: Research and Ratings*, www.moodys.com/researchandratings/market-segment/financial-institutions/banking/005001000/ 005001000/-/-1/0/-/0/-/-/-/-/-/-/-/en/global/pdf/rra (archived at https://perma.cc/83CS-5ZSZ)

FURTHER READING

Chapter 8

Fintechnews (2019) Fintech Events and Conferences in the Middle East taking place in H1 2019, fintechnews.ae/3456/events/fintech-events-conferece-in-the-middle-east-2019/ (archived at https://perma.cc/85UY-ZWPR)

King, N (2017) FinTech comes to the fore in the GCC, Gulfbusiness.com, gulfbusiness.com/fintech-comes-fore-gcc/ (archived at https://perma.cc/HP8U-NJD7)

Chapter 9

BNP Paribas (2020) Fintech: Start-ups which improve banking and finance, bnpparibas/en/hottopics/fintech/briefing (archived at https://perma.cc/GCT7-LNKJ)

BNP Paribas, Plug and Play (2020) www.plugandplaytechcenter.com/bnp-paribas-plugandplay/ (archived at https://perma.cc/2SMN-68MQ)

Café de la Bourse (2019) Startup: La France ouvre les bras au secteur fintech, Café De La Bourse, www.cafedelabourse.com/actualites/startup-france-ouvre-bras-secteur-fintech (archived at https://perma.cc/WCA2-MQCB)

Choose Paris Region (2020) Setting international companies up for success, investparisregion.eu/en/news/paris-region-info/paris-region-presents-its-regional-artificial-intelligence-plan-ai-2021-and (archived at https://perma.cc/97FE-M2V5)

Clot, A (2019) La Fintech, Secteur D'excellence Française, France FinTech, francefintech.org/alain-clot-la-fintech-secteur-dexcellence-francaise/ (archived at https://perma.cc/BRP9-K8P4)

FinTech Finance, www.fintech.finance/ (archived at https://perma.cc/848F-TLHN)

FinTech Global (2019) FinTech investment in France has grown almost ten-fold since 2014, FinTech Global, fintech.global/fintech-investment-in-france-has-grown-more-than-ten-fold-since-2014/ (archived at https://perma.cc/U2SK-3GTV)

French Tech Ticket (2019) Questions on the French Tech Ticket Program Season 2, French Tech Ticket,www.frenchtechticket.com/7/faq (archived at https://perma.cc/2U3W-ZJFW)

Kesitys (2019) Gamma-Hedging: France, Kesitys, www.kesitys.com (archived at https://perma.cc/3RX4-K4Z6)

Kramer, L (2018) Fintech: Trends and Developments in France, *The In-House Lawyer,* www.inhouselawyer.co.uk/legal-briefing/fintech-trends-and-developments-in-france/ (archived at https://perma.cc/VCG8-RB7F)

La French Tech (2020) www.gouvernement.fr/en/la-french-tech (archived at https://perma.cc/V3DG-K6M6)

Levin, K (2019) Overview of the current legal market in France and recent developments, www.inhouselawyer.co.uk/legal-briefing/fintech-trends-and-developments-in-france/ (archived at https://perma.cc/VCG8-RB7F)

Norton Rose Fulbright (2019) French Inpatriates Tax Regime (2019), www.nortonrosefulbright.com/en/knowledge/publications/2298c717/french-inpatriates-tax-regime (archived at https://perma.cc/N2XW-E7FN)

Plessis, A (2003) The History of Banks in France, www.fbf.fr/en/french-banking-sector/history-of-banks-in-france/the-history-of-banks-in-france (archived at https://perma.cc/VB2F-J6RM)

Saiidi, U (2019) We went inside the world's largest start-up campus, located in Paris, *CNBC,* www.cnbc.com/2019/01/10/station-f-in-paris-inside-the-worlds-largest-start-up-campus.html (archived at https://perma.cc/635H-M42C)

Skinner, C (2019) How will UK fintech fare in the future? [blog] thefinanser.com/2019/04/how-will-uk-fintech-fare-in-the-future.html/ (archived at https://perma.cc/7DA6-M2T9)

Special Expatriate Tax Regime (2018) www.impots.gouv.fr/portail/international-particulier/special-expatriate-tax-regime (archived at https://perma.cc/DB3Z-49YV)

Taylor, C (2019) San Francisco has rising competition when it comes to big fintech startups, *CNBC,* www.cnbc.com/2019/04/09/london-threatening-san-franciscos-fintech-unicorn-lead-research-says.html (archived at https://perma.cc/A8C7-MSWM)

Thiteux, V (2019) Paris, France: Business and Fintech Landscapes, B-Hive, b-hive.eu/news-full/2018/6/13/paris-france-business-fintech-landscapes (archived at https://perma.cc/2TJ7-M4UV)

WEF (2018) The Future of Jobs report, www.orientamentoirreer.it/sites/default/files/materiali/2018%2009%2017%20WEF-Future-of-Jobs-2018.pdf (archived at https://perma.cc/UJ98-QSM9)

Chapter 12

Cheung, E (2019) Greater Bay Area: 10 facts to put it in perspective, *South China Morning Post,* www.scmp.com/native/economy/china-economy/topics/great-powerhouse/article/3002844/greater-bay-area-10-facts-put (archived at https://perma.cc/Z5JT-4AKE)

China Law Blog (2019) The Shenzen Model City Initiative, www.chinalawblog. com/2019/10/the-shenzhen-model-city-initative.html (archived at https://perma. cc/UPZ9-K5X7)

Deloitte (2017) A tale of 44 cities. Connecting Global FinTech: Interim Hub Review, Deloitte and Company, www2.deloitte.com/content/dam/Deloitte/uk/Documents/ Innovation/deloitte-uk-connecting-global-fintech-hub-federation-innotribe- innovate-finance.pdf (archived at https://perma.cc/GT2C-C5QE)

Feifei, F (2019) Fintech opens new doors for talents, *China Daily Hong Kong,* www.chinadailyhk.com/articles/81/61/61/1563942510300.html (archived at https://perma.cc/3L5R-8YEW)

Fintech Association of Hong Kong (2019) *The GBA Fintech Report 2019,* ftahk.org/ system/files/2019-07/The%20Hong%20Kong%20-Macau%20-%20 Guangdong%20GBA%20Fintech%20Report%202019%20-%20FTAHK%20-% 20Final%20May_2019.pdf (archived at https://perma.cc/UQ4U-3LBZ)

Greater Bay Insight (2019) *Coming up: Shenzhen's new fintech trick,* greaterbayinsight.com/coming-up-shenzhens-new-fintech-trick/ (archived at https://perma.cc/D2FJ-RPQ9)

Greater Bay Insight (2019) *Guangzhou sees future in blockchain,* greaterbayinsight. com/guangzhou-sees-future-in-blockchain/ (archived at https://perma.cc/ QB55-RLLL)

Han, HQ (2018) *FinTech in China: An Introduction,* Wharton Fintech, medium. com/wharton-fintech/fintech-in-china-an-introduction-6b11abd9cb64 (archived at https://perma.cc/BD9V-JCQ2)

Hays (2018) Navigating Asia's changing workforce: Understanding tomorrow's workforce today, cthr.ctgoodjobs.hk/doc/trends/2018-hays.pdf (archived at https://perma.cc/B3L8-5ZWL)

International Comparative Legal Guides International Business Reports (2019) *Fintech 2019: Laws and Regulations, China,* iclg.com/practice-areas/fintech- laws-and-regulations/china (archived at https://perma.cc/Q65V-E8AA)

Iskyan, K (2016) China's middle class is exploding, *Business Insider,* www.businessinsider.com/chinas-middle-class-is-exploding-2016-8?r=US&IR=T (archived at https://perma.cc/T973-ASZJ)

Liang, S (2019) *Venture Capital Funding Report 1H19,* EqualOcean, equalocean. com/auto/20190703-number-of-investments-in-china-fell-by-48-and-dollar- amount-fell-by-60-in-1h19 (archived at https://perma.cc/C9FX-6A5R)

Lingqing, Z (2017) Fintech reimagines new service models, *China Daily,* www.chinadaily.com.cn/a/201811/07/WS5be25b2da310eff303287227.html (archived at https://perma.cc/Q7ZP-7FD3)

Malet-Bates, G (2019) Growth in China and Hong Kong: Green Shoots or Greenwashing? *The Fintech Times,* thefintechtimes.com/china-greenwashing (archived at https://perma.cc/9CDU-CHTL)

Mullen, J (2018) European companies are worried about China's tech ambitions, too, *CNN Business,* money.cnn.com/2018/06/20/technology/china-tech-european-companies/index.html (archived at https://perma.cc/B3V4-UNSW)

Rivers, M (2018) Inside China's Silicon Valley: From copycats to innovation, *CNN Business,* edition.cnn.com/2018/11/22/tech/china-tech-innovation-shenzhen/index.html (archived at https://perma.cc/HEY9-49NX)

Sender, H (2016) Hong Kong's welcome mat to fintech start-ups looks worn, *Financial Times,* www.ft.com/content/92a72046-a545-11e6-8b69-02899e8bd9d1 (archived at https://perma.cc/FR8J-U2U2)

South China Morning Post (2019) China Internet Report 2019, www.scmp.com/china-internet-report (archived at https://perma.cc/9JUL-DWKM)

Wakefield, J (2019) China is getting smarter – but at what cost? *BBC,* www.bbc.co.uk/news/technology-50658538 (archived at https://perma.cc/A5V8-4BTQ)

Wang, X (2017) A Chinese Company That Lends To Borrowers With No Credit Scores, *Forbes,* www.forbes.com/sites/xiangwang/2017/03/22/a-chinese-company-that-lends-to-borrowers-with-no-credit-scores/#5f9b7f6d2d9f (archived at https://perma.cc/MA4Y-ZFZ4)

INDEX

NB: page numbers in *italic* indicate figures or tables

From 4 December 2025 the EU Responsible Person (GPSR) is:
eucomply oÜ, Pärnu mnt. 139b – 14, 11317 Tallinn, Estonia
www.eucompliancepartner.com